Die Hard!

Die Hard!

Dramatic Actions from the Napoleonic Wars

PHILIP J. HAYTHORNTHWAITE

'Die Hard, 57th, die hard!' — Exhortation by
Lieutenant-Colonel William Inglis to his battalion
at the Battle of Albuera, 16 May 1811

ARMS AND
ARMOUR

Arms and Armour Press
An Imprint of the Cassell Group
Wellington House, 125 Strand, London WC2R 0BB

Distributed in the USA by Sterling Publishing Co. Inc.,
387 Park Avenue South, New York, NY 10016-8810.

British Library Cataloguing-in-Publication Data:
a catalogue record for this book is available from the British Library

ISBN 1-85409-245-6

Designed and edited by DAG Publications Ltd.
Designed by David Gibbons; edited by Michael Boxall;
Printed and bound in Great Britain by
Hartnolls Limited, Bodmin, Cornwall

CONTENTS

INTRODUCTION

The French Revolutionary and Napoleonic Wars represent the most intense period of military activity in Europe between the conclusion of the Thirty Years' War and the beginning of the First World War; indeed, until the war of 1914–18 it was the Napoleonic conflict which was referred to in Britain as the 'Great War'. During this period there occurred many of the greatest and most celebrated battles in history, and at least two of the greatest military commanders of all time exercised their skills in theatres of operations which extended from Lisbon to Moscow, from Copenhagen to Cairo.

During this period of conflict, innumerable battles, sieges and lesser actions were fought, many with great ferocity. The intensity of the fighting often bore no direct relevance to the importance of the action in the wider scheme of the course of the wars; some of the bitterest conflict occurred in more obscure actions, or in fights which formed episodes of a more substantial battle. This book contains accounts of a selection of the most desperate actions of the period, from decisive battles to sieges, actions of lesser importance and significant episodes within a larger action; it was just as likely for small actions, which normally rate only a footnote in the histories of the era, to produce deeds as remarkable as any which occurred in the great battles. It is not suggested that the actions described were exclusively the most dramatic or hard-fought, but included are some which by all contemporary standards were remarkable in terms of the outcome or the determination with which one or both sides contested the field. For a truly hard-fought action, the troops of both combatants had to exhibit a degree of exertion beyond that which might have been expected, unless one side was in some way markedly inferior in terms of numbers or situation, in which case such efforts were required to redress the disparity.

Using a remark attributed to the great Turenne, Voltaire stated that *'Dieu est toujours pour les gros bataillons'* – God is always on the side of the big battalions. In the 18th and early 19th centuries, some military theorists accepted some premises as fact, with a certainty which led to such instructional comments as 'The number of men necessary to carry on a siege with vigour, is founded upon fixed principles, always remaining the same; varying however in certain contingencies and of which the commander of the army is alone capable of judging.'[1]

There were certainly cogent reasons to support such a belief, not least the fact that while the minutiae of systems of manoeuvre varied between armies, the essential aspects of contemporary warfare were conducted in similar ways irrespective of the nationality of the troops involved. It was perhaps the existence of such common principles, or what might be termed the rules of military probability, that led to the suggestion that it was possible to estimate the outcome of a battle conducted under certain conditions and with a given number of facts. Such calculations were never more than the broadest principles: for example that artillery fire was most effective when taking its target in enfilade; that cavalry could not break well-formed squares; that troops of certain categories could only sustain a certain amount of fire before breaking, and so on. It was against these doctrines that generals exercised their skills, and indeed the outcome of many battles may be attributed to such skills, allied with the system of organisation and discipline which pertained in their armies. A number of factors, however, rendered such calculations liable to be overturned; as Napoleon himself was wont to remark, a general's luck was one of many intangibles which could radically and unexpectedly alter the outcome of a battle.

Undoubtedly, generalship could be a major factor in determining the outcome of an action, but some victories were won despite, rather than because of, the efforts of the commanding general; and in some cases the deciding factor was not superior numbers, or tactical system, or military genius, or 'luck', but the desperate or dogged courage of the individual soldier which had the most profound effect, for no matter how brilliant the plan, the finest of strategies could not succeed without the determination and discipline of the general's followers. The occasions when troops exhibited heroism and determination beyond all expected levels were legion, and resulted in many of the most desperate, sanguinary conflicts of the era, and because of this produced results on the battlefield which could scarcely have been imagined if the accepted balance of probability were taken as a guide to the outcome of a set of given circumstances, in which troops behaved as might have been predicted by the aforementioned military theories. It is with such unexpected outcomes that this book is largely concerned.

Much more difficult is to attempt to explain *why* such deeds were performed, and how it was that the fortitude of some troops might have confounded the predictions of those attempting to use accepted standards as a guide to the outcome of actions. Writing in *Colburn's United Service Magazine* in 1843, a correspondent signing himself 'A General Officer' stated that 'When civilians will write military history, and venture to advance opinions of their own on technical points of which the Profession alone are able to judge, they, generally, talk nonsense';[2] even more difficult must it be for those so removed from the mores and practices of the period to comment upon the subject of morale. Indeed, it is even difficult to equate the conditions of the Napoleonic era with those pertaining at the beginning of the 20th century. There is, for example, little evidence of 'shell shock' or psychological problems attributable directly to the stress of being under fire during the Napoleonic period. To use Lord Moran's comparison of courage resembling a bank-account which suffered withdrawals throughout protracted combat, which caused a gradual seeping away of courage, it is interesting to reflect upon the exposure to danger undergone by soldiers of the Napoleonic Wars. Calculations are extremely difficult to approximate, but to take the case of those men who were awarded the maximum number of clasps for the British Military General Service Medal: James Talbot and Daniel Loochstadt were each awarded 15 clasps, each representing a battle. In the case of Talbot (of the 45th Foot), in the fifteen actions for which he was awarded a clasp, he was probably under enemy fire for no more than a total of 24 hours, spread over eight years; in these actions his regiment suffered some 123 men killed in action (plus the eventual deaths of many of those originally returned as 'wounded'). Arduous although Taylor's service undoubtedly was, the time spent actually under fire could easily have been exceeded by a few days' service on the Western Front during the First World War, so that while Taylor would have experienced hours of extreme hazard, it would not have been the same kind of continual, wearing exposure to bombardment which produced so many of the psychological casualties of the First World War.[3]

It was believed at the time that certain nations possessed identifiable characteristics, which led to comments like those of the Prince de Ligne on the abilities required of a general: 'Whenever it falls to the lot of an individual to be entrusted with the command of an army composed of lively materials, such as are to be found among the English, the Italians, the French, and the Hungarians, it must be his study to repress his own ardour in order to keep under the natural effervescence of his followers. When a man is put at the head of an army made up of colder elements, such as Germans, Russians, or Dutchmen, he must, like Prometheus, endeavour to steal a spark of celestial animation, to give them motion and activity.'[4]

The events of the Napoleonic Wars would lend some credence to such beliefs, although whether it was essentially a matter of inherent national characteristics, or more a product of the various aspects of each nation's military system, is a matter of debate, and any such contemporary opinions are open to distortion as a result of national bias. Despite the very different backgrounds or sources of recruits from which the soldiers of various armies were drawn, some factors were universal, exemplified by an aphorism written on a wall of a French barracks in Lisbon, concerning the qualifications necessary to make a good soldier:

'Le courage d'un Lion,
La force d'un cheval,
L'appetit d'un souris,
Et l'humanité d'une bête' [5]

– the bravery of a lion, the strength of a horse, the appetite of a mouse, and the humanity of a brute.

Nevertheless, the universal inherent reaction to combat was that expressed by the French officer Elzéar Blaze, who remarked that the best battle he ever witnessed was Bautzen, because he wasn't in it but watched it in safety, from a distance! Blaze articulated the futility of the entire process, and postulated what would have been the reaction of a man who lived in the moon were he to arrive on earth and be told that 'Yonder are one hundred thousand men, who are going to fight at the command of an individual for interests which they know nothing about, and which not one of them cares about. Some go by force, others voluntarily; but all take a pride in running into the greatest possible dangers. They will get themselves killed, perhaps mutilated, crippled, which is frequently worse than death. They will endure all privations, all fatigues, all inclemency of the weather [and] will come back wounded, racked with pains, in rags; and, by way of reward, they will be permitted to admire the statue of their general erected in some public place. What would the man in the moon say to this? ... he would say that the inhabitants of the earth are fools, and that their sovereigns are arrant knaves.'[6]

But there is little evidence that many soldiers dwelt upon such thoughts; probably more common was the type of philosophy expressed in a reported conversation with an old French sergeant: 'At first starting I said to myself, The Almighty has created you, and sent you into the world to love and serve Him by loving and serving your country. Go a straight road, and look always before you. Obey your superiors, be friendly to your equals, remember that those under your command are men, and you will be happy – and so it has turned out.'[7]

Even if such philosophy were widespread, it could be no more than a minor contributory factor in the maintaining of morale which permitted the great exploits of heroism that occurred. Discipline was undoubtedly of crucial importance. The armies of the period were drilled and disciplined until, ideally, they could march and fight like automata, irrespective of the dangers to which they were exposed; indeed, retaining formation and performing the manoeuvres ordered might actually in some circumstances be simply a matter of self-preservation, in that greater safety could be found in formed bodies than for troops who were scattered and vulnerable. Nevertheless, it required an extraordinary level of composure to stand fast, under fire, while comrades were struck down left and right.

The discipline and system of manoeuvre which was instilled into the armies of the period not only enabled soldiers to perform their duties under duress, to the extent of overcoming the inherent human instinct to flee from danger, but was even held to produce a kind of mass heroism: 'In large masses, the standard of courage which is established by discipline, may be often inferior to that produced by fanaticism or any other peculiar excitement; but the latter never lasts long, neither is it equable, because men are of different susceptibility, following their physical and mental conformation.'[8] The 'heroism of discipline' was perhaps founded upon the fact that if a soldier's comrades were standing firm, then he should also, against any inherent reaction to remove himself from danger. Blaze recalled an old fable of a prince who possessed an enchanted ring, which when turned made the wearer invisible; and stated that at the first shot, any soldier of whatever nationality would immediately turn the ring, were it not for the presence of his fellows: 'I am there because you are there, and because you know that I am and ought to be there; but devil take me if I would stay there if you knew nothing about it!'[9]

The distinction made between the courage of individuals and that of troops in mass almost seemed to suggest that a unit took on the characteristics of a sentient entity, whether this were entirely the product of discipline or not. Referring to the experience of the Napoleonic Wars, a paper published in 1843 expressed the concept thus:

'... whenever two bodies of infantry meet, it is ... the least daring *mass* which gives way. Now as it may perfectly well happen that individual courage does not suffice to constitute the courage of the mass, so the courage of the mass may exist without individual courage. Of the former position innumerable examples have been afforded us. We see warlike tribes of savages, the meanest of whose warriors show a fearlessness and contempt of death which is not possessed by the bravest in the disciplined armies which his tribe unsuccessfully endeavoured to oppose. Yet, when formed into a body, we have seen these crowds of heroes swept away like chaff before the wind, by these civilised masses – an aggregate of comparative cowards, united into a strong and daring body, against valorous individuality forming a body cowardly and timid ... Of the second the Russian soldier furnishes the most remarkable instance; for the Infantry of which he forms a part is brave, though he, generally speaking, is not so. Uninspired by any military enthusiasm, or any patriotic feeling, or even by the spirit of natural pugnacity, which for its own sake invests the very act of strife and contention with charms in the eyes of certain races of men, the Russian private will do his duty – he will stand passively to be cut to pieces, or he will advance as he is directed; his arm may be unnerved, indeed, by his individual terrors, but still he *keeps his place* – the man is there, at his post, forming part and parcel of a *brave and formidable whole* – a whole which stands unawed by danger, or which itself advances threatening.'[10]

Despite such assertions, the determination of the individual must have been a significant factor in the creation and maintenance of a unit's morale. This morale was held to originate from a number of factors, not least the national attributes of the army in question, which as noted above were defined reasonably clearly in the opinions of the time, for example:

'The genius of the French is essentially military, and a great majority of her population have a taste for the arts of war ... The love of glory is stronger among the French than among ourselves, and more *pervading*; with them it reaches the lowest classes ... There is also more of patriotism ... among the masses in France, and a greater feeling of individual concern in the national character and honour. These sentiments and an indispensable chivalry unknown to the lower orders of Englishmen, will always make it easier to fill the ranks of the French army than the British. The same characteristics will make it easier to preserve discipline in a French army especially in circumstances of hardship and privation ... [but] in cool, *persevering* courage – that courage which decides the final success of the day, we believe our countrymen to have greatly the advantage ... though the English soldier wants the love of glory which distinguishes the French, he is actuated by a strong "sense of duty" – a principle more to be relied on in the long run, than "*l'amour de la gloire*". He has perfect confidence in his officers, and believes himself, according to the traditional saying, to be "worth two Frenchmen", or any other foreigners: for all of whom he has but a light regard.'[11]

Contemporary writings, and some later, especially by those to whom the idea was appealing, make much of the concept of 'glory', and the nobility of spirit which could be encountered only on the battlefield, and expressed only through the medium of combat, and forming an important source of motivation for the soldier. The very concept of 'glory', in a process which involved violent death, mutilation, weapons capable of inflicting the most dreadful of injuries and generally only the most rudimentary medical treatment, is one very difficult to comprehend according to modern standards, but during the period in question it did play a part. Blaze admitted that without the 'idea of glory in the profession of arms ... not a creature would follow it; nay it is astonishing that any one will at any price'.[12] Conversely, George Napier could write that 'There is never any personal animosity between soldiers opposed to each other in war ... and I hope always will be the case. I should hate to fight out of personal malice or revenge, but have no objection to fight for "fun and glory".'[13] (It is noteworthy that Napier wrote this with the experience of the Peninsular War, when both British and French armies were fighting in a country not their own and to a degree in a mutually chivalrous manner; personal animosity was unquestionably a serious motivation among those nations whose own homelands had been ravaged by an invader: Napier's description would not have been appreciated to the same degree by those engaged in the guerrilla war in Spain, in Russia in 1812, or among some of the Germans involved in the 'War of Liberation' in 1813, for example, where patriotism and a desire for revenge were undoubtedly motivating factors on the part of those involved.)

A typical contemporary commentary on the concept of patriotic exertion might be Robert Burns' *Song of Death* (written in 1791 but broadcast more widely in the early part of the French war, and reprinted in *The Anti-Gallican* in 1804:[14]

13

'In the field of proud honour – our swords in our hands,
   Our King and our Country to save
While victory shines on life's last ebbing sands,
   Oh! who would not rest with the brave'.

It might be thought that ideals of patriotism or the quest for glory might not be foremost in the thoughts of the individual when actually under fire, and in imminent danger of death, and indeed this was articulated by some; Wilhelm Heinemann, who served with the Westphalian army in Russia in 1812, stated that the courage of the rank-and-file emanated not from self-confidence or patriotic sentiments of national honour, but that troops went into action on a tide of a kind of despair.[15]

The devotion to, or confidence in, a particular leader could produce extraordinary effects; never was this more marked than in the near idolatry accorded to Napoleon, which led even those dying on the battlefield to raise the cry of '*Vive l'Empereur!*', and to inspire men to great levels of heroism in even the most distressing circumstances. Oratory on the part of such a leader might inspire those who heard him, although this was dependent largely upon the susceptibility of the listeners; it was thought, for example, that Napoleon's harangues could hearten and embolden his followers, but Thomas Brotherton of the British 14th Light Dragoons averred that if such speeches had been addressed to British soldiers, their universal reaction would have been 'Fudge!'[16]

Perhaps a more realistic reaction to the more melodramatic sentiments of patriotic or personal exhortation would have been something like the words ascribed to Charles Lever's 'Mickey Free' in *Charles O'Malley, The Irish Dragoon:*

'To the tune of a fife
   They dispose of your life,
You surrender your soul to some illigant lilt,
   Now I like Garryowen,
When I hear it at home,
   But it's not half so sweet
When you're going to be kilt.'[17]

One of the most powerful emotions was regimental pride, if harnessed properly, especially if the regiment had a special standing or distinguished history. The morale effect of recalling past events as deeds to be emulated was appreciated at the time, hence the display of battle-honours upon regimental flags (most obviously in the French army, to a lesser extent in the British), even if the events commemorated had occurred in previous wars (for example, in the song of the British 15th Light Dragoons, which began with a reference to the action at Emsdorf in 1760:

> 'Emsdorff's [*sic*] fame unfurl'd before ye,
>   Brave Fifteenth, your standards rear,
> Guided by your ancient glory,
>   Shew what dauntless Britons are.'[18]

The consequence of the effect of *esprit de corps* was demonstrated by a writer who spoke to many British officers who had served at Waterloo, and remarked that although many had been expected to be beaten, every one thought that though they expected neighbouring units to give way, all had said 'certainly not my own corps'. Indeed, the morale effect of regimental pride was probably nowhere better exemplified than in the British Army, about which the same writer remarked that 'Our regiments, accustomed to act and live alone, are not taught to dread the failures of adjoining corps in combined operations; they cannot yield readily to the belief, that the defeat of a corps in their neighbourhood can license themselves to flee: penetrate an English line, you have gained but a point; cut into a continental line, even a French one, and the *morale* of everything in view, in vicinity, is gone. The English regiment will not give way, because the English regiment of the same brigade has done so, but will mock the fugitive, and in all likelihood redouble its own exertions to restore the fight – a true bull-dog courage against all odds – if well led.'[19]

Associated with other motivations was that of a sense of duty, which could produce examples of amazing fortitude, such as that of the French Colonel Jean-Baptiste Sourd, who was badly sabred on the day before Waterloo. On seeking medical attention it was found that his right arm could not be saved, so during its amputation (by Larrey) the colonel dictated a letter to Napoleon to the effect that he wished to remain in command of his regiment, even if that meant declining promotion to general; on completion of the operation, Sourd signed the letter with his left hand and immediately rode off to rejoin his regiment.

Many unexpected factors could cause a huge boost to morale, even something as mundane as the delivery of beef and biscuit after four days of existing on nothing but leaves (this occurred in the Pyrenees to the British 82nd: Lieutenant George Wood noted that the arrival of rations 'gave us such spirits, that, woe to the enemy who should dare oppose us!')[20] Perhaps less surprising, the influence of stirring music could have a similar effect: Coignet recalled how at Austerlitz the band of the Imperial Guard struck up a well-known song, '*On va leur percer le flanc*' as the formation began to advance: 'While this air was played, the drums ... beat a charge loud enough to break their drumheads in. The drums and music mingled together. It was enough to make a paralytic move forward!'[21]

In the final analysis, however, it was probably the courage of the individual which was one of the most decisive factors, perhaps of the type Napoleon himself described as 'two o'clock in the morning courage ... unprepared courage, that which is necessary on an unexpected occasion'.[22] John Kincaid, an officer of great experience, remarked that in battle, soldiers 'are apt to have a feeling that they are but insignificant characters – only a humble individual out of many thousands, and that his conduct, be it good or bad, can have little influence over the fate of the day. This is a monstrous mistake ... for in battle, as elsewhere, no man is insignificant unless he chooses to make himself so ... men in battle may be classed under the disproportionate heads – a very small class who consider themselves insignificant – a very large class who content themselves with doing their duty, without going beyond it – and a tolerably large class who do their best, many of whom are great men without knowing it.' He then quoted an example of how a single individual could affect the whole: 'We were engaged in a very hot skirmish ... when we were at length stopped by [enemy] regiments in line, which opened such a terrific fire within a few yards that it obliged every one to shelter himself as best he could among the inequalities of the ground and the sprinkling of trees which the place afforded. We remained inactive for about ten minutes amidst a shower of balls that seemed to be almost like a hail-storm, and when at the very worst, when it appeared to me to be certain death to quit the cover, a young scampish fellow of the name of Priestly, at the adjoining tree, started out from behind it, saying, "Well! I'll be hanged if I'll be bothered any longer behind a tree, so here's at you", and with that he banged off his rifle in the face of his foes, reloading very deliberately, while every one right and left followed his example, and the enemy, panic struck, took to their heels without firing another shot. The action required no comment, the individual did not seem aware that he had any merit in what he did, but it is nevertheless a valuable example for those who are disposed to study causes and effects in the art of war.'[23]

In the accounts which follow, the coverage of each action is not uniform; in some cases an entire battle is described, in others only one aspect which serves to emphasise the intensity of the fighting, concentrating less on tactical analysis than upon what might be termed the 'personal experience' as recounted by participants. Such accounts demonstrate the desperate nature of the actions described, and the endeavour and heroism displayed; and may dispel any idea, which might be assumed from the way in which some histories have been written, that the warfare of the period was largely a matter of tactical and strategic theory and not underlaid by the human price for each victory. This was articulated by Moyle Sherer, one of the most thoughtful of the contemporary memorialists, who described his emotions on seeing the battlefield of Albuera: '... thousands of slain, thousands of wounded, writhing with anguish, and groaning with agony and despair ... Look at the contraction of this body, and the anguish of these features; eight times has some lance pierced this frame. Here again lie headless trunks, and bodies torn and struck down by cannon shot; such death is sudden, horrid, but 'tis merciful. Who are these that catch every moment at our coats, and cling to our feet, in such humble attitude? The wounded soldiers of the enemy, who are imploring British protection from the exasperated and revengeful Spaniards ... Some readers will call this scene romantic, others disgusting; no matter; it is faithful; and it would be well for kings, politicians, and generals, if, while they talk of victories and exultation, and of defeats with philosophical indifference, they would allow their fancies to wander to the theatre of war, and the field of carnage.'[24]

NOTES

1. *Journals of the Sieges undertaken by the Allies in the Years 1811 and 1812, with Notes*, Lieutenant-Colonel J. T. Jones, London, 1814, pp. 334–5.
2. 'Alison versus the Duke of Wellington', in *United Service Magazine* 1843, II, p. 433.
3. Lord Moran's theory appears in *The Anatomy of Courage*, Lord Moran of Manton, London, 1945.
4. Quoted in 'On the Purchase and Sale of Commissions', in *British Military Library or Journal*, London, 1799–1801, II, p. 401.
5. 'Recollections of the Peninsula', Lieutenant-Colonel Wilkie, in *Colburn's United Service Magazine*, 1843, III, p. 427.
6. *Lights and Shades of Military Life*, ed. Lieutenant-General Sir Charles Napier, London, 1850, pp. 421–2.
7. 'Gascony on Stilts, or, The Serjeant-Major of the Landes', anon., in *Colburn's United Service Magazine*, 1844, I, p. 391.
8. *History of the War in the Peninsula and in the South of France*, W. F. P. Napier, London 1832, II, p. 50.

9. *Lights and Shades, op. cit.*, pp. 422–3.
10. 'Military Strength and Condition of the Russian Empire', anon., in *Colburn's United Service Magazine*, 1843, II, p. 193.
11. 'England and the French Press', 'E. W.', in *United Service Magazine* 1842, I, p. 104.
12. *Lights and Shades*, p. 421.
13. *Passages in the Early Military Life of General Sir George T. Napier*, ed. General W. C. E. Napier, London, 1884, p. 177.
14. *The Anti-Gallican*, London, 1804, pp. 235–6.
15. This remark can be found in translation in *1812: Napoleon in Moscow*, P. Britten Austin, London, 1995, p. 245.
16. *A Hawk at War: The Peninsular War Reminiscences of General Sir Thomas Brotherton*, ed. B. Perrett, Chippenham, 1986, p. 77.
17. *Charles O'Malley, The Irish Dragoon*, C. Lever, 1841, chap. XCIV.
18. *British Military Library or Journal*, I, p. 324,
19. 'Waterloo and the Waterloo Model', anon., in *United Service Journal*, 1839, II, p. 202.
20. *The Subaltern Officer*, G. Wood, London, 1825, pp. 205–6.
21. *The Note-Books of Captain Coignet*, ed. & intr. Hon. Sir John Fortescue, London, 1929, p. 124.
22. *Memoirs of the Life, Exile and Conversations of the Emperor Napoleon*, Count de Las Cases, London, 1836, I, p. 251.
23. *Random Shots from a Rifleman*, Sir John Kincaid, London, 1835; Maclaren's edn., London, 1908, pp. 210–11.
24. *Recollections of the Peninsula*, 'by the Author of "Sketches of India"' (Moyle Sherer), London, 1823, pp. 221–3.

'Into Perils Nobly Courted'
VILLERS-EN-CAUCHIES

24 April 1794

The first important campaigns of the French Revolutionary Wars are probably best remembered for the preservation by arms of the infant French republic, which by the end of 1794 was no longer in danger of being overrun by the coalition of European monarchies which had been assembled to prevent the export of the revolution which had overthrown the Ancien Régime in France, and to restore the king of France to his throne. In the Netherlands, 1794 was a decisive year which saw the French triumph over a multi-national Allied army, part of the leadership of which led the future Duke of Wellington to remark that it demonstrated 'what one ought not to do, and that is always something'.[1] Perhaps because of the discomfiture of the Allies, or because of the greater prominence accorded to subsequent events, the actions of the Netherlands campaign are not especially well known, and their neglect has tended to obscure a quite remarkable cavalry action fought at Villers-en-Cauchies on 24 April 1794. It is remembered by one British regiment, but for many of the subsequent years under a mis-spelled name; in one of the first published accounts it was given an entirely different name;[2] it has been given an incorrect date;[3] and the identity of the Austrian unit present, and the names or status of some of those distinguished in the action, may all be found with conflicting details in various sources.

At the commencement of the Netherlands campaign of 1794, the Allied forces were commanded by Prince Friedrich Josias of Saxe-Coburg, comprising a powerful if mixed concentration of Coburg's own Austrians, Hessians, Hanoverians, Dutch and British, the latter commanded by Frederick Augustus, Duke of York, son of King George III and an earnest, if not especially inspired, field commander. If the French army had been riven apart by the effects of the Revolution, and then re-assembled in a less than perfect state of equipment and discipline, then the Allied forces were equally mixed in quality, and in many cases lacked experienced leadership: the Duke of York, for example, was aged only 28, and although he had studied in Prussia his lack of combat or command experience was hardly redressed by personal bravery or the organisational ability which he demonstrated later in his career. By general consent, the Austrian troops were among the best of the Allied forces, and measured against them some of the other contingents appeared distinctly mediocre. This view was expressed most eloquently by John Gaspard Le Marchant, later an outstanding British commander and military theorist, who was killed at Salamanca in 1812, but who served in the Netherlands as a captain in the 2nd Dragoon Guards (Queen's Bays); comparing his own British troops with their Austrian comrades, in June 1793 he remarked that 'our friends the Austrians ... are at present, as superior to us as we are to the train-bands in the city', i.e., to the London Militia.[4] In view of the general opinion of the London Militia at that time – 'Bold daring old Watchmen and wooden legg'd Sailors,/Butchers, Barbers, and Tinkers, Tomturdmen and Taylors',[5] the comparison is quite telling; but it referred more to lack of experience in active campaigning than to want of spirit or morale, as was demonstrated on numerous occasions in the Netherlands campaign despite the manifest imperfections in leadership.

The campaign of 1794 opened in April, with the Allied forces taking the initiative despite the best efforts of the French to strike first. The Allied army received an augmentation of uncertain value in mid-April with the arrival of the Holy Roman Emperor, Francis II (later Francis I of Austria), who just three years before had succeeded his father Leopold II, at the age of 24; as nominal commander-in-chief of all the empire's military forces, his approval was necessary for the plan of campaign to be followed during his presence in the region. Prince Friedrich Josias proposed to initiate the campaign by besieging Landrecies, because he considered the wings of the Allied army too weak to attempt a general offensive against a French force estimated to number about 300,000 men; and with the emperor's approval this plan was put in motion even though a policy of isolated sieges could not be expected to achieve a decisive result. Such a scheme also tended to negate perhaps the Allies' greatest advantage over their opponents, the possession of a much superior force of cavalry, in open terrain over which large formations of cavalry could be used most effectively. This had been demonstrated a couple of miles from Villers-en-Cauchies on 12 September 1793, when at Avesnes-le-Sec nine squadrons of Coburg's Austrian cavalry, approximately 2,000 strong, had routed a French division of some 7,000 men, inflicting about 2,000 casualties and capturing 2,000 more and twenty guns, while sustaining a loss of only 69 men, a quite brilliant achievement in the annals of cavalry service.

In the immediate front of Coburg and the Emperor, the French forces of General Jean Charles Pichegru were not concentrated, but disposed in separated units, giving opportunity for them to be overwhelmed in succession; but the Allied command retained its old tactics and advanced in no less than eight columns, the commanders of which were enjoined not to advance precipitately, but to consolidate any captured positions instead of pursuing any defeated enemy forces. The areas in which the British operated featured many place names that were and would become famous in British military annals; the fortress of Bouchain, for example, stood before the 'Non Plus Ultra' lines and had been captured by Marlborough in 1711; Landrecies was the scene of an action involving the 4th (Guards) Brigade of the 2nd Division on 25 August 1914; Le Cateau and Solesmes, again in 1914; Cambrai figured large in the campaigns of 1917 and 1918; Le Quesnoy in the Battle of the Sambre, 1918; St-Quentin in 1918. Among these, Villers-en-Cauchies deserves to occupy a distinguished place.

On 16 April 1794 a great review of Allied forces was held before the Emperor near Le Cateau, in preparation for the advance, initially upon Landrecies on the Sambre; in addition to the French forces there, others were deployed to the south and west, with greater concentrations at Maubeuge and Cambrai. Beginning on 17 April, the Allies' advance initially encountered only limited opposition, which was swept aside, and the siege of Landrecies was begun on 20 April.

On 23 April a strong French force marched out from Cambrai in three columns, evidently intent upon disrupting the siege of Landrecies; they probably numbered about 15,000 strong, although the figure quoted by the Austrian commander was 24,000. Concentrating at a place called 'Caesar's Camp' (which the Duke of York referred to as 'Camp de Caesar'), the French drove in the outlying Allied (Hessian) positions. The Austrian commander in this sector, Lieutenant-General Otto, was informed of the movement by the colonel in command of his cavalry vedettes, the Hungarian Baron Andrew Szentkerestzy (whose name appears in most contemporary reports as 'Sentkeresky'; other versions include 'Lentkeresky' and 'Sentheresky'). Otto at once joined him and reconnoitred in person, finding that some 10,000 French had advanced as far as Villers-en-Cauchies. The only force at his immediate disposal was Sentkeresky's vedettes, two Austrian and two British squadrons; so he immediately fell back some four miles to the village of St-Hilaire, reported the enemy movement to the Duke of York, and requested support. The Duke immediately dispatched the cavalry brigade of the British Major-General John Mansel (two squadrons from each of the Royal Horse Guards, 3rd Dragoon Guards and 1st (Royal) Dragoons), together with two squadrons of the Austrian Zeschwitz Cuirassiers and two of the British 11th Light Dragoons; but it was after dark before these reinforcements joined Otto, so action against the French advance had to await the daylight of the following morning.

Accordingly, between 4 and 5 o'clock on the morning of 24 April Otto moved forward with his advance-guard, still consisting of Sentker-

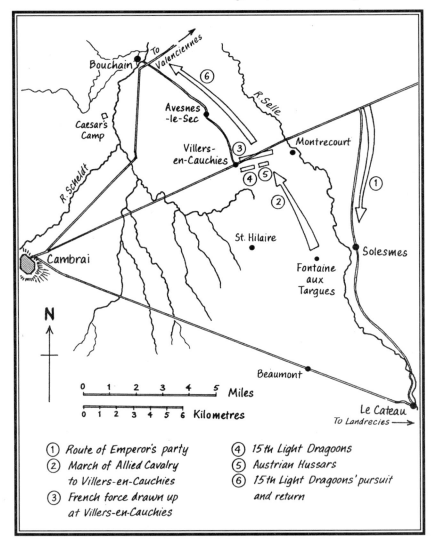

22

esky's four squadrons, until by Villers-en-Cauchies they came upon what appeared to be a force of French cavalry. So comparatively obscure was the action which followed that conflicting accounts exist even as to the identity of Otto's two Austrian squadrons. It has been assumed from an early date that the regiment concerned was the Leopold Hussars (as early as 1801 they were described as 'the Imperial Corps Leopold Toscano',[6] but it has been conjectured that, as Otto's report merely described them as 'two hussar squadrons', this identification arose from the fact that Sentkeresky was the regimental colonel, and this identification has been repeated in a number of accounts). Austrian sources indicate that the unit involved was in fact the Archduke Ferdinand Hussars, one of whose members, Rittmeister (Captain) Daniel, Freiherr Meschéry de Tsoor, was decorated for the action; yet his presence would seem not to be positive proof of the participation of his regiment, as Otto's account (which spells his name 'Mezery') notes that he was serving in the role of ADC rather than in his regimental capacity.

No such confusion surrounds the identity of the other two squadrons of the Allied vanguard: they belonged to the British 15th Light Dragoons, and were commanded by Major William Aylett. He had under his command seven other officers from the 15th: Captain Robert Pocklington, Captain-Lieutenant Edward Michael Ryan, Lieutenants Granby Thomas Calcraft and William Grant Keir, and Cornets Charles Burrell Blunt and Robert Wilson. The seventh was Edward Gerald Butler, about whose status there is some question, for at the time of the action he was captain of an independent company, and transferred as a lieutenant to the 11th Light Dragoons some three weeks later. It has been speculated[7] – probably correctly – that he had joined the 11th in an unofficial capacity (not unusual for an officer in imminent expectation of receiving a commission), but not being officially a member of the regiment was free to join the 15th in their advance-guard duties in the expectation of a better opportunity for action. The 15th was a regiment not unused to the type of service they were about to undertake, for at Emsdorf on 16 July 1760, in concert with Luckner's regiment of Hanoverian hussars, they had made several remarkable charges which had resulted in the capture of the entire French force against which they were opposed. As if to inspire their successors to emulate this remarkable feat, the 15th carried the honour 'EMSDORF' on their appointments, the battle-honour and date being affixed to the sides of their helmets as an ever-present reminder of the offensive power of cavalry.

The total strength of Otto's command appears to have been only 272 men, according to Otto split between 160 of the 15th and 112 Austrians, although another early account states that the force consisted of 86 members of the Leopold Hussars and 186 of the 15th.[8] Using this force as a vanguard for Mansel's brigade and the other four squadrons, Otto advanced northwards down the valley of the River Selle towards the suspected position of the French, although it is clear that he had no exact knowledge of the whereabouts or composition of the enemy in his immediate vicinity. The whole force, including Mansel's heavy cavalry, had spent the night in a state of readiness at a farm called Fontaine au Targue near Solesmes, and the two contingents certainly marched north at about the same time; but for some reason the vanguard outdistanced the main body. Why Mansel's command failed to keep contact with Otto's vanguard is unclear; the Duke of York's report merely noted that 'General Mansel's brigade did not arrive in time,'[9] but another early report suggested that Mansel's brigade 'lost time by missing the direct road to the scene of the action'.[10] Whatever the cause, Otto's four squadrons were left without support when they came upon a body of French cavalry between the villages of Montrecourt and Villers-en-Cauchies.

The French were obviously two or three times the number of Otto's strength, but when pressured on their left flank they retired somewhat precipitately and re-formed to their rear, their right flank protected by the village of Villers-en-Cauchies and their left by a bank of thick woodland. For Otto, the prudent course of action would have been to await the arrival of support; but instead he received news which probably changed entirely his intended course of action. The Emperor Francis, he was informed, was on the road from Brussels to Le Cateau, and thus in danger of being intercepted by the French. It must be very doubtful that the Emperor's party was in immediate danger, given the initial reaction of the French cavalry to the sight of Otto's small force, and it must have been unlikely that the French had any inkling of the Emperor's vulnerability; but the consequences of his death or capture were so profound that Otto decided that his only course of action was to attack immediately with the few troops he had, and not await the arrival of Mansel, who was nowhere in sight. Otto assembled his officers, explained the situation to them, and declared that there was nothing else for it but to attack, whereupon British and Austrian officers crossed their swords in a solemn pledge that they would charge home, believing that such a reckless manoeuvre was necessary to preoccupy the French sufficiently to allow the Emperor to escape. Otto added that as their numbers were so few, it would be impossible to take prisoners. British sources have sought to explain the savagery of the fight by stating that the French National Convention had decreed that no quarter should be given to the British; but in fact this decree was not issued until a month after the action at Villers-en-Cauchies. Instead, Otto's order was based upon sound tactical reasoning: that the Allied contingent was already small enough without having to detach men to superintend any prisoners who might be taken. Brutal though the 'no prisoners' instruction might seem, it is likely that the Austrian officers never gave it a second thought, and that only the British might have queried it. In the previous year, Le Marchant had written of his utter revulsion at the Austrians' refusal to grant quarter, and of their murder of French prisoners taken by the British; and added that the British practice was only to harm those enemies who did not surrender, in order to preserve life as much as possible. Perhaps understandably, the Austrians were less concerned with such scruples at a time when they were striving to defend their own possessions from invasion.

The French (light cavalry, *chasseurs à cheval*) were drawn up in line between Villers-en-Cauchies and the woodland; the Allied force, commanded by Sentkeresky and with the ADC Meschéry present, deployed in three bodies. On the right flank, the two Austrian squadrons formed up, presumably acting together because of their comparative weakness in numbers; in the centre a squadron of 15th Light Dragoons commanded by Captain Edward Ryan, and on the left the other 15th squadron under Captain Robert Pocklington; Major Aylett exercised supreme command over the British element of the force. The order 'March!' was given, whereupon Otto detached a small number of Austrian hussars to move into the wood upon which the French left flank was anchored, believing that French troops might be concealed there. Although it weakened even further the Allied force, this was a necessary diversion of resources which prevented the possibility of a countercharge in the flank, for as the hussar detachment threw out its skirmishers, who began to fire into the wood, a considerable body of concealed French cavalry (which Cornet Robert Wilson estimated as two squadrons) withdrew from the trees.

The main body of the Allied cavalry moved forward in line at a trot, over open ground and towards the waiting line of French *chasseurs*. French skirmishers advanced to meet them, firing from the saddle at quite close range; Wilson, riding on the extreme left flank, narrowly escaped death when a carbine-shot grazed his helmet just above his ear, stripping off a piece of silver edging. The French skirmishers must have dispersed or retired to their own main line as the Allied troops increased their pace, from trot to gallop. A popular theory of cavalry tactics was that to receive a charge at the halt was fatal, in permitting the attackers' impetus to overthrow a static line; so the charging British and Austrians must have expected the French to move before contact was made. Move they did, but in a quite unexpected direction; instead of advancing to meet the charge, the French line divided at the centre, turned towards their flanks and began to gallop away, half towards Villers-en-Cauchies and half towards the cover of the woodland on the left flank. As the line of French *chasseurs* opened at the centre, the attackers met a horrifying sight: behind the French cavalry stood a formation of infantry with artillery in front, having been deliberately 'masked' by the cavalry. The numbers of French troops assembled here are in doubt; estimates range between a total of 10,000 (including the cavalry) to 3,000 infantry, but whatever the case, the charging Anglo-Austrian cavalry was hugely and apparently hopelessly outnumbered. Nor were the troops opposing them the semi-trained conscripts found in some French armies at this period; it is clear from the way they awaited the charge that they were disciplined and competent troops. The French infantry, six battalions in strength, were described as being arrayed in a three-deep line, but it is possible that they were formed in two oblong 'squares' with the artillery in advance and between them, a formation which to the chargers would have given the impression of a line.

The exact sequence of events is somewhat confused at this stage of the action, for the situation would have appeared differently to those chargers in Ryan's central squadron from those in Pocklington's left-flank squadron and the Austrians at the right; but what is not in doubt is the fact that despite the revelation of the force which confronted them, the chargers made no attempt to rein-in or break their stride, but continued towards the huge mass at full tilt. Cornet Wilson recalled that the French infantry and artillery appeared as if by magic, but by that time the chargers' speed was probably almost at its maximum, and no matter how intimidating the sight ahead of them, they might not have had time for reflection before their mounts carried them into the middle of the French. Even had the leaders of the charge had opportunity to re-assess their situation, they might have realised that charging home would have been no more destructive than endeavouring to halt in front of the infantry, losing their impetus and permitting the French to shoot them down at will.

Sited some way in front of their infantry, the French artillery was able to deliver a salvo of canister-shot as soon as the French cavalry had cleared their frontage. Ryan's central squadron, however, dashed on with hardly a check, through the battery, sabring the gunners, and plunged on towards the infantry. Four guns were captured, but it proved possible to take away only three of them. Between the guns and the infantry was a sunken road with steep banks, but the cavalry cleared it with scarcely a check, and at this moment the infantry fired, the front rank dropping to one knee with bayonets angled upwards at the level of a horse's breast, the classic position of 'prepare to receive cavalry', with the second and third ranks behind them also presenting a hedge of bayonets which under normal circumstances would be impenetrable to cavalry, to say nothing of the musketry which could be delivered.

This fire was now directed into the central squadron of the attackers, but so rapid had been the progress of the charge that on the flanks the French cavalry, even at a gallop, had not been able to clear the enemy's frontage before the 15th and the Austrians were upon them; thus, on the flanks some French cavalrymen were brought down by the fire of their own infantry, while the charge of the Austrians on the right and Pocklington's squadron on the left fell in part not only upon the infantry, but upon the French cavalry which had not yet completed its movement to the flanks, so compounding the confusion. Against disciplined infantry in square, or in line with secured flanks, few cavalry charges could ever have been expected to press home to a range at which the cavalrymen could use their sabres; but so determined were the 15th and their Austrian comrades that on this occasion they did. When twenty yards from the French, the British officers cried *'Vive l'Empereur!'*, and their men following gave the more usual British 'huzza!' The former exclamation, which later in the Napoleonic Wars became the universal acclamation of support for Napoleon, was presumably used by the British on this occasion – and perhaps the only time when British officers charged shouting a slogan in French! – to express solidarity with their Austrian comrades, as presumably French would have been the language in which Britons and Austrians would have conversed, at a time when few Britons spoke German and few Austrians understood English.

A consistent complaint about British cavalry performance in action, which plagued British commanders throughout the period, was their lack of control, the exuberance of both officers and men carrying them on with more excitement than sense, not to mention a frequent lack of tactical awareness and training in the vital skills of maintaining formation during a charge and of rallying after the first shock. In this case, however, despite the speed of the charge and the emptying of saddles by artillery and musketry, the 15th maintained their formation (Wilson described the charging body as 'solid') and, undaunted by the appearance of the infantry, smashed into the French formation all along the line. A number of horses were mortally struck by the French volley, but it was delivered at such close range that the impetus of the falling mounts carried them right into the French ranks, destroying all cohesion among the infantry. (It could be that the French volley was aimed too low, for although Calcraft's horse was shot twice, and the mounts of Blunt, Wilson and Butler likewise wounded, their riders were unscathed.) The only salvation for foot-soldiers facing horsemen was to present a united front; once broken, they were almost defenceless against maddened horses and sabres capable of striking off limbs at a stroke.

If an infantry formation were broken, slaughter could be the result; which was what now occurred. In the first shock of the impact, as horses and riders crashed into the infantry, the British lost their commander, Major Aylett being run through the body with a bayonet, and his horse was twice wounded; but overturned by a tide of racing horses and whirling sabres, the French infantry formation was reduced to chaos. Some part began to flee in the direction of Cambrai, doubtless hastened in their flight by the Austrian squadron, which had now come up on the right, having been unable to keep pace with the 15th's charge; Robert Wilson claimed that the 15th's horses were so superior to the lighter hussar mounts of the Austrians that they gained three yards in every ten. Otto reported that after this first overthrow of the French line, elements of the Imperial and Hessian outlying detachments, which had been pushed in by the original French advance, joined in the pursuit of that part of the French force which fled towards Cambrai. For the 15th Light Dragoons, however, the exploit had only just begun.

After smashing through the infantry, the 15th appear hardly to have checked, but continued to charge onwards; though, as Wilson was careful to report, they still retained their formation and quite deliberately closed up the gaps in the ranks occasioned by the artillery- and musket-fire and by the brief sabre-versus-bayonet fight as they clove through the infantry line. Having emerged from the wreck of the infantry, the 15th saw before them a mass of French cavalry, the troopers who had moved from in front of the infantry now attempting to reform upon a supporting body in the rear. The French *chasseurs* must have presumed that they would have had adequate time to rally on the flanks and re-form before (as they must have expected) being launched to pursue the defeated Anglo-Austrian troopers; but the unprecedented success of the Allies in riding through the infantry in so short a time left the French cavalry with no time to steady themselves before the 15th Light Dragoons were upon them. Indeed, Wilson recorded that the French cavalry made hardly any resistance before beginning a panic-stricken flight. The pursued thought only of escape, and the pursuers of inflicting the maximum damage while the opportunity existed, for the 15th were still acutely aware of the great disparity in numbers; indeed, in pursuing the *chasseurs* the men of the 15th found themselves quite surrounded by enemies running before them like a flock of sheep, and permitting the Britons to slash and carve away almost without resistance. The carnage became horrific; Wilson described it as 'a dreadful massacre' and noted that one of the 15th's farriers single-handedly *killed* twenty-two Frenchmen. (An early map of the scene of the action shows the presence of a ravine in the rear of, and almost parallel to, the French line, where, it was stated, great numbers of French were trapped and killed in their attempts to escape.)

Leaving the Austrians to pursue elements of the shattered French force westwards towards Cambrai, the 15th (now commanded by Pocklington) continued to chase the fugitive cavalry northwards, along the road to Bouchain. In the course of a four-mile gallop they overtook a French column of fifty guns and ammunition-wagons which was on the march (early reports suggest that it was advancing to the relief of Landrecies, others that it was retiring upon Bouchain); the 15th thoroughly cut it about. Had the troops not been so few in number the whole artillery train could have been captured, but as they neared Bouchain the guns of the city began to fire, and a relief-force issued out, probably to save the artillery train.

At this point Pocklington considered it prudent to break off the pursuit, and to extricate his command from its imminent danger. With horses 'blown' after a four-mile gallop, it would have been unlikely that the 15th could have outdistanced a chase mounted by the fresh French troops from Bouchain, so they attempted by stealth that which would have been difficult by force. The 15th re-assembled in good order, and began to retrace their steps at a steady trot, although French units were appearing on their flanks and in their rear. By virtue of the 15th wearing blue uniforms, it was presumed that the French thought that they were part of the relief-force from Bouchain, not realising that they were British; such confusions were not uncommon in the warfare of the period.

Back at Villers-en-Cauchies, despite the havoc that had been wrought among the infantry and artillery, with part apparently being pursued by the Austrians towards Cambrai, the French force had been so large that the remainder had been able to rally in the area of their original position. That the whole force had not been routed is evident from the early accounts, one of which describes 'the enemy's infantry, which they [the Allied cavalry] had broken but could not entirely destroy through the want of men, drawn up in order of battle',[11] while Wilson stated that the original charge had perforated, but not dislodged, the original formation. Other accounts state that a fresh force had come up, and it is not impossible that the original formation had been reinforced. It was evidently against this formation that Mansel's brigade finally attempted to act.

The actions of the main body of the Allied cavalry are unclear, but having lost contact with Otto's four advanced squadrons, it has been speculated that Mansel, hearing the sound of gunfire as Otto's charge went in, marched towards it. Either he was a very long distance behind, or had not especially hurried, for it appears that the disorganised French who remained on the field had had time to re-form, or to be reinforced, before Mansel's brigade came within range. Apparently the only certain fact is a report that the British brigade behaved badly, and that the 3rd Dragoon Guards lost 38 men and 46 horses killed, and nine men wounded or missing. It is conceivable that Mansel led his command into heavy French fire which so damaged the 3rd and caused the whole to retire in confusion, with the Royal Dragoons being the first to rally and cover the withdrawal of the remainder.[12] What is not in doubt is that the devastating charge of the 15th and the Austrian hussars was not supported as it should have been, or the entire French force would have been destroyed.

This left the 15th deprived of support and effectively four miles behind enemy lines. Pocklington formed a rearguard under Captain Ryan, who was accompanied by Butler, and an early plan shows the 15th as having deployed a screen of skirmishers to bring up the rear, to discourage pursuit. The course of the withdrawal is another matter which is unclear; Wilson stated that they retired at a steady trot, without interruption, but another account has it that 'every inch of ground was disputed',[13] which must be less likely, for if there were French troops on all sides, as Wilson suggests, the tired little party of Britons would surely have been overwhelmed.

Arriving again in the vicinity of Villers-en-Cauchies, Pocklington found his way barred by the re-formed and possibly reinforced French infantry through which they had recently ridden, and with more French troops now pressing up hard from Bouchain. The scarlet coats of Mansel's brigade were visible in the distance, beyond the French line, but obviously they could be of little use in helping extricate the 15th from what was potentially the most hazardous situation to have faced them that morning. After a quick conference with Ryan, Pocklington determined to charge once again, first against their pursuers to check the force which had followed them from Bouchain; and then, wheeling, the 15th once more hurled themselves against the line of infantry. Again they received some musketry, but on this occasion it was largely ineffective; probably because those Frenchmen who had been ridden-through by the initial charge, although re-assembled, would still have been somewhat shaken by the experience and not especially willing to face yet another charge. Once again, the 15th burst through the line and rode to safety, bringing to an end one of the most remarkable and hard-fought actions in the whole history of cavalry service.

Just as the numbers engaged were hugely disproportionate, so were the casualties sustained; French losses were estimated at some 800 dead and 400 wounded (the Duke of York's dispatch somewhat over-estimated the carnage by stating that the French lost '1,200 men killed on the field'.[14] Set against this, the 15th lost some seventeen men and nineteen horses killed, an officer (Aylett), seventeen men and eighteen horses wounded, and the Austrians some 31 casualties.[15] Low though these casualties appear, they represent almost one-quarter of the entire strength. Three French guns were also brought off the field by the Allied detachment.

By any standards, this was a quite astonishing achievement, and even if the action had not been necessary, it being very unlikely that the Emperor would have been intercepted by the French, much was made of the victory, the Emperor deciding to honour all eight of the British officers involved. In his testimonial to Ryan, written in December 1797, Count Maximilian de Merveldt implied that the 15th had saved the Emperor's life, and had 'rescued his Imperial Majesty from the danger that menaced his person, who, being on the road ... was cut off by the patroles [sic] of the enemy ... The courageous conduct of this regiment, animated by its brave officers, is so much more the meritorious, as the main column of the allied army did not arrive to its support; but this brave regiment, abandoned to itself, still relied on its own valour, attacked the enemy, so much stronger, and whose bravery alone prevented the melancholy consequences above stated'.[16] In gratitude, the

Emperor announced that he would appoint all eight officers as knights of the Order of Maria Theresa, the principal Austrian decoration of military distinction, founded in 1757 as a reward for officers for especially heroic or meritorious service.

This did not immediately come to pass, for as Aylett was informed in March 1798, 'His Majesty regrets, that the statutes of the Order of Maria Theresa ... forbids [sic] the cross of this order, strictly national, being conferred on officers so worthy of being decorated with it; but wishing to give you, as also your honourable companions, a public mark of his particular esteem, his Majesty has commanded a medal to be struck, to perpetuate the remembrance of this brilliant action, and has ordered me to offer to them the only impressions which have been struck, except one, which is placed in the Imperial Cabinet of Vienna'.[17] Suspended from a gold chain, the medal was circular, struck in gold, and bore a portrait bust of the Emperor on the obverse; the reverse was lettered 'FORTI.BRITANNO / IN EXERCITU.FOED / AD CAMERACUM / XXIV.APR.MDCCXCIV'. Permission for the medal to be worn in uniform was granted by the King in January 1798. Following a change in the constitution of the Order of Maria Theresa, the knighthood of the order was finally bestowed upon the eight officers in November 1800. This in itself was a singular honour, for between the inauguration of the decoration and the end of the 19th century, no more than two crosses were awarded to any Austrian regiment for a single action, which presumably reflects the extraordinary feat performed by the 15th.

It is even more remarkable when compared with the honours bestowed upon Austrian officers who took part in the action. One cross of the Order of Maria Theresa was awarded, to Captain Meschéry (who was also greatly distinguished in the action at Beaumont, two days later), and the same was proposed for Sentkeresky. It was debated by a twenty-strong panel at headquarters, only seven of whom voted for Sentkeresky receiving the Order; the other thirteen (including Otto) voted against, and thus denied the highest honour, Sentkeresky had to be satisfied with a lesser decoration. This was a considerable disappointment to the eight British officers, who ordered for him a presentation sword in memory of the action, and as a token of *their* esteem. The sword was sent to him in 1796, accompanied by letters from Pocklington and Ryan, dated two years to the day after the action, which expressed their admiration and respect for their Hungarian comrade. Retiring from active service in 1805, Sentkeresky (a Protestant, despite the largely Roman Catholic nature of the Hungarian officer corps) presented the sword to the college of the Reformed Church at Maros-Vásárhely.

Evidently the officers of the 15th thought that their men should receive some memento of the action, so in 1798 eleven silver-gilt medals were produced unofficially, and probably at the officers' expense, for presentation to quartermasters, sergeants and corporals who had been distinguished in the fight. Circular, and suspended from a ribbon of the Order of Maria Theresa (white with red edges), the medals' obverse was inscribed 'IMP.CAES. / FRANCISCUS.II / P.F. AUG.', and the reverse 'FORTITUDINE' (the motto of the Order of Maria Theresa) over 'VILLERS EN COUCHE / 24th APRIL 1794'.

The eight British officers enjoyed quite distinguished careers, using the title 'Sir' even though their knighthoods were Austrian. Probably the most famous was Robert Wilson, a mercurial character described by Wellington as 'a very slippery fellow', who was known for raising the Loyal Lusitanian Legion during the Peninsular War, for his career in radical politics, and for his military writings, not least concerning his service as British attaché to the Russian headquarters at the time of Napoleon's retreat from Moscow. Like Wilson, Aylett, Calcraft, Keir and Butler all achieved the rank of major-general, Calcraft being awarded the Gold Medal for Talavera.

The name of the action became one of the 15th Light Dragoons' (later 15th Hussars') most revered battle-honours, and like 'Emsdorf' was unique to the regiment; it first appeared in the *Army List* in 1818, misspelled as 'Villiers en Couche', the spelling only being corrected to 'Villers-en-Cauchies' in 1911. Further to commemorate the action, an Austrian pattern of lace was used by officers of the 15th Hussars.

A footnote to the action concerns the larger and more famous victory at Beaumont (or 'Le Cateau-Cambresis') two days later, on 26 April. In renewed hopes of raising the siege of Landrecies, Pichegru launched a major attack, commanded by General Chappuis, in two columns along and to the south of the Cambrai–Le Cateau road. Advancing under cover of fog and having pushed in the Allied outposts, the 10,000 French presented a major threat to the maintenance of the Allied siege. Viewing the advance, once the fog lifted, from Inchy, near Beaumont, Otto and the Duke of York realised that it had to be stopped as a matter of urgency, and determined to use their cavalry to accomplish it. Command was given to the 23-year-old Karl Philipp, Prince Schwarzenberg, who was later to enjoy a distinguished career, especially in leading the Austrian army against Napoleon in 1813–14. He formed his command of six Austrian squadrons, the Zeschwitz Cuirassiers, and twelve or thirteen British, including Mansel's brigade, into three lines. Using folds in the terrain to cover their approach, these attacked in succession upon the flank of the main French column, while a subsidiary force under Lieutenant-Colonel Stephanic, comprising two squadrons of the Austrian Ferdinand Hussars and two each of the British 7th and 11th Light Dragoons, attacked the smaller French column. Both French bodies were overturned and destroyed, losing some 4,000 casualties, 500 prisoners and 33 guns. The Allies lost only about 400 casualties; Schwarzenberg immediately received the cross of the Order of Maria Theresa (and the Zeschwitz Cuirassiers a gift of £20 from the Duke of York for each of the 22 guns they captured), but although the victory was a great success, it included a sad consequence of the action of two days previously. Smarting under suggestions of cowardice following his inaction at Villers-en-Cauchies, Mansel determined to disprove such imputations, and it was even reported that he swore not to return alive from the charge. Consequently, he dashed ahead of the Allied cavalry at Beaumont and was killed as he rode into the French force. The 3rd Dragoon Guards, his own regiment (Mansel having been appointed their lieutenant-colonel in 1775, prior to his promotion to major-general in 1790), was equally eager to disprove any suspicions of cowardice, to the extent that five of the six British officers who became casualties in the attack belonged to them, including Mansel's son, a captain, who was captured in a vain attempt to rescue his father.

Both actions at Beaumont and Villers-en-Cauchies demonstrated the offensive power of a cavalry attack, when delivered in the correct circumstances, and, most significantly, with the maintenance of discipline. Although more significant, the attack at Beaumont was the less remarkable, considering the number of troops involved and the more deliberate nature of the attack, which was handled most expertly by Schwarzenberg. The charge at Villers-en-Cauchies was the more extraordinary by virtue of the numbers involved; against such odds it would never have been considered feasible by all existing tenets of cavalry service. For the attack to succeed, and still more for the 15th to extricate themselves from virtually the midst of the French force, their discipline must have been of a high order, as confirmed by Wilson's statement that once the infantry line had been pierced, the 15th deliberately closed the gaps in its ranks, even though moving at a gallop, so as to hit the French cavalry in a cohesive body. With the more usual perception of a cavalry charge, in which order and cohesion were lost in the excitement of the moment, once through the infantry line the disorganised troopers would have been easy prey to a counter-charge by the French cavalry.

More remarkable, perhaps, was the fact that the charge was pressed home at all, against such huge odds, even if the troops had been spurred on by the belief (albeit mistaken) that the salvation of the Emperor was in their hands. This would imply either bravery of almost fanatical proportions, or a level of morale which refused to be shaken even when faced with a task which by conventional standards must have seemed little better than suicide; but the explanation is probably rather more commonplace. An early account of the action commented: 'It may be asked, how so small a body of men could be ordered to attack in the face of so formidable a force? This is answered by observing, that the French did not, at first, appear in such numbers.'[18] This must have been the case: that until the French cavalry unmasked the troops behind them, the Allied troopers must have believed themselves to be embarked upon a much less hazardous enterprise. By the time that they realised that their opponents were very much greater in numbers, it was too late to break off the attack. Having penetrated the infantry line, the realisation of, and exultation in, the extent of the achievement would presumably have been all that was needed to sustain the unit in its pursuit of the broken troops; while simple self-preservation would have aided their resolve to extricate themselves from the potential trap at the conclusion of the action. Perhaps regimental *esprit de corps* also had a part to play, with the inspiration of previous exploits behind them. It may not be coincidence that the song composed for the 15th on the anniversary commemoration of the battle began:

> 'Emsdorff's [*sic*] fame unfurl'd before ye . . .
> 'Mid the Battle's rage transported,
> Numbers vanish in your eyes;
> Into perils nobly courted,
> O'er the ranks of death ye rise.'[19]

NOTES

1. *Notes of Conversations with the Duke of Wellington*, 5th Earl Stanhope, London, 1888, p. 182.
2. *The British Military Library or Journal*, 1799, referred to it as 'the Affair of Landrecies'.
3. 'The 15th Light Dragoons at Villers-en-Cauchies, 24th March 1794', Sir Charles Oman, in *Journal of the Society for Army Historical Research*, XVII, 1938, pp. 12–14.
4. 'New Light on the Flanders Campaign of 1793: Contemporary Letters of Capt. J. G. Le Marchant', ed. Lieutenant-Colonel A. H. Burne, *SAHR Journal*, XXX, 1952, p. 117.

5. 'The City Militia' by 'P. H.', quoted in *The Honourable Artillery Company 1537-1926*, G. Goold Walker, London, 1926, pp. 189–90.
6. 'Sketch of the Action fought on the 24th of April, 1794', in *British Military Library or Journal*, London, 1799–1801, II, p. 176.
7. 'A Note on the 15th Light Dragoons and Villers-en-Cauchies Medal', E. J. Martin, in *Bulletin of the Military Historical Society*, VI, 1955, p. 43.
8. 'Sketch of the Action ...', *op. cit.*, p. 176.
9. *London Gazette*, 30 April 1794.
10. 'Sketch of the Action ...', p. 177.
11. Ibid.
12. This, at least, is the construction put upon it by Fortescue.
13. 'Sketch of the Action ...', p. 177.
14. *London Gazette*, 30 April 1794.
15. Slightly different statistics are given by Fortescue.
16. 'Copies of the Official Testimonies ...', *British Military Library or Journal*, London, 1799–1801, I, p. 106.
17. Ibid., p. 107.
18. 'Sketch of the Action ...', pp. 177–8.
19. 'Verses sung on the Anniversary Day ...', *British Military Library or Journal*, London, 1799–1801, I p. 324.

— 2 —

Victory from Defeat
MARENGO

14 June 1800

On 14 June 1807, when endeavouring to encourage his army on its march towards the Battle of Friedland, Napoleon encountered Marcellin de Marbot. 'Have you a good memory?', asked the Emperor; 'what anniversary is it today?' 'Marengo', replied Marbot. 'Yes', said Napoleon, 'and I am going to beat the Russians as I beat the Austrians'; and, never a man to miss an opportunity of recalling the past as an encouragement for the present, as he passed his troops he called out repeatedly, 'Today is a lucky day, the anniversary of Marengo.'[1] Whether the reference to luck was intentional or not, it was certainly accurate: for Marengo must have been among the luckiest days of his life, when victory was dependent more upon the resilience of his army, great good fortune, and the determination of his subordinates, than upon Napoleon's own military genius, despite his later attempts to claim the glory for himself by manipulating the facts.

One of Napoleon's best-known remarks was that every French soldier carried in his knapsack the baton of a Marshal of France; a typical but obvious exaggeration intended to convey the belief that ability was the only requisite for an individual wishing to rise to the highest rank. In early 1800 his own career seemed proof of the fact: from being an obscure captain of artillery in 1793, via a series of stunning victories and an abortive attempt to conquer the Middle East, by the end of 1799 he was established as effective ruler of France, First Consul (of three) in a system in which the other two were of little consequence. Nevertheless, First Consul Bonaparte needed a success to consolidate his position, for despite his earlier victories, France remained at war with the European powers constituting the Second Coalition, with active theatres of war on the 'German front' and in northern Italy. It was in the latter region, the scene of his triumphs in 1796–7, that Bonaparte decided to exercise his personal skill in the campaigning season of 1800.

The need for Bonaparte's personal intervention in northern Italy was urgent, for the campaigning of 1799 had undone virtually all of his earlier successes. Unlike earlier campaigns, the French and the satellite Italian states established in the wake of Bonaparte's successes were opposed in 1799 by more than just their previous Austrian enemies; for Tsar Paul I of Russia, generally regarded as insane and described by the British *Gentleman's Magazine* in December 1800 as 'odious in the mind of every impartial person',[2] had committed Russian troops to drive out the French. Commanded by the old and distinguished Field Marshal Alexander Vasilievitch Suvarov, Count of Suvarov-Riminsky, the Austro-Russian forces duly overran the territory held by the French, so that by the beginning of 1800 the only lands remaining in French hands were western Piedmont (the Italian border with southern France), and the coast from Nice to Genoa, where General André Masséna's French 'Army of Italy' still held out. They numbered about 40,000, and were faced by an Austrian army about 100,000 strong with a further 20,000 reserves, commanded by General Michael Melas. Fortunately for the French, there was no longer a Russian presence in northern Italy, or indeed in the war; despite Suvarov's successes in 1799, Allied reverses in Switzerland and the Netherlands, together with his fury over the British possession of Malta (of whose Order of St. John he had proclaimed himself head), had caused the unstable Tsar to withdraw his forces from the war.

Despite the threat to Masséna's Army of Italy, Bonaparte decided against reinforcing them directly, and instead created a new 'Army of Reserve', concentrated at Dijon, under the nominal command of General Louis-Alexandre Berthier. That officer, for many years Napoleon's chief of staff, was ideally suited for that rôle, but was undistinguished in independent command (somewhat ungenerously, Napoleon remarked that he 'was not fit to command five hundred men';[3] but he was appointed to lead the Army of Reserve because Bonaparte himself was officially prohibited from commanding troops by virtue of his position as First Consul. In effect, however, Bonaparte was in sole command of the army, and with it intended to trap Melas between his own forces and those of Masséna; but in the event Melas moved first, resuming the offensive and in April 1800 besieging Masséna in Genoa with some 22,000 men, the remaining French forces falling back beyond Nice. This virtually extinguished the French presence in northern Italy, but Melas' westward advance towards Nice actually benefited Bonaparte's plan, by lengthening the Austrian line of communications; although it was a plan requiring the greatest audacity if Bonaparte were to succeed.

Audacious the plan certainly was; for Bonaparte advanced into Italy by crossing the Alps from Switzerland, largely via the Great St.

Bernard Pass, which was regarded as the least practicable route, unsuitable for artillery and transport. Such physical difficulties as climate and terrain presented no obstacle to Bonaparte's determination and ingenuity; with the Alpine tracks and deep snow precluding the use of normal artillery carriages, the gun-barrels were laid in hollowed tree-trunks and dragged like sledges by teams of men. Gun-carriages were taken to pieces and manhandled; transport wagons were unloaded, sent through the pass empty and their contents carried on mule-back or by soldiers. Smaller detachments marched down the Little St. Bernard and Mount Cenis Passes, and reinforcements were dispatched down the Simplon and St. Gotthard Passes by the French commander of the 'Army of the Rhine' in Switzerland and Alsace, General Jean Moreau. Because Bonaparte's Alpine route was so unlikely, only weak Austrian detachments had been posted to cover the Italian end of the passes, which were easily pushed aside as Bonaparte and his army, after some ten days of struggling against snow and avalanches, fell (to use his own phrase) like a thunderbolt upon the Austrians. By late May some 40,000 Frenchmen were firmly established in Lombardy, in a position to move south and east to sever Melas' communications with Austria. It was for this manoeuvre, rather than what happened in the battle that resulted, that Bonaparte deserves greatest praise, for the transportation of his army through the Alps and into northern Italy was one of the most remarkable achievements of his career, testimony to organisational skill and strategic awareness of the highest order. The later stages of the operation, however, were to depend more upon the army's ordinary soldiers and some of its subordinate commanders, rather than upon the genius of its leader.

Learning of the arrival of the French from the Alpine passes, Melas hurried back from Nice, where he had been confronting what remained of the Army of Italy which had not accompanied Masséna to Genoa. The latter force, Bonaparte calculated, would occupy much of the Austrian resources, allowing him to destroy the remainder piecemeal as he advanced to Masséna's relief. As Bonaparte's army fanned out through Lombardy, however, news was received of Masséna's capitulation: on 4 June, after a most appalling siege, starvation had compelled the French to yield Genoa, Masséna being allowed to take his 8,000 survivors to rejoin the French forces around Nice. This considerably disordered Bonaparte's plans, for no longer did the Austrians have to maintain a large force to cover Genoa; but by this time Bonaparte's army was widely spread throughout Lombardy, considerably reducing the number of troops immediately available. Those accompanying Bonaparte himself were organised in three corps, commanded by General Jean Lannes, one of his closest friends, a colleague of considerable duration and a brave and accomplished officer; General Claude Victor, who was experienced in campaigning in Italy; and General Louis Desaix.

It was Louis Charles Antoine Desaix who was to play perhaps the most significant role in the eventual battle, and few would have doubted his suitability for such distinction. Born into an impoverished but noble family (the name was properly Desaix de Veygoux), he was commissioned into the French army in 1783, but embraced the principles of the Revolution; a British comment to explain what might have been considered the abandonment of his birthright was that he was simply 'a good citizen [who] loved and respected his country even in the persons of those who overwhelmed it with their acts of injustice'.[4] Desaix's military talents were soon recognised, and after excellent service in 1795–6 his fame was equal to that of Bonaparte and Moreau; but he became a loyal follower of the former and accompanied him to Egypt. In his conquest of Upper Egypt 'he acquired a distinction more honourable than the triumph of arms, for the inhabitants gave him the title of "the Just Sultan"'.[5] He was detained in Egypt for some time, and only joined Bonaparte's army on 11 June, by which time the first major action against the main Austrian army had taken place.

Responding to Bonaparte's arrival, Melas marched northwards to Turin; and then, learning of the threat to his communications, advanced eastwards and ordered a concentration around Alessandria. On 9 June Lannes, commanding the advance-guard of Bonaparte's army, was marching south from Pavia when unexpectedly he encountered the Austrian General Peter Ott at Montebello. With only some 6,000 men against Ott's 17,000, Lannes was repulsed, but Victor's arrival swung the action towards the French, and Ott retired upon Alessandria. It was against the Austrian forces at this place that Bonaparte directed the movements of his army, ordering a concentration at the village of Marengo, a couple of miles east of Alessandria.

If Bonaparte's planning is open to criticism, it should be noted that he possessed only limited knowledge of his enemy's position. When concentrating around Marengo on 13 June, his reconnaissance was so imperfect that he could have had no clear idea of the size of the Austrian force on the far side of the River Bormida; indeed, the fact that they were in Alessandria, and not in the plain to the east of the Bormida, where the terrain was ideal for the superior force of Austrian cavalry, must have convinced Bonaparte that they had no fixed intent to engage him. The retirement of the Austrians over the Bormida into Alessandria upon the appearance of the French, and reports that the Austrians had destroyed the bridges over the river must have confirmed him in this view. In reality, the bridges had not been destroyed – three were in place – and this failure in reconnaissance caused Bonaparte to weaken his position even further. Convinced that Melas was intending to retire, on the afternoon of 13 June Bonaparte ordered Desaix south, in command of Boudet's division, with the aim of blocking Melas' route to Genoa; and he determined to send Lapoype's division north, to cover the crossing over the Po. When these detachments were deducted, Bonaparte was left with less than 24,000 men and 23 guns, against which Melas could deploy about 31,000 Austrians with a massive artillery force of about 100 guns.

On 13 June, Bonaparte's vanguard halted when it came under fire from Austrian artillery on the far bank of the Bormida, and no further action occurred as a violent rain storm beat down. Jean-Roche Coignet, a grenadier in the French 96th *Demi-Brigade de Ligne*,[6] wrote of the misery experienced by the French army at this time, weary and half-starving after their great march, and of their intense disappointment at finding their rations, when they finally arrived, consisted of nothing but damp and mouldy bread, which starvation forced them to consume. He also told a story of how on that day the 24th *Demi-Brigade Légère* (like Coignet's, a unit of Chambarlhac's division) was sent forward to contact the Austrians retiring across the Bormida, and was left in a deliberately exposed position as a punishment for misbehaviour at Montebello. In the evening the survivors of the 24th heaped insults upon the rest of the division for having left them unsupported for so long; but, added Coignet, their losses 'did not prevent their fighting still better the next day'.[7] The pouring rain of that evening must have been thoroughly unpleasant for the troops, in their exposed position, devoid of shelter; but along with other factors, it may have been instrumental in saving the day on the morrow, for by causing the River Scrivia to flood, it delayed Desaix's march south, so that he made less progress than Bonaparte had intended.

Throughout the night of 13/14 June the French forward picquets reported movement in Alessandria, but these were taken as evidence that the Austrians were packing up before retiring. Bonaparte spent some of the night with Victor's men, camped around Marengo, but finally retired to bed in the belief that his army was safe. Lannes' corps was bivouacked farther east, and beyond them was Bonaparte's Consular Guard and Monnier's Division, that part of Desaix's corps which had

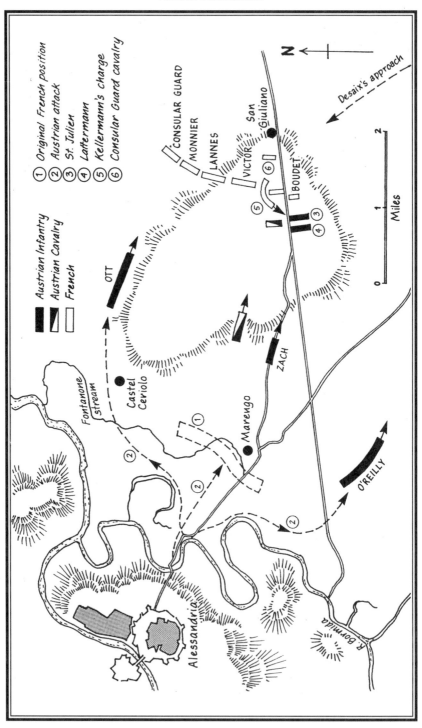

remained behind when their commander and Boudet's division was sent south. Should any action begin, it was upon Victor's corps and the (comparatively) small cavalry force of Joachim Murat that the first blow would fall.

When the blow *did* fall, it came as a complete surprise, and indeed it was a very considerable time before Bonaparte realised what was happening. Fearing a union between Bonaparte's army and the remainder of the Army of Italy advancing from around Nice, and desirous of immediately re-opening his communications to the east, Melas had decided to risk everything in an all-out attack upon Bonaparte's army. Accordingly, preparations were made through the night of 13/14 June – the sounds being heard by Victor's picquets – and early in the morning of 14 June the entire Austrian army was put into motion, marching out from Alessandria towards the bridges over the Bormida, and the bridgehead on the far bank which was still in Austrian hands. In numerical terms, Melas had an advantage of about 29 per cent over Bonaparte, but more significant was the huge Austrian preponderance in artillery, and the fact that whereas the Austrians were concentrated in order of battle, the French were scattered and unprepared. Once over the Bormida, the Austrians deployed in three columns: a central column under Melas in person, with his chief of staff, General Zach; a column under General O'Reilly, which moved south to form the Austrian right wing; and some 7,500 men under Ott which formed the Austrian left wing, and advanced upon the village of Castel Ceriolo, north of the French dispositions, which Melas believed (erroneously) to be in French hands.

Sunday, 14 June, dawned fine and clear, and the Austrians marched at first light. Coignet, who was not with the French picquets but with Victor's main body around Marengo itself, reported that skirmish-fire was heard as early as three o'clock, and that the French drums beat to arms at four; but other sources state that it was as late as six a.m. before the Austrian artillery opened upon the French position. Nevertheless it was not until about nine o'clock that the Austrian attack got into full swing because the cramped position around the bridgehead made rapid deployment difficult. O'Reilly's force, before swinging south to form the Austrian right wing, pushed straight on and drove back the forward French elements, enabling the first of Melas' main body to deploy under cover of O'Reilly's firing-line. This delay between the initial advance and the first serious fighting should have given the French the time to respond; but so convinced was Bonaparte that Melas could have no really aggressive intention, that he refused to believe that the

43

Austrian advance was anything more than diversionary skirmishing, to cover a retreat. Accordingly, Bonaparte sent off Lapoype's command as planned, and wrote to Desaix urging him to press on in a southerly direction. This lack of appreciation of the true situation, perhaps excusable on the grounds of insufficient reconnaissance, condemned Bonaparte's army to a desperate day's fighting, and brought his own career to the brink of disaster.

Initially, the brunt of the fighting was borne by the divisions of Victor's corps, Gardanne's on the right and Chambarlhac's on the left, fifteen battalions together numbering less than 9,000 men with only five guns, holding a line around Marengo roughly along the steep-sided Fontanone stream which ran north to south between Marengo and the Bormida, and at first quite unsupported. The fighting was intense, and it is surprising that these units were able to hold on so long, giving barely any ground. Coignet's account gives an indication of their ordeal, for his 96th *Demi-Brigade* was engaged from the first main salvo from the Austrian artillery. Coignet was very unimpressed by the conduct of his divisional general, Jacques Antoine, baron de Chambarlhac de Laubespin; as a shell burst amid Coignet's company and killed seven of his comrades, the general's orderly was struck dead by a bullet; whereupon Chambarlhac 'galloped off at full speed. We saw him no more all day.'[8] (Coignet's comments provide a reminder of the effect exercised by a general's presence, for the sizes of such formations were sufficiently small for a general's actions to be noted by most of his men.) Instead, a little general with big moustaches came up – Coignet never discovered his identity – and ordered the 96th's grenadiers forward to act as skirmishers, urging them not to halt even when loading, but to blunt the attack until reinforcements arrived. He promised to recall the grenadiers by drum-beat when fresh troops had come up, but this he failed to do; consequently Coignet and his comrades were fired upon by Austrians in front and by the main French line in their rear. Coignet hid behind a tree to escape the cross-fire as musket-balls so shattered the willow that branches fell on top of him. When the French firing-line advanced he was able to rejoin his unit, but his grenadier company was no more: mown down by both sides, Coignet counted only fourteen survivors out of 170. The company captain, with nothing left to command and wounded in the arm, attached himself to the moustachioed general as ADC for the rest of the day.

For at least two hours the outnumbered French kept the Austrians at bay, the fighting ebbing and flowing as the firing-line swayed back, then forward. The first Austrian division, that of General Haddick, suffered heavily as it crossed the Fontanone stream, and Haddick was mortally wounded; but as one division retired, another took up the assault. Coignet's regiment was at first in a field of standing wheat, which the flashes of musketry set ablaze, the flames running up the stalks of wheat and causing some men's cartridge boxes to explode; this caused much commotion, and the French had to fall back to re-form their shrinking ranks. They fired away their ammunition, but more was distributed; and the constant firing caused the musket-barrels to become so hot that they dare not load any more, for fear that the hot metal would cause a premature ignition of the powder. Water canteens were not issued to the French army, so those wishing to carry a drink with them had to provide their own flask or gourd; but with raging thirst afflicting men in action (partly the result of the constant presence of gunpowder in the mouth, from the biting open of cartridges), even those who had water might not have had sufficient to cool their musket-barrels, or would not have wasted so precious a commodity in this way. As Coignet reported, only one alternative was left: the soldiers urinated on their muskets to reduce the temperature to permit them to continue to load and fire, and this would also have had the effect of freeing the barrel and lock of burned powder, the residue of which could clog up the action after protracted firing.

By mid-morning the fighting was so fierce that despite any preconceived ideas concerning Melas' intentions, it was now obvious to all that this was a major attack, so Lannes' corps and Murat's cavalry was moved forward to bolster the line. Although styled a corps, Lannes' force consisted of but one division, that of General Watrin, twelve battalions strong, in all some 5,000 men, and it took post at the right of the existing firing-line. At about 11 a.m., when Lannes' men had been in action for perhaps an hour, Bonaparte arrived from the rear to assess the situation. What he found must have appalled him: for although the line was still holding, casualties were severe and away to the right, in the direction of Castel Ceriolo, there was imminent danger that Ott's flanking movement would take the French at their most vulnerable point, and roll up their line from the right flank, while the Austrian cavalry ranged into the rear of the French position, severing their communications. Bonaparte's very appearance put heart into the French troops – Coignet remarks that 'we felt ourselves strong again',[9] but even his inspiring presence could not forestall the disaster facing the army.

At last realising his error, Bonaparte sent ADCs in an urgent bid to recall both Lapoype and Desaix; it was said that his summons to the latter betrayed his sense of desperation by imploring 'for God's sake come up'. The plea to Lapoype was in vain: the messenger did not reach him until six p.m., by which time it was too late for him to be of any assistance.

Some relief to the pressure on Victor's men was provided by the French cavalry brigade on the left flank, commanded by François Etienne Kellermann, son of François Christophe de Kellermann, duc de Valmy, one of the greatest heroes of the Revolutionary Wars, whose victory at Valmy saved the infant French republic and whose reward, long after the end of his active career, was to be the appointment as Marshal by Napoleon. His son François Etienne was unimpressive in looks ('a little man, of unhealthy and insignificant appearance, with a clever look, but false'),[10] and later having an unsavoury reputation as an unbridled looter, but though not the most famous of Napoleon's cavalry leaders was probably the most capable. Allied to personal bravery and the ability to inspire his men, his most important characteristic was 'that quickness of perception which enabled him to seize the exact moment for throwing his command on the enemy'.[11] That command was only small – about 800 in all[12] – to which were added some 320 men of the 8th Dragoons from the other cavalry brigade, which were placed under his orders. An Austrian cavalry force having crossed the Fontanone above Marengo with the intention of attacking the French left flank, at about noon Kellermann engaged them with the 8th Dragoons, who after initial success were repelled; he then led forward his own brigade and drove away the Austrians, temporarily relieving some of the pressure upon Victor's embattled men.

Although Victor's corps was nearing the end of its endurance, Bonaparte decided to commit his last resources on the extreme right of his position, to prevent the Austrians from falling upon his right flank. He ordered up the Consular Guard to extend the right of the existing line, and Monnier's division to move yet further to the right towards Castel Ceriolo. Including its cavalry, the Consular Guard was less than 1,250 strong; the infantry, less than 1,000, but they were regarded as the élite of the army, and came on as such, marching in square formation, the men singing in accompaniment to their band, 'On va leur percer le flanc'. Distinguished by the bearskin caps which became the symbol of Napoleon's Imperial Guard (as the Consular Guard was re-titled in 1804), their demeanour was as 'a redoubt built of granite'.[13] So impressive was their conduct that it was said when Austrian officers asked of prisoners, how many were the men in the large caps, they believed it true when they were told that there were 4,000 of them. Probably never

46

had the Guard more deserved the epithet accorded them by Coignet on another occasion, 'a marching rampart'.[14] Although they suffered severely from Austrian fire, they eased the pressure on what had been the right flank (Watrin's division), and allowed Monnier's eight battalions (some 3,600 men) to deploy on the extreme right.

Along the front, fighting subsided temporarily as the Austrians re-grouped for another attack; but Monnier's attack on Castel Ceriolo, which stopped Ott's flanking movement in its tracks, at about 2 p.m., coincided with the loss, at last, of Marengo village. Pressed to breaking-point and beyond, and almost out of ammunition, Victor's men retired in disorder, withdrawing towards the village of San Giuliano, which lay on the road east from Marengo. Had Austrian cavalry been able to get among them at this stage great slaughter would have ensued, but Kellermann covered their retreat by an orderly withdrawal of his cavalry, dropping back troop by troop. Lannes' left flank was uncovered by Victor's retreat, so his men had to fall back as well, at first in echelon of squares in good order ('Never, perhaps, did the most experienced officer witness such regularity in movement, precision in evolution, or commanding firmness throughout every part of the retreating line';[15] yet when the Austrian artillery began to rake these formations, they too began to disintegrate, and the cry *Tout est perdu – sauve qui peut!'* ('All is lost – every man for himself!') was heard. Thanks in part to Bonaparte's activity – 'The First Consul ... ran along the ranks, exhorting the soldiers to regain their ground, and at length succeeded in stopping the retrograde movement of the line'[16] – they managed to rally around San Giuliano, behind some troops who had remained steady, and covered by the cavalry.

During this stage of the battle, Coignet had his second miraculous escape: an Austrian cavalryman sabred him, the blow landing across the back of his neck and shoulder, cutting off his epaulette and pieces of his coat and shirt, nicking the skin but being mostly absorbed by his thick queue of hair, which was almost cut through. Stunned, Coignet fell in a ditch as the whole of Kellermann's cavalry charged over him. Abandoning all his kit and musket, Coignet jumped up as Kellermann's troopers retired, grabbed hold of a horse's tail and was pulled along for some way before he collapsed again; but when thus dragged out of the immediate zone of combat, he recovered his breath, re-equipped himself and rejoined his comrades. One of his unit's captains, amazed to see him alive, minus his queue and with his shoulder laid bare, shook his hand and told him to go to the rear with the rest of the walking wounded; but

Coignet declared that he preferred to stay in the ranks and take his revenge on the Austrians for the beating he had taken.

Although Bonaparte spent this period attempting to infuse his troops with the will to stand firm, by the inspiring nature of his presence, Coignet glimpsed him in a moment of contemplation, disconsolately sitting on a bank and idly flicking up stones with the end of his riding-whip, before remounting and resuming his gallop along the ranks, encouraging and cajoling.

Conforming to the retreat of the left and centre, the Consular Guard and Monnier's division fell back from Castel Ceriolo; as ammunition ran low, a grenadier named Brabant began to load and fire an abandoned 4-pounder cannon; covering the withdrawal of his comrades he continued to fire into the Austrian ranks until, with one hand shattered, he grew too weak from loss of blood to serve the gun any longer. (Contrary to some accounts, and to Napoleon's 'revised' official version, which stated that Castel Ceriolo was held deliberately as a pivot upon which the rest of the army could swing, the early accounts make it clear that the right wing *did* retire: 'they were necessarily obliged to evacuate the village. During their retreat in the rear of the army, whose movements they strictly followed, they were surrounded by detached parties of the enemy's cavalry ...')[17] During this retreat, the 72nd *Demi-Brigade* of Monnier's division was retiring in line when menaced by Austrian cavalry from both front and rear; the front two ranks held firm and the rear rank faced about, so that both attacks were driven off.

To Melas it seemed that the battle was won, and, tired and elderly as he was, having been in the saddle since midnight and slightly wounded, he handed over command to his chief of staff, Zach, and returned to Alessandria to rest and dispatch messages of victory. Thereupon a further lull fell over the battlefield, as the Austrians again reorganised to march in column down the road to San Giuliano, confident that the defeated French would be unable to resist.

At this moment came Bonaparte's salvation. His second message to Desaix, imploring him to return, reached him at about 1 p.m., Desaix not having made the expected progress due to the delay caused by the swollen River Scrivia. Some sources state that Desaix had already reversed his course upon hearing the cannonade from Marengo, and was already 'marching towards the sound of gunfire' when the message arrived; but whatever the case, he pressed on to Bonaparte's relief by forced march. In expectation of his arrival, Bonaparte sent Louis-François Lejeune, the renowned artist, who was serving as a staff officer, to see if Desaix were approaching; riding south, he found Desaix's command 'marching as gaily as if they were bound for a ball'.[18] Outdistancing his men, Desaix galloped up, mud spattered, and greeted Bonaparte at about 3 p.m. 'What do you think?', asked the First Consul. Desaix pulled out his watch and consulted it. 'This battle is completely lost,' he said, 'but there is time to win another.'[19]

Bonaparte continued to urge his troops to hang on, riding down the line and calling to them that they had retreated far enough, that help was at hand, and, 'Mes enfants, remember that it is my practice to sleep upon the field of battle';[20] in other words, he wished to bivouac where they were, and not retreat another step. The promises of reinforcement had the French troops straining to espy them; then, suddenly, 'Finally came the joyful cry, "Here they are, here they are!" That splendid division came up, carrying arms. It was like a forest swayed by the wind ...'[21] This description by Coignet exemplifies the relief with which the French army greeted the appearance of Desaix at the head of Boudet's division, marching at full speed as if on parade, 'carrying arms' with muskets held vertically at the shoulder, the upright musket-barrels swaying with the movement like trees moving in the breeze. The division consisted of only three *demi-brigades*, 9th Light, 30th and 59th Line, nine battalions of some 5,300 men, who must have been half-exhausted after their day's marching and counter-marching; but they put heart into the French army as they took station on the left flank of Bonaparte's new line; the shattered units of Victor and Lannes held the centre, with the Guard and Monnier's division, having retired from Castel Ceriolo, holding the right. As the Austrians formed up to advance in column – marching with ordered arms 'as though they were on their way home',[22] so confident were they that the battle was won and that the French were in flight – and as their attack would proceed down the road to San Giuliano, it was plain that Desaix's men would bear the brunt. They formed in echelon and in *ordre mixte*, a deployment in which line and column alternated to maximise firepower while not sacrificing the impetus of the column; and, importantly, they were not unsupported. Kellermann's command – or what remained of it, after his earlier charges – was at hand, and for the first time in the battle there was also a concentration of French artillery.

The French artillery commander was Auguste de Marmont, who at the age of 26 was already a *général de brigade* and a close associate of the First Consul. Upon Bonaparte's order he collected some guns from the artillery reserve, reinforced by eight pieces which had come up with

Desaix. As the Austrian columns advanced, led by Zach with the brigades of Lattermann and Saint-Julien (the former a concentration of grenadiers), Marmont's improvised battery opened upon them, causing considerable havoc; Saint-Julien's brigade broke but Lattermann's grenadiers continued on. After some minutes, Desaix led his troops forward, at the head of the 9th *Demi-Brigade Légère*. Almost immediately he was shot through the heart, conceivably by an accidental shot from his own side. There were stories that he exclaimed 'Dead!', or, more theatrically, said to the son of the Consul Lebrun, 'Tell the First Consul that I die with regret, because I feel that I have not done enough to be remembered by posterity.'[23] Such stories are probably apocryphal; according to the surgeons who embalmed the body, the shot had so shattered the heart that they doubted if he could have spoken even a single word. Although it has been stated that Desaix's death was not at first noticed, the loss of their leader appears to have shaken severely the men following, and one unit – perhaps the 9th *Demi-Brigade Légère*, though Marmont thought it was the 30th – hesitated and even began to recoil.

As the smoke temporarily rolled away Marmont saw a body of troops some fifty paces from the disordered French; at first he thought them friendly, but then realised that they were Austrians. He directed part of his artillery – perhaps as few as four guns – to pour salvo after salvo into their flank. Lejeune thought that the Austrians compounded their own difficulties, by pressing forward too closely, leaving insufficient room for manoeuvre, and presenting a fatally closely packed target. The column staggered, as Boudet's division steadied and resumed its advance; and at that moment an Austrian ammunition wagon was hit and exploded, throwing their ranks into even greater confusion.

At this critical moment, when the fate of the battle hung in the balance, Kellermann made his most decisive charge. Having been hovering around the French left flank, he wheeled his surviving troops behind Boudet's left and centre and erupted upon the left flank of the wavering column, and swept away the Austrian ranks in chaos. Whether by luck or design, the charge was delivered at exactly the most effective moment; a few moments earlier or later would not have had the same devastating effect. Virtually the whole of Zach's central column dissolved, as Kellermann rallied, then charged a body of Austrian cavalry and sent them tumbling back into the main body, carrying with them ever greater confusion. Kellermann himself described the action: 'The Austrians advanced to follow up their success, in all the disorder and security of victory. I see it; I am in the midst of them; they lay down their arms. The whole did not occupy so much time as it has taken me to write these six lines.'[24] Kellermann rallied again, quickly requested that Bonaparte reinforce him with the mounted part of the Consular Guard, and uniting these to the survivors of his own command charged again, completing the total rout of the Austrian centre, as the exhausted French infantry made a final effort to support the drive against the enemy's centre. Nothing could stop the rout; the ardour with which the French pressed the attack may be surmised by Coignet's remark that, as the drums began to beat the charge, instead of raising the usual cheer or shout, the French gave forth a howl of fury. Zach was captured in the first charge, thus depriving the Austrians of their commander at the crucial moment. Weidenfeld's grenadier brigade managed to blunt the French pursuit, but the remainder fled for their lives, back through Marengo, over the ground so recently fought over, and towards the bridgehead over the Bormida.

No such catastrophe overtook the right and left columns of the Austrian army, but when they observed the collapse of their centre, they too retired; Ott in particular, on the Austrian left flank, withdrew in good order and safely resisted the pressure from Bonaparte's advancing right flank. The Austrian flanking columns eventually formed an organised rearguard to cover the bridgehead, although Bonaparte's army was too exhausted to mount an offensive against it; but the main (central) column of the Austrian army was in irremediable chaos. They packed into the bridgehead with such a crush that the crossing became choked, and some of the fugitives threw themselves into the water; Coignet remembered that when the French pursuit was called to a halt at about nine in the evening, the leading elements could hear the cries of drowning men, which so horrified him that it became one of his most vivid memories of that tumultuous day. Some flavour of the panic in the Austrian ranks may be gleaned from the remarks of an officer of the 28th *Demi-Brigade* of Watrin's division, who had been captured earlier in the day and was swept along in the rout: 'I have witnessed some defeats in the course of my military career, but I never saw anything that resembled this', as the crush to cross the Bormida bridge was so great that he was actually lifted off his feet and borne along for as much as 500 paces.[25]

As evening and the exhaustion of the French troops brought an end to the slaughter, the extent of the Austrian defeat became clear. Melas had lost about 14,000 men, including 8,000 prisoners, and the morale of the remainder must have been fatally shaken. The French army had the satisfaction of victory, but their initial emotion as fighting ended must have been one of utter weariness, the main body having experienced a day-long fight, a withdrawal and then an advance, and Boudet's division a protracted forced march before being hurled into the battle. Coignet, who had had nothing all day save a mouthful of spirits given him by his captain, was one of the luckiest; at 10 p.m. he was invited to share the captain's supper as he had a gash over his eye dressed, where an Austrian bayonet had caught him during the final advance, and then had his mangled queue put in order, for the loss of part of his hair seems to have been what most upset him. Next morning he was able to repay his captain's kindness with a loaf of bread, cadged from the Consular Guard (which always had the best rations), and on the way passed the field hospital where the Guard's casualties were undergoing amputations; it was bad enough, he remarked, to hear the screams and cries all around, but even worse was the sight of the battlefield, where French soldiers and Austrian prisoners were dragging dead men and horses into piles for burning, to avert the pestilence associated with decaying bodies. It was reported that as he passed groups of wounded, Bonaparte remarked that 'It would be a satisfaction to participate in the pains of these soldiers, and one regrets not being wounded to have that consolation.'[26] The story is probably apocryphal, like so many reported in the immediate aftermath of battles; for none could seriously have expressed such views with sincerity if they had seen stricken soldiers being treated in the charnel-house of a hospital. The French had lost about a quarter of their total force.

Melas held a council of war, which decided that further resistance was hopeless; a temporary armistice was granted by Bonaparte (who as head of state had complete power to conclude treaties), on condition that the Bormida bridgehead was surrendered. On 15 June this agreement was turned into the Convention of Alessandria, by which Melas surrendered all remaining Austrian holdings in Piedmont and Lombardy, and withdrew his forces eastwards, beyond the River Mincio. On 16 June, the day before Bonaparte left the army for Paris, and a week before the Army of Reserve was officially absorbed into the Army of Italy, the heroes of Marengo paraded before their chief, decked out in oak-leaves as a substitute for the laurels of victory. Coignet reported that General Chambarlhac re-appeared for this parade, but took himself off when the 96th fired a volley in his direction! (Nevertheless, he was promoted to *général de division* in 1803, and served in a number of staff appointments, being elevated to the rank of baron in 1811, retiring in 1815 after he refused to serve under the Bourbons.)

As Bonaparte remarked, in one day he had recovered Italy; but Marengo was not an entirely decisive blow, for the war continued until Moreau won his great victory at Hohenlinden (3 December 1800), which, together with pressure from the revitalised Army of Italy advancing towards the Julian Alps, persuaded the Emperor to sue for peace (25 December), concluded on 9 February 1801 by the Peace of Luneville. For Bonaparte, the results were even more rewarding; in August 1802 he was proclaimed Consul for Life, but a short step from his coronation as Napoleon I, Emperor of the French, in December 1804. Without Marengo, it is unlikely that these events would have occurred, perhaps proving the veracity of Napoleon's usual question hearing the merits of a commander: 'But is he lucky?'. Few generals of the period can have benefited more from good luck than Bonaparte himself at Marengo.

Perhaps it was not entirely out of character that in later years Napoleon endeavoured to adjust the official record in order to portray himself in the most favourable light. Successive revisions of the authorised account of the battle implied that it had all gone to plan, and that by using the Guard and Monnier's division as a pivot, Bonaparte had deliberately fallen back before the Austrians to draw them into a trap.

The dispatch of Desaix away from Marengo was reported as a deliberate ploy, to permit him to proceed south or return to Marengo if an action developed there; the fact that he was recalled almost in panic when a battle began unexpectedly was quietly concealed. Just as the retirement of the right flank was re-written so that Castel Ceriolo could be regarded as a deliberately held pivot, so the identity of its commander was changed in the later official accounts. The unfortunate Monnier fell out of favour with Napoleon, so in the official version one of his brigadiers, Claude Carra Saint-Cyr (who had actually led only the two battalions of the 19th *Demi-Brigade Légère* which constituted his brigade), was elevated to the rank of right flank commander.[27]

Similarly, Bonaparte was less than generous to those subordinates who were really responsible for his salvation. He acknowledged Kellermann's contribution on the evening of the battle, but in a somewhat cursory manner, and then pointedly congratulated Jean-Baptiste Bessières, commander of the Consular Guard cavalry, implying that it was Bonaparte's own guards who had accomplished the greatest success. Kellermann was said to have remarked that he was glad the First Consul was pleased, for it (by implications Kellermann's actions) would put a crown on Bonaparte's head. Kellermann remained resentful and repeated this claim in a letter, which fact was divulged to Bonaparte. It may have cost

Kellermann his promotion to Marshal; yet whenever his rapacious conduct was reported in the future, Napoleon would remark that he could remember nothing but Marengo, so perhaps Kellermann's charge did receive more recompense than its aggrieved leader cared to admit.

When adjusting the account to make Desaix's march to Marengo appear to be part of the plan, Napoleon was more generous towards the fallen hero; the cynic might have remarked that he could afford to be, a dead hero no longer being a rival, even though Napoleon later stated that Desaix 'lived only for noble ambition and true glory: his character was formed on the true ancient model', and that his death was the greatest loss that he (Napoleon) could have sustained, for 'they would always have preserved a good understanding between them. Desaix would have been faithful with secondary rank, and would have remained ever devoted and faithful'.[28] Indeed, so noble was Desaix's character regarded that even in the land of his enemies it could be remarked that he was 'esteemed by the French Soldiers, honoured by the Austrians, and loved by all who knew him'.[29]

Marengo may be seen as the beginning of Napoleon's greatest period, for a defeat there might have prevented him from ever becoming emperor. It could be argued that the successes which flowed from Marengo were not undeserved, despite the fact that Napoleon had been surprised, had performed unimpressively tactically and had been saved by good fortune and by the abilities of his subordinates; for whatever the tactical failings, the campaign was a strategic triumph at least as far as the audacious Alpine crossing was concerned. In the final analysis, however, the victory and its far-reaching consequences depended less upon the inspiration of genius and the timely intervention of Kellermann, Marmont and the lamented Desaix, as upon the dogged courage of men like Grenadier Brabant and by the troops of Boudet's division who fought a battle after an exhausting forced march. Bonaparte's Order of the Day of 24 June proclaimed that the day of Marengo would remain famous throughout history; despite its commemoration as a place-name as far away as Wisconsin, it is perhaps a little bizarre, and surely a little sad, that it is known best from the dish 'chicken à la Marengo', a concoction of chicken, tomatoes and mushrooms cooked in oil, based upon the ingredients which formed Bonaparte's supper on the night of the battle.

NOTES

1. *The Memoirs of Baron de Marbot*, trans. A. J. Butler, London, 1913, I, p. 225.
2. *Gentleman's Magazine*, December, 1800, p. 1195.

3. *The Court and Camp of Bonaparte*, anon., London, 1831, p. 242.
4. *The Monthly Review*, London, 1804, p. 541.
5. Ibid.
6. From 1794 the term *Demi-Brigade* had replaced 'Regiment' as the name of the basic infantry unit, 'regiment' supposedly having monarchist associations which were eliminated after the Revolution.
7. *The Note-Books of Captain Coignet*, ed. Hon. Sir John Fortescue, London, 1928, p. 74.
8. Ibid., p. 74
9. Ibid., p. 76.
10. *The Recollections of Colonel de Gonneville*, ed. C. M. Yonge, London, 1875, I, p. 250.
11. *Achievements of Cavalry*, General Sir Evelyn Wood, London, 1897, p. 24.
12. Statistics vary, some mentioning only half that figure, although the latter may in some cases relate to reduced numbers later in the battle, after casualties had been incurred.
13. 'Other Interesting Particulars respecting the Battle of Marengo', by 'C. J.', in *British Military Library or Journal*, London, 1799–1801, II, p. 422.
14. Coignet, p. 154.
15. 'French Account of the Battle of Marengo', by 'Citizen Foudras', in *British Military Library or Journal*, London, 1799–1801, II, p. 419.
16. 'French Account', p. 420.
17. Ibid.
18. *Memoirs of Baron Lejeune*, trans. & ed. Mrs. A. Bell, London, 1897, I, p. 21.
19. *Memoirs of Napoleon Bonaparte*, M. de Bourienne, London, 1836, I, p. 361; this suggests that the time was about 2 p.m., whereas it was actually about an hour later; see, for example, *The Campaigns of Napoleon*, D. G. Chandler, London, 1967, p. 293. Other sources suggest that it was as late as 4 p.m., for example Wood, *op. cit.*, p. 35.
20. 'Other Interesting Particulars', p. 422.
21. Coignet, p. 78.
22. Ibid., p. 79
23. 'Other Interesting Particulars', p. 422.
24. *History of Europe from the Commencement of the French Revolution to the Restoration of the Bourbons*, Sir Archibald Alison, Bt., Edinburgh & London, 1860, V, p. 380; the source of Kellermann's MS note to this effect is detailed in ibid., p. 383.
25. 'Other Interesting Particulars', p. 423.
26. Ibid. p. 422.
27. An excellent account of the re-writing of the history of Marengo is 'Adjusting the Record: Napoleon and Marengo', in *On the Napoleonic Wars: Collected Essays*, D. G. Chandler, London, 1994, pp. 82–98.
28. *Memoirs of the Life, Exile and Conversations of the Emperor Napoleon*, Count de Las Cases, London, 1836, I, p. 148.
29. *Monthly Review*, London, 1804, XLV, p. 541.

— 3 —

'The Snow shall be their Winding-Sheet'
EYLAU

6–7 February 1807

'Few, few shall part where many meet;
The snow shall be their winding-sheet;
And every turf beneath their feet
Shall be a soldier's sepulchre'

These lines from the poem on the Battle of Hohenlinden by Thomas Campbell (1777-1844) are applicable equally to Eylau, 'the bloodiest day, the most horrible butchery of men that had taken place since the beginning of the Revolutionary wars'.[1] It was also remarkable for being fought in the depths of a most bitter winter.

Napoleon's victory at Jena and Auerstädt on 14 October 1806 effectively removed Prussia from the Fourth Coalition ranged against him; but to prevent any Russian attempt to relieve Prussia, Napoleon immediately marched into Poland. He intended to destroy the Russian army of General Levin Bennigsen (a Hanoverian in Russian service), but after Bennigsen avoided his trap, Napoleon put his army into winter quarters. Campaigning in winter was not usual, as the weather could ruin transportation and communications; and the winter of 1806/7 in Poland was especially cruel. The French supply system, which still depended to some extent upon widespread foraging, broke down completely and compelled Napoleon to institute a complete overhaul of his methods of supply, while the army in Poland suffered from both cold and hunger.

Napoleon's hopes for a period of recuperation for his army were undone in late January 1807, when Bennigsen took the field in unseasonable weather with the intention of improving his situation for the time when the spring campaign would begin. The conditions for the Russian army were as bad as for Napoleon, but it was believed that the Russian troops were more resilient; recruited from serfs who had spent their lives in virtual slavery, they were inured to a life of hardship and brutality even before they were conscripted into the army, where deprivation and physical beatings were not uncommon. Nevertheless, they retained an unswerving loyalty to their Tsar, officers and motherland, in the service of which they bore the most awful privations without a murmur of discontent, and fought with a determined heroism which impressed, even awed, those who witnessed it. Despite the continuing handicap of an officer corps which some described as the least educated militarily in Europe, reforms and improvements under Tsar Alexander I (in all but commissariat and the care for the well-being of the soldier, which remained deplorable) transformed the Russian army from what one observer had described as 'exactly the hard, stiff, wooden machines which we have reason to figure to ourselves as the Russians of the Seven Years' War'[2] into a modern army. These improvements, furthermore, were made without affecting the morale or determination of the Russian soldier, who remained a being separate from the usual rules of military behaviour, according to some commentators. Marcellin de Marbot, for example, wrote of the almost inhuman behaviour of Russian troops at Golymin, shortly before Eylau: 'although our soldiers fired upon them at twenty-five paces, they continued their march without replying, because in order to do so they would have had to halt, and every moment was precious. So every division, every regiment, filed past, without saying a word or slackening its pace for a moment. The streets were filled with dying and wounded, but not a groan was to be heard, because they were forbidden. You might have said that we were firing upon shadows. At last our soldiers charged the Russian soldiers with the bayonet, and only when they pierced them could they be convinced that they were dealing with men.'[3] Against such troops, a desperate fight was guaranteed.

Moving out of winter quarters, Napoleon's attempt to trap Bennigsen failed when the interception of a French courier revealed his plans to the Russians. Bennigsen retired after an indecisive action at Ionkovo on 3 February 1807, followed by Napoleon, whose forces were considerably separated. With Bernadotte's corps delayed by the late arrival of orders thanks to the wretched condition of the roads, and with the corps of Ney and Davout away on the left and right flanks respectively, under his immediate command Napoleon had only the corps of Marshals Soult and Augereau, and Murat's reserve cavalry, totalling about 45,000 men and 200 pieces of artillery. By contrast, Bennigsen's forces were concentrated, about 67,000 strong with 460 guns, the only outlying detachment being a division under General Lestocq, the last remnant of the Prussian field army, about 9,000 strong, which was retiring in front of Ney.

Despite Napoleon's careful planning, the major action which developed began more as the result of chance than deliberation. Bennigsen drew up his army just north and east of the town of Preussisch-Eylau, occupying a line roughly along some low hills; to the south-west was more dominating high ground, roughly along the line which was to be occupied by the French. Pine woodland was spread throughout the area,

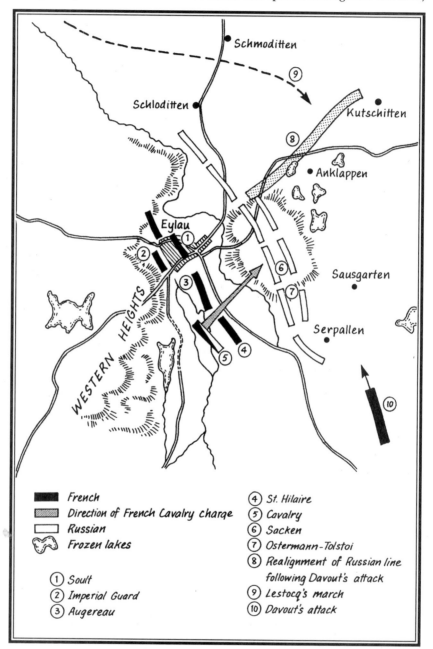

French

Direction of French Cavalry charge

Russian

Frozen lakes

① Soult
② Imperial Guard
③ Augereau

④ St. Hilaire
⑤ Cavalry
⑥ Sacken
⑦ Ostermann-Tolstoi
⑧ Realignment of Russian line following Davout's attack
⑨ Lestocq's march
⑩ Davout's attack

and between the hills were a number of streams which formed ponds in places, frozen and largely covered with snow. Soult's corps and Murat's cavalry reached the Eylau area early in the afternoon of 7 February, and before evening were joined by Augereau and the Imperial Guard; it was evident that Bennigsen was prepared to stand and fight, but contrary to the 'official' version which stated that Napoleon initiated the action that afternoon to secure the town of Eylau as shelter for his troops, it appears that he decided upon the prudent course of awaiting the arrival of Ney and Davout. This plan was frustrated by part of the French baggage-train, however, which entered Eylau and began to unpack within range of the Russian forward positions, and was duly attacked. The skirmishing increased from mid-afternoon as both sides fed in troops, until full-scale street-fighting was taking place in Eylau, possession of the cemetery in particular being bitterly disputed until it finally fell into French hands. After each side had suffered about 4,000 casualties, the Russians withdrew to their original position, leaving Eylau in French possession but littered with dead and wounded.

The night of 7/8 February was wretched in the extreme, recalled by some participants as exceeding everything in misery save the carnage of the morrow. Already the ground was covered with snow and frozen so hard that the ponds could be crossed by artillery and baggage without those concerned even being aware that they were walking on water, but on that night the temperature dropped even lower. It was measured by Dominique-Jean Larrey, chief surgeon of the Imperial Guard; in the evening of 7 February it was the equivalent of 14° Fahrenheit – 18 degrees of frost – but by early morning had fallen to 2° Fahrenheit, or 30 degrees of frost.[4] Some French troops found shelter in the buildings of Eylau, which were not entirely proof against the weather, as the doors were broken-up for firewood; others, like the entire Russian army, spent the night in the open. For several days many had had nothing to eat but potatoes and melted snow, the French supply system being so bad that even Napoleon had to order each mess of his Guard to supply him with a piece of wood and a potato, so that he and his staff might have something warm to eat; seated upon a bundle of straw, he baked his potatoes himself and apportioned them to his staff when they were done. Charles Parquin of the 20th *Chasseurs à Cheval* made himself a comfortable bed from a pile of straw and a dead Russian for a pillow; others spent the night on the move, endeavouring not to freeze and to find food, like Jean-Baptiste Barrès of the Guard. Although suffering from partial snow-blindness, by assiduous foraging he was able to find himself a piece of partially cooked sheep's liver. He recalled that after days of marching in this weather, he and his comrades were suffering severely; but, he remarked philosophically, they were young and used to it. Ironically, the very bitterness of the cold was the cause of saving some lives, if it took others; Larrey and the other surgeons, working through the night on the casualties of the day's fighting, found that the cold so inhibited the flow of blood that many men were saved from bleeding to death.

Dawn brought little relief to the miseries of the night, for although the temperature rose somewhat, there was a piercing north wind which blew the snow that fell intermittently throughout the day so hard into the troops' faces that at times it was literally blinding. The cloud seemed scarcely to clear the tree-tops, the snow piled so deep underfoot as to inhibit the movement even of mounted men, the wind so howled that it drowned shouted words of command, and the day was so gloomy that the Russians were unable even to discern the town of Eylau. The weather was so appalling that Davout later remarked that it exhibited many of the characteristics of a battle at night.

Napoleon's plan for the battle of 8 February depended upon the arrival of Davout's corps on his right flank. The main French position, upon the high ground known as the 'Western Heights', was held by two divisions of Soult's corps on the left (with Eylau approximately in the centre of their position) and Augereau's on the right, with Soult's third division, that of Saint-Hilaire, to the right of Augereau. Napoleon determined to use Soult's troops to make a 'pinning' attack to divert Russian attention and thus delay a mass assault, until Davout arrived on the Russian left flank; whereupon Augereau and the cavalry would join Davout in an attack on the Russian left and roll up their line. Ney's arrival on the Russian right would it was hoped complete the encirclement of Bennigsen's army, and as usual the Imperial Guard would be held in reserve. The Russians were deployed in a line more or less parallel to the French, along the low ridges about 1,200 yards east, with a massive concentration of artillery in the centre, including two batteries of 60 and 70 guns. Folds in the terrain afforded some protection to the French, but intermittently during the blizzard the Russians were clearly visible upon the snow-covered slopes of their position.

At about eight in the morning the Russians began to bombard Eylau town; the French replied in a furious interchange of artillery fire. After about an hour Eylau was ablaze, the smoke adding to the gloom of the day, though the noise of bombardment was curiously muffled by the falling snow. About half an hour into the battle, Napoleon ordered Soult to advance against the Russian right and right-centre, to divert attention from Davout's arrival on their left; the Russian right wing responded and in a fierce struggle Soult's two divisions were pushed back. As Davout's leading elements (Friant's division) came up on the left, they encountered stiff opposition from the Russian left-wing cavalry. Napoleon realised the danger of allowing the Russians to dictate the course of the battle on his centre-left, with the possibility of his line being divided if Eylau were taken; so to give the Russian command another problem, a diversion was needed. For this, he ordered Augereau's corps to attack virtually straight ahead against the Russian left-centre, with Saint Hilaire's division of Soult's corps attacking similarly on Augereau's right, to link up with Davout's advance. This he had intended to do to break the Russian left, and win the battle; but instead of striking the decisive blow, he had to use these troops to stabilise a deteriorating situation.

One of Napoleon's longest-serving companions, Pierre François Charles Augereau, duc de Castiglione, was a man of humble stock, who remained unpolished despite his title and Marshal's rank; although of martial bearing his reputation for looting tended to overshadow his military abilities, hence a somewhat unflattering early assessment: 'In the military career of this marshal we have found little to praise beyond fiery and indomitable courage; and his private character appears to have been, in every point of view, detestable.'[5] On the day of Eylau he was seriously unwell, stricken by a fever, and on the previous day had asked to be relieved of duty, but had been persuaded to remain for one more day; it was said that he was so ill that he had almost to be held in the saddle, but he determined to carry out his orders. Perhaps his illness contributed to what happened, or perhaps it was just the weather; but his two divisions marched off into the snow and into oblivion.

It was about 10 a.m. when Napoleon's diversionary attack was ordered. Saint-Hilaire duly marched his division against the Russian left wing, commanded by General Count Ivan Ostermann-Tolstoi. Saint-Hilaire was supposed to have co-operated with Augereau, but found himself opposing Ostermann-Tolstoi alone, and thus was unable to make much headway. Instead of keeping contact with Saint-Hilaire and marching against Ostermann-Tolstoi, Augereau's two divisions veered to the left. In the reduced visibility of blinding snow, it might have helped the units to remain in contact had they advanced in close formation; but according to Augereau, the first brigade of each division deployed, with the second supporting them in squares. For whatever reason, Augereau's men marched straight into the centre of the Russian position, where

Count Sacken commanded, and more significantly, right into the mouth of the 70-gun battery. With visibility reduced to fifteen yards at times, they came under fire not only from the Russian guns, but from some French batteries as well, which were unable to see but probably presumed that Augereau's men were where they should have been. The division of General Desjardins led the attack, followed by that of General Heudelet; as the storm of shot fell upon them, Desjardins was killed and Heudelet seriously wounded. Augereau himself was struck in the arm by grapeshot, and was bruised when his horse fell with him. The divisions staggered as immense numbers fell to the artillery-fire; and then Bennigsen launched against them two columns of infantry and the cavalry within striking distance. (Bad though the conditions were, the Russians would have been able to see more clearly than the French, who had the blizzard in their faces). Both divisions were devastated, and those who survived the slaughter fell back to where the injured Augereau was trying to rally them around the cemetery of Eylau. Of perhaps 7,000 men in each division, or slightly less, as few as two or three thousand may have rallied around their commander; Augereau acknowledged some 5,200 casualties, but at the end of the day there were as few as 700 men in each division still under arms. A major part of Napoleon's army had been destroyed, probably in no more than half an hour.

At this point it is appropriate to consider what is probably the most famous story concerning Eylau, as recounted in the memoirs of Marcellin de Marbot, who was at the time serving as ADC to Augereau. His story, written with himself as the hero (his account is not the most self-effacing of documents!) concerns one of the units leading Augereau's advance, the 14th Line. This regiment had suffered a heavy loss earlier in the campaign, when on Christmas Eve the French army was crossing the River Wrka (or Urka) in the face of the enemy. The 14th was the first unit over a bridge constructed under fire, their vanguard of skirmishers being led by the regimental commander in person, Colonel Savary (brother of Napoleon's aide, later duc de Rovigo). Hardly had the colonel ridden over the bridge than a Cossack dashed from the cover of nearby woodland, ran a lance through Savary's heart, and escaped back into the woods. He was the fifth colonel of the 14th to be killed in action, emphasising its reputation as being an unlucky regiment.

According to Marbot, when leading Augereau's advance at Eylau, the 14th reached a low hillock before the full weight of the Russian artillery was brought to bear upon the remainder of the corps. While the rest retired, the 14th clung to this eminence, and as the blizzard slackened temporarily, those in the French line could see the 14th on their hillock, waving their 'Eagle' to show that they were still resisting, or (as Marbot thought) asking for assistance. The gilt-bronze, sculpted Eagle which crowned the pole of French army colours symbolised the almost mystic attachment between the unit and its emperor, in whose name the Eagles were presented, and its loss in action was the worst disgrace which could befall a unit; as Napoleon himself noted, 'The loss of an Eagle is an affront to the reputation of its regiment for which neither victory nor the glory acquired on a hundred fields can make amends.'[6] According to Marbot, Napoleon observed their gesture of defiance and instructed Augereau to send a courier through the swarms of Cossacks to order the 14th to withdraw. The first two officers to be sent never made it; then it was Marbot's turn. He was riding a fleet-footed but evil-tempered mare named Lisette, which had already bitten a groom to death. Marbot determined to trust to the speed of his horse; having seen the previous couriers gallop off sword in hand, he decided to ride unarmed in the hope that the Cossacks would ignore him.

Surprisingly, his scheme worked, and he arrived to find the remains of the 14th in square, surrounded by a rampart of dead, over which he was able to clamber only with difficulty. Finding the senior surviving officer, Marbot conveyed the message which ordered him to retire; the major in command replied that their ranks were so thinned that it would be impossible, and that a huge column of Russians was even then bearing down upon them. Instead, he handed Marbot the Eagle and asked him to return to Napoleon, 'bid him farewell from the 14th of the Line, which has faithfully executed his orders, and bear to him the Eagle which he gave us, and which we can defend no longer: it would add too much to the pain of death to see it fall into the hands of the enemy.'[7] With that, the survivors of the 14th set up a shout of 'Vive l'Empereur!'; it was, thought Marbot, the modern equivalent of the gladiatorial cry 'Ave, Caesar, morituri te salutant'.[8]

As Marbot tried to break off the gilt-bronze head of the Eagle, so that he could leave behind the unwieldy and valueless pole, a Russian roundshot carried off the rear peak of his hat, the concussion of the shot leaving him conscious but stunned and paralysed, with blood flowing from his nose and ears. He remained in the saddle but was powerless to help himself as the Russian onslaught fell upon the 14th, and he was surrounded by fighting men. A Russian grenadier, attempting to bayonet a French quartermaster who had fallen under Marbot's horse, overbalanced and ran his bayonet into Marbot's cloak; then transferred his attention to Marbot himself, stabbing him in the arm. The next thrust went into

Lisette's thigh, which galvanised the mare into action; turning on the grenadier, she bit off his entire face. A Russian officer seized Lisette's bridle; kicking and rearing at the mêlée around her, she grabbed the officer by the midriff and dashed away from the hillock, pausing only to drop the mutilated officer and stamp him to death, then galloped off towards Eylau, with Marbot unable to raise a hand but held in tight by the peaks of his hussar saddle.

Perhaps because Marbot's story was so colourful, the fate of the 14th has become almost legendary; but it seems certain that there was no Thermopylae-like 'last stand' as he implied. At least part of the 14th was able to retire in good order, though suffering about 50 per cent casualties, which were terrible enough; and the 14th's plight was remarked on by other witnesses – Coignet, for example, noted that they were 'cut to pieces; the Russians penetrated their square, and the carnage was terrible'.[9] The attention of other writers, however, was not focused upon the 14th as might have been expected had their end been as dramatic as implied by Marbot, but upon other regiments which had suffered severe losses, such as the 43rd, or upon the death of Colonel Semelé of the 24th and the destruction of his regiment. What does not seem in doubt is that the 14th's flag and pole *were* captured by the Russians, but events surrounding the Eagle itself are more variously reported, from its having become detached on the previous day and kept with the regimental baggage, to its having been shot off the pole but recovered by another regiment, being claimed after the battle by both the 14th and 44th (the latter also having lost its Eagle) and eventually being restored to its rightful owners. Some have reckoned Marbot's story a fabrication, but while it is obviously embroidered, it is not impossible that he did suffer his injury when carrying a message to part of the unit in the no man's land between the two armies; and the 14th's declaration of devotion to Napoleon, and their attempt to save their Eagle, would not be untypical of the veneration with which both were regarded in the French army.

The slaughter of Augereau's corps, and the repulse of Saint-Hilaire, was witnessed by Napoleon from the vantage-point of Eylau church tower; and there now occurred the potential for even greater disaster, in a threat to the person of the Emperor himself, as Russian columns, perhaps 6,000 strong, followed the debris of Augereau's corps into the streets of Eylau itself. To the rear of the town, the Imperial Guard had been held in reserve throughout the morning, under artillery fire; as Coignet remarked, it was the greatest suffering imaginable to stand and be killed without the opportunity of fighting back. But stand they did, heartened by such gestures as that of a quartermaster-sergeant whose leg was taken off by a shot; he remarked to his comrades that his three pairs of boots would now last him twice as long, and taking a pair of muskets as crutches, hopped away to the field hospital. Barrès saw files on either side mown down, then helped carry to hospital a friend who had lost a leg; on the way back he had to check his stride every half-dozen steps to avoid bouncing roundshot or spinning lumps of shell, and two of his friends were killed before the carrying-party rejoined the ranks. One shot smashed the pole of a Guard Eagle; Lieutenant Morlay inserted what was left of the splintered pole into the muzzle of a musket, so that the flag could still be carried. It was to these troops that now fell the task of repelling the Russian incursion.

Under General Dorsenne, two Guard battalions (2nd Grenadiers and Chasseurs) moved up with fixed bayonets, considering that their honour would best be served by a charge without firing; but before they arrived Napoleon's own escort had to charge the head of the Russian column to buy time. As the Guard attacked with the bayonet, Bruyère's brigade from the French left-wing cavalry screen assailed the Russians from the rear: they gave way and temporarily the French centre was secured. (If Marbot's story is to be believed, some of the Guard must have fired, for he claimed to have received a volley from them as he galloped on, helpless, out of the gloom; he presumed that they must have thought him the leader of a Russian cavalry charge. His cloak and saddle were pierced with musket-balls, but neither he nor Lisette were hurt, and the mare dashed through the French line before her strength gave out and she collapsed, rolling upon Marbot who was knocked unconscious.)

During this desperate period, Napoleon's conduct was especially remarked upon; General Henri-Gatien Bertrand, for example, said that he was never so impressed by the Emperor's calm demeanour as on this occasion. Napoleon was afoot, and gave Berthier a 'reproachful look' when the faithful chief of staff ordered horses to be brought for their escape; instead, he stood fast as the Russians approached, saying only 'What audacity! what audacity!', and never moved as the Guard drove them back, although those around him were 'much alarmed'.[10] Rarely had Napoleon been in such imminent danger, and later admitted that one of the deaths which had most affected him was that of his aide, General Corbineau, who was smashed to pieces by a roundshot while the Emperor was speaking to him.

Napoleon's situation was now critical. On his left, Soult's men were being mauled, and Ney's reinforcement was still hours away; on the right, Saint-Hilaire was repulsed and only the leading elements of Davout's corps had come into action; in the centre, Augereau's corps was to all intents destroyed, leaving only the Guard and Murat's cavalry reserve to hold the line. The cavalry had been intended to act as the blow which would destroy the Russian army once it had been weakened by Davout's arrival; but instead, Napoleon had to use it for a more defensive attack, to prevent the Russians breaking the line before Davout could lend his full assistance. At about 11.30 a.m. Murat was ordered to charge.

Joachim Murat, Napoleon's brother-in-law, Grand Duke of Berg and later King of Naples, was the most flamboyant of Napoleon's old comrades, the *beau sabreur* supreme, always gorgeously dressed in uniforms of his own devising (at Eylau he wore a fur-edged, gold-braided green frock-coat, white breeches, and a red cap with a fur head-band and a panache of white feathers), but was the most dashing of cavalry commanders. Now, at the head of some 80 squadrons (about 10,700 men in all), he led one of the greatest cavalry charges in history, towards the centre of the Russian position; although as one of the witnesses commented, in parts of the field the snow and marshy ground made movement at more than a walk virtually impossible. Murat led the immense column of horsemen with his own cavalry reserve, the 1st-3rd Dragoon and 2nd Cuirassier Divisions, followed by Jean-Baptiste Bessières and the Guard cavalry.

They had already been under fire, an ordeal which had produced one of the most memorable exhortations ever addressed to soldiers in such circumstances. General Louis Lepic, colonel of the *Grenadiers à Cheval* of the Guard, had almost missed the action because of an attack of rheumatism in the knees on the previous day, but Larrey's treatment had got him sufficiently mobile to lead his command. Now, sitting under fire, some of his bearskin-capped grenadiers ducked and flinched as the shot screamed past them. 'Heads up, by God!', shouted Lepic. 'Those are bullets, not turds!'[11]

First, the huge charge rode down the Russians retiring from Eylau, then divided into two wings, Emmanuel Grouchy's dragoon division scattering the Russian cavalry which was harassing the beleaguered men of Saint-Hilaire's division. Grouchy's horse was killed, but he re-mounted and rode on, wheeling his men to the left against the Russian centre, supporting the other column. General Jean Joseph Ange, comte d'Hautpoul, led his cuirassiers through the 70-gun battery, sabring the gunners, then through the Russian first line of infantry, then the second, and emerged in front of the Russian reserve at the rear of their position; d'Hautpoul had his right thigh broken by grapeshot, an injury which proved fatal after he refused to permit Larrey to amputate it. Following the first waves came the Guard cavalry, led by six squadrons of the *Chasseurs à Cheval* under General Nicholas Dahlmann, who also received a mortal wound, and died next day.

Having rallied in the Russian rear, the French cavalry were surprised to find that the Russian units through which they had ridden had actually re-formed and were now facing them, tribute to the courage of the ordinary Russian soldier. Despite their tiredness after the charge, the French cavalry formed a single column and charged back the way they had come, again breaking through the Russian lines, again cutting-up the surviving gunners, until they regained Napoleon's line. Casualties among the French cavalry were probably about 1,500, or about 14 per cent of those engaged; but their great charge had saved Napoleon from possible defeat, by temporarily wrecking Bennigsen's centre and in concealing from him the true weakness of Napoleon's centre. Perhaps for the first time, the cavalry had demonstrated their value to Napoleon as an independent and decisive force in its own right, rather than as a supporting arm or one to be reserved to complete a victory which was already half-won by the efforts of other arms.

As the cavalry re-assembled behind Napoleon's front line – where they continued to take casualties from the continuing Russian bombardment – it was noticed that Lepic was not at the head of his Grenadiers. He arrived a little while later with a small party with whom he had penetrated the Russian lines, declined a call that he surrender, and cut his way free. Napoleon greeted his arrival with a remark that he had feared Lepic had been captured; no, replied Lepic, the only report he would ever receive would be of his death, never of his capture!

Over this sector of the battlefield there now descended an atmosphere of exhaustion, both sides being shaken by the severity of the fighting and the appalling loss of life. Although Napoleon still possessed the Guard largely intact, as usual he declined to commit it because it represented his last reserve, a practice which gave rise to the somewhat ironic nickname 'immortals', bestowed upon the Guard by the rest of the army, those for whom Napoleon showed no such qualms about getting them killed. An artillery duel continued, but the main focus of the fighting switched farther south, where Davout's command now came up in strength and began to pressurise the Russian left flank. As the afternoon wore on, the Russian left was forced back, eventually at right-angles to its original position, the centre also pulling back to maintain a solid line. In addition to Davout's three divisions, there was only limited cavalry support from Napoleon's centre, for the troops engaged in the bloody fighting of the morning were hardly in a state to renew a serious contest with the equally ravaged Russian forces in their immediate front; so that while Davout advanced a considerable distance on the right, the centre and left edged forward only a short way. With snow still blinding the combatants and visibility reduced at times to no more than ten paces, Davout deliberately kept his units closed-up, even closer than the prescribed distance between battalions, so that they would not lose touch with one another and suffer the fate that had befallen Augereau's corps earlier in the day.

Even at this point, with the Russians seemingly on the point of breaking before Davout's drive, the carnage of the day was not ended. By late afternoon, by hard marching and by evading Ney's attempt to engage him, Lestocq arrived with his Prussians in the rear of Bennigsen's beleaguered line. Ney was still some distance away; it might have been expected that the sounds of conflict would have spurred on his command, but so fierce was the howl of the wind and so deadening the falling snow, that even the roar of the massed cannonade at Eylau was unable to be heard those few miles away; even when Lestocq came within sight of the battlefield, he could see the smoke and flashes of gunfire, but could hear not a sound of the conflict. Lestocq's troops arrived within range of supporting Bennigsen's army as early as 1 p.m., but had to rest after their exertions, so that it was probably about 4 p.m. before they had traversed the length of the rear of the Russian line and were ready to reinforce Bennigsen's collapsing left flank. Gathering up Russian units which had been withdrawn for reorganisation, Lestocq counter-attacked Davout and recaptured about half the ground Davout had gained, as the French right flank was pushed back. Then, at about 7 p.m., Ney's corps finally made its appearance and fell into line on the left of Soult's men, extending Napoleon's left flank. Furious fighting continued on both flanks until by about 10 p.m. both armies had fought themselves to a standstill, and conflict ceased right along the line.

For those who had survived, the night of 8/9 February was even worse than the one before, for cold and hunger was now blended with the shock of a battle the like of which few had ever experienced. Most of the wounded lay unattended; many, like the dead, stripped by the horde of scavengers which accompanied every army (many of them members of the army) and who descended like jackals upon the fallen, even before the battle was over. Just as the sun was setting, it was one of these predators who roused Marbot from his unconsciousness; he came to his senses wearing nothing but his hat and right boot, which a driver of the transport corps was endeavouring to pull off, to be frustrated by an old wound on

Marbot's foot having swollen with frost-bite. The scavenger made off with the rest of Marbot's clothes, but the grey astrakhan trimming on the pelisse was recognised by Augereau's valet, who made the transport man take him to Marbot. Augereau had finally turned over command of the debris of his corps in mid-afternoon, and was preparing to leave the army by sledge, being too ill to ride; so when Marbot was found, he had him tied on to the sledge beside him, and by careful medical attention Marbot was eventually restored to health. Even his horse survived to accompany him in his convalescence; the cold had staunched the bayonet-wound in her leg until Marbot's servant was able to bind it up with a shirt taken from a dead body.

Marbot's survival was exceptional; for most who lay on the field there was no such salvation. They were not entirely devoid of help – Larrey worked at Eylau for almost a week, treating the wounded and arranging for their evacuation – but for most, succour came too late. Jean-Roch Coignet of the Imperial Guard wrote that it was impossible to convey any idea of that terrible time; apart from the cold and hunger, little rest was possible throughout the night as the cries of the unattended wounded blended into one, unbearable, incessant shriek.

There appears to have been considerable despondency in the French camp; even Napoleon seems initially to have been uncertain whether to hold his position or retreat. During the night he toured some of the casualty stations with Soult, remarking despondently that the Russians had done them great damage; whereupon Soult made his celebrated rejoinder, that the reverse was also true, as 'French bullets were not made of cotton-wool either.'[12] Soult was all for standing fast, but in the event it is likely that the Russians made up Napoleon's mind for him. At about 11 p.m. Bennigsen held a council of war at Anklappen, a village in the left rear of his line which Lestocq's counter-attack had recovered from Davout. Despite the advice of subordinates such as Ostermann-Tolstoi and Lestocq (the latter called to the conference while actually planning to renew his attack), who believed that one more push would secure the victory which they believed was almost won, concerned about his lack of rations and ammunition, Bennigsen chose instead to retire, and by midnight the Russian retreat had begun. Davout was actually planning his own withdrawal when it was reported to him that the Russians could be heard marching away; his notification of this convinced Napoleon that he should hold his ground. Similar movements were reported by the French left wing, and daylight revealed that the Russians had indeed departed. Some attempt was made by Murat's cavalry to follow them, but the French army was in no state to attempt a proper pursuit.

The artist Louis Lejeune, serving as a staff officer, only joined the army on 8 February, and recalled how he and his friends spent the night in the snow, fervently wishing for the return of daylight, in the expectation of renewed fighting. When morning came, they must have wished that it had not revealed the sight which met their eyes. Through the low cloud, threatening more snow, the dim light fell upon a field piled with dead, many of whom lay in ranks as they had fallen, so that it was possible to discern the events of the previous day from the piles of bodies. 'Never was spectacle so dreadful as that field presented ... above fifty thousand men lay in the space of two leagues, weltering in blood ... broken gun-carriages, dismounted cannon, fragments of blown-up caissons, scattered balls, lay in wild confusion amid casques, cuirasses, and burning hamlets, casting a livid light over a field of snow. Subdued by loss of blood, tamed by cold, exhausted by hunger, the foemen lay side by side amidst the general wreck.'[13]

Fresh snow had partially covered some of these dreadful sights, but elsewhere the snow was churned to mud, marking the course of the heaviest fighting, and besmirched with huge stains of blood which, one witness remarked, had in places curiously turned to yellow where the bloody snow had been trampled by charging men and horses. Elsewhere, the dead and wounded were piled on top of one another, where the injured had crawled together for warmth during the night, only to die of cold before morning. Barrès of the Imperial Guard walked over the battlefield and observed parties of Frenchmen and Russian prisoners beginning to remove the wounded; wherever one looked, he recalled, there was nothing but corpses, and the maimed and injured dragging themselves aimlessly through the snow, in search of help, with no sound but the screams of those still alive. He turned away, sick with horror.

Such scenes were universal after a battle, but not even the most experienced members of the French army could recollect anything so terrible as the sights and sounds of Eylau. The shock and damage to morale was evident when Napoleon toured the field on the day after the slaughter; as usual there were shouts of '*Vive l'Empereur!*', but even more of 'Long live peace!' or 'Bread and peace!' More pathetic was the reaction of wounded Russians who reached up to kiss Napoleon's feet and stirrups as he rode past, as they would have acknowledged their own Tsar, perhaps overlooking the fact that Napoleon had been one of the causes of their misfortune. Napoleon was not immune from such dire sights, remarking in his Bulletin that they were calculated 'to inspire princes with a love of peace and a horror of war', and elsewhere writing that 'The land is covered with dead and wounded; this is not the noble portion of war. One is pained, and the soul is oppressed at the sight of so many victims.'[14] It is greatly to Napoleon's credit that he insisted that the Russian wounded be given the same consideration as the injured French; but for all his revulsion at the sight of such carnage, he appears not to have made any commitment to avoid such horrors in the future.

It is difficult to calculate the Eylau casualties, not least because it has been claimed that 'The official accounts of this great battle on both sides are so much interwoven with falsehoods as to furnish no clue whatever to the truth. That of Napoleon is distinguished by more than his usual misrepresentation.'[15] Even if this is an exaggeration, the calculation of losses is fraught with hazard, partly because the first statistics gathered after the battle counted only those men still with the colours, and not all those who for whatever reason were separated from their units. Ostermann-Tolstoi, for example, was able to count only 2,170 men in his whole command on the night of the 8th, implying an impossible level of slaughter. Similarly, the numbers Augereau was able to rally at the cemetery would imply that his division had lost about 80 per cent; Augereau admitted a loss of 5,200, excluding prisoners, or about 35 per cent, which is certainly too low, about 8,000 casualties being more likely, or over half those engaged. Napoleon's claim of 1,900 dead and 5,700 wounded is certainly one of his more imaginative figures, intended to put a victorious sheen upon what was at best a drawn battle; more realistic estimates of French casualties ranged from 10,000 to 28,000. Including the forces which came up later in the day, the losses were probably about 25,000, or 35 per cent of the entire force.

One method of gauging the scale of a victory or defeat was by the numbers of flags captured or lost, but here also the truth is obscured, principally by a claim that the unprecedented number of twelve Eagles were lost by the French. This statement appears to have originated with Bennigsen's first report, but though he later adjusted the claim to five, the story persisted. One account described the loss of six identified Eagles (including that of the 14th Line, based on Marbot's story), mentions two more of unidentified regiments (but evidently counts them twice, as the captors are given as those of two of the identified Eagles), and adds the loss of four cuirassier Eagles during Murat's charge, which are not mentioned elsewhere.[16] Napoleon's admittance of the loss of only one Eagle (belonging to the 18th Line) was an even greater falsification than Bennigsen's initial and probably genuinely mistaken claim of twelve. The actual French loss was probably four or six Eagles, plus the staff and flag of the 14th Line, which was severe enough without need of exaggeration.[17] Several other Eagles had near escapes, like that of the 1st Battalion 7th *Léger*, which had a wing shot off.

Russian losses are equally difficult to estimate; Bennigsen admitted 12,000 dead and 7,900 wounded, a curious calculation in that fatalities hardly ever outnumbered the wounded, but not impossible given the climatic conditions which must have caused many deaths from exposure among those who might otherwise have survived their injuries. Napoleon's estimate of enemy casualties was perhaps similarly understated (7,000 dead and 12–15,000 wounded); the actual losses were probably between 15,000 and 24,000, probably rather less than those suffered by the French.

Despite fourteen hours of slaughter, no decision had been reached. Perhaps the most accurate comment on the terrible day was that uttered by Ney, when he rode over the field next day: 'What a massacre; and no result.'[18] That was not how Napoleon portrayed it; despite the appalling losses, he had been left in possession of the field, so proclaimed a victory, which was suitable for public consumption even if the army knew better. Nevertheless, the battle left its mark upon Napoleon. Some three weeks after the action he castigated his brother Joseph for complaining about the rigours of fighting in Italy by listing his recent trials: 'I myself have been a fortnight without taking off my boots, in the middle of snow and mud, without bread, wine or brandy, living on potatoes and meat, making long marches and counter-marches without any sort of comfort, fighting with our bayonets frequently under grapeshot; the wounded obliged to be removed in sledges, in the open air, to a distance of fifty leagues. To compare us with the army of Naples, making war in that beautiful country, where they have bread, wine, oil, linen, sheets to their beds, society, and even women, looks like an attempt at a joke ... We have war in all its fierceness and all its horrors ... The army of Naples has no cause for murmuring. Say to them ... "your Emperor has been living for weeks upon potatoes, and bivouacking in the snows of Poland ..."'[19]

Despite such misery and the slaughter of Eylau, the war continued; Napoleon returned his army to winter quarters to recuperate, which somewhat ironically allowed the Russians to take possession of Eylau and the surrounding area, which Napoleon's army had suffered so to defend. Not until Napoleon's decisive victory at Friedland (14 June 1807) was the war concluded, by the Treaty of Tilsit, one of the high points of Napoleon's success. Even if the losses of Eylau had been uniquely terrible in the eyes of even the most hardened campaigners, they cannot have been unexpected, given the accepted courage and calibre of both contending armies, the heroism of the Russian soldier which was acknowledged even by his enemies, and the fact that the French army was near the peak of its efficiency. That the battle was contested so bitterly, that the remnant of Augereau's corps was able to rally after their ordeal, and that the Russians were able to mount a counter-attack upon Davout, after both sides had endured such hard marching on miserable rations and in appalling weather, is sufficient tribute to the morale and resolution of the troops of both armies.

It is perhaps indicative of the effect which Eylau had upon the French army that at the conclusion of the retreat from Moscow in 1812, after experiencing all the horrors of that catastrophe, and with Cossacks not far away, Adrien Bourgogne of the Imperial Guard and his comrades still found time to break their journey to safety to view the battlefield, and to read the inscriptions upon the wooden crosses which stood there, including one which read:

'Here rest twenty-nine officers of the brave 14th, who died on the field of honour.'[20]

NOTES

1. *Memoirs of a Napoleonic Officer*, J.-B. Barrès, ed. and intr. M. Barrès, trans. B. Miall, London, 1925, p. 101.
2. *Narrative of some Passages in the Great War with France*, Sir Henry Bunbury, 1854; London, 1927 edn., p. 127.
3. *Memoirs of Baron de Marbot*, trans. A. J. Butler, London, 1913, I, p. 200.
4. These statistics are a conversion from the original readings which were recorded on the scale of temperature devised by René Réaumur (1683–1757) which took the freezing-point of water as 0° and the boiling-point as 80°; see, for example, *Napoleon's Campaign in Poland 1806–07*, F. L. Petre, London, 1901, 1907 edn., (r/p with intr. by D. G. Chandler, London, 1976), p. 173.
5. *The Court and Camp of Bonaparte*, anon., London, 1829, p. 133.
6. 55th Bulletin of the *Grande Armée*, 1807.
7. Marbot, I, pp. 213–14.
8. 'Hail, Caesar, those who are about to die salute you': the greeting of Roman gladiators on entering the arena.
9. *The Note-Books of Captain Coignet*, ed. and intr. Hon. Sir John Fortescue, London, 1929, p. 144.
10. *Memoirs of the Life, Exile and Conversations of the Emperor Napoleon*, Count de Las Cases, London, 1836, I, pp. 335–6.
11. Quoted in *The Anatomy of Glory*, H. Lachouque and A. S. K. Brown, London, 1962, p. 88. This incident formed the subject of the memorable painting by Edouard Détaille, *'Haut les têtes! La mitraille n'est pas de la merde'*, exhibited at the *Salon* of 1893. It appears on the cover of the study of Détaille's art, *Edouard Détaille: l'héroisme d'un siècle*, J. Humbert, Paris, 1979.
12. Quoted in *Soult: Napoleon's Maligned Marshal*, Sir Peter Hayman, London, 1990, p. 77.
13. *History of Europe from the Commencement of the French Revolution to the Restoration of the Bourbons*, Sir Archibald Alison, Edinburgh and London, 1860, VII, p. 360.

14. *History of Napoleon*, M. Laurent d'Archeche, London, 1840, I, p. 428.
15. Alison, VII, p. 359.
16. *The War Drama of the Eagles*, E. Fraser, London, 1912, pp. 153–69.
17. See *Les Aigles Impériales*, General J. Regnault, Paris, 1967, and *Drapeaux et Etandards de la Révolution et de l'Empire*, P. Charrié', Paris, 1982 .
18. Quoted in *Napoleon's Campaign in Poland 1806–7*, (r/p with intr. by D. G. Chandler, London, 1976), p. 201.
19. This translation from *The Confidential Correspondence of Napoleon Bonaparte with His Brother Joseph, sometime King of Spain*, London, 1855, I, pp. 231–3.
20. *The Memoirs of Sergeant Bourgogne 1812–13*, A. J. B. F. Bourgogne, trans. and ed. P. Cottin and M. Hénault, London, 1899 (r/p with intr. by D. G. Chandler, London, 1979), p. 322.

To the Last Ditch
THE SIEGES OF SARAGOSSA
June 1808 to February 1809

Perhaps in part because of the large number of British accounts which condemned it, the Spanish army of the Napoleonic Wars is often regarded as 'nothing better than mere rabble ... more like an armed mob than regularly organised soldiers'.[1] There is much truth in such assertions concerning the regular army, which had suffered years of neglect and poor leadership; yet such criticisms tend to obscure the real Spanish contribution to the Allied victory in the Peninsular War, in the resistance of the civilian population and the operations of guerrilla bands which tied down a major part of French resources. Nothing demonstrates more clearly the determination of the Spanish people than the defence of Saragossa.

Situated on the right bank of the River Ebro, the city of Saragossa (Zaragoza) was a Roman colony, Caesarea Augusta (from which the modern name derives), and was a location of importance from an early date: ecclesiastical councils were held there in AD 380 (to deal with the Priscillian heresy) and in 592 (to resolve problems arising from the conversion of the West Goths from Arianism to orthodox Christianity), but it was also the scene of military operations. Captured in AD 452 by the Suebi, by the Visigoths in 476 and by the Moors in 712, it resisted a siege by Charlemagne, but the Moors were expelled in 1118 by Alfonso I of Aragon. As capital of Aragon it grew in importance, and in 1710 was the site of a battle in the War of the Spanish Succession in which the Allied army of Marshal Guido Starhemberg (with British forces under General James Stanhope) defeated the Marquis de Bay's Spaniards. None of these actions, however, were as famous as the sieges of 1808–9.

Napoleon's occupation of Spain in 1808, and his attempt to install his brother Joseph Bonaparte as king in place of the deposed Charles IV and his equally ineffective son Ferdinand aroused widespread public hostility which erupted spontaneously throughout Spain. From the very outset the conflict between the French occupiers and the Spanish partisans or guerrillas was marked by atrocity and massacre on both sides, a level of revolting brutality which contrasted sharply with the more 'civilised' mode of warfare obtaining between the British and French armies in the other part of the Peninsular War. In a war which involved the ravaging of the country, the massacre of civilians, prisoners and the injured and in which both sides behaved with barbarity, it is not surprising that the fight was waged with extreme bitterness and hatred. A testament to the torment endured by the French occupiers of the country is the fact that one estimate puts their losses to guerrillas and similar civilian bands at one hundred men per day throughout the war, but statistics alone can never convey the horror and destruction which was a feature of much of the Franco-Spanish hostility during the war.

The first outbreak of violence against the French, and in support of the Spanish royal family, occurred in Madrid on 2 May 1808, followed by savage reprisals (as immortalised by Goya's powerful depictions of these events). Within days spontaneous risings flared elsewhere, the most vehement support coming from the ordinary population; most of the nobility and civic authorities were seemingly unwilling to act lest insurrection against the French brought about civil unrest. Thus when rebellion began in Saragossa on 24 May, its leaders were two local farmers, Don Mariano Cerezo and Jorge Ibort, alias 'Tio Jorge'. When important citizens and local demagogues aroused the population of the city, a mob converged on the residence of the military governor and endeavoured to persuade him to lead them against the French occupation. The governor, Captain-General of Aragon Don Jorge de Guillelmi, was an experienced veteran but at 72 years of age was past active service and unenthusiastic about the scheme; and the military forces in Saragossa were too few to suppress serious civil disorder, and were probably in sympathy with the insurgents. Guillelmi delivered up to the mob the city armoury of 25,000 muskets and 65 pieces of artillery, and, pleading indisposition, resigned on the following day. By public acclamation he was replaced by a 28-year-old local nobleman, José de Palafox y Melzi.

A member of one of the oldest families in Aragon, with close connections to the Spanish royal family (his mother had been one of the Queen's attendants), Palafox was a man of unquestioned loyalty; as an officer in the royal bodyguard, he had plotted to rescue the royal family from its exile in France, but returned home when the plan proved impossible. Defence of a principle to the very end was not unknown in his family: a kinsman, Juan de Palafox de Mendoza (1600–59) had been a bishop in Mexico and had almost ruined his career by taking as high as the Pope protests against Spanish cruelty against the natives. Palafox was thus regarded as a natural leader, and was appointed Captain-General on 26 May.

William Napier, never especially generous towards the Spanish and universally critical of the civil and religious despotism which he thought characterised the Spanish establishment, in his history tended to regard Palafox as a mere figurehead who was not even completely trusted by his followers (presumably because of his aristocratic background), and a tool of 'a stern band of priests and plebeian-leaders'.[2] This is surely unfair, and a more accurate evaluation might be that if Palafox were to some extent merely articulating genuine public sentiment, he was truly the head, if not exactly the heart and soul, of the resistance of Saragossa.

Palafox quickly calmed the fevered atmosphere of the city, establishing a new civil administration, a provisional *Junta* comprising civic, church and military leaders; but the formation of an army was more difficult. The only regular soldiers in the region were about half the regiment of King's Dragoons (300 men with only 90 horses), a weak battalion of the Volunteers of Aragon, about 500 deserters from other garrisons who had left their units when the insurrections began, and a number of retired officers. Upon this nucleus Palafox formed an army composed of patriotic volunteers and conscripts (the latter virtually all able-bodied men aged between 16 and 40), in units regularly organised. By November his 'Army of Aragon' had risen to at least 33,000 in number, all newly raised corps save for a small minority of regulars, six infantry battalions, two weak dragoon corps, and one old militia unit.

Not content to await the approach of the French, within days of taking command Palafox sent a small force of some 2,000 men to Tudela, a town of recognised strategic importance on the Ebro, northwest of Saragossa; command of this force was given to Palafox's elder brother Luis, Marquis of Lazan. Knowing that Aragon contained very few regular troops, the French forces in the region (the 'Corps of Observation of the Pyrenees' under Marshal Jean-Baptiste Bessières) expected only limited resistance. Accordingly, Bessières sent his chief of staff, General Charles Lefebvre-Desnouëttes, with some 6,000 men, to deal with the revolt in Aragon. These experienced troops were too much for Lazan's recruits; he was defeated at Tudela on 8 June and at Mallen on 13 June, and when Palafox personally led out a force to oppose the French at Alagon, seventeen miles from Saragossa, he too was overthrown. Wounded in the arm, he returned to Saragossa with those of his troops who had not deserted and fled.

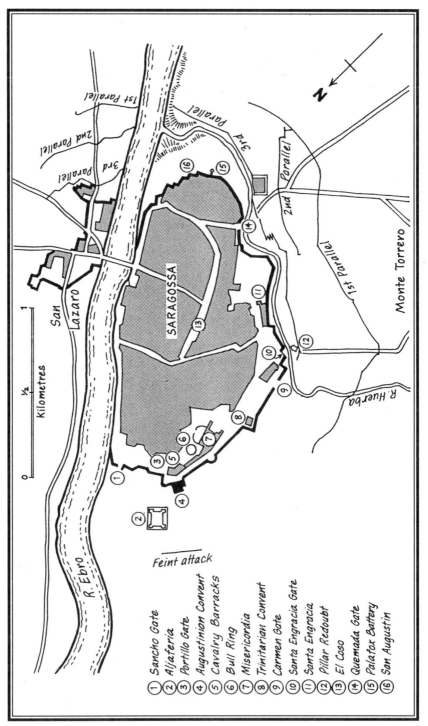

Feint attack

SARAGOSSA

R. Ebro

San Lazaro

Monte Torrevo

R. Huerba

1st Parallel

2nd Parallel

3rd Parallel

1st Parallel

2nd Parallel

3rd Parallel

Kilometres

0   ½   1

① Sancho Gate
② Aljaferia
③ Portillo Gate
④ Augustinian Convent
⑤ Cavalry Barracks
⑥ Bull Ring
⑦ Misericordia
⑧ Trinitarian Convent
⑨ Carmen Gate
⑩ Santa Engracia Gate
⑪ Santa Engracia
⑫ Pillar Redoubt
⑬ El Coso
⑭ Quemada Gate
⑮ Palafox Battery
⑯ San Augustin

Having dispersed the Spanish forces with such ease, Lefebvre-Desnouëttes imagined that he had only to attack Saragossa for the city to fall. Indeed, it did not appear a robust fortification. Where the city did not back on to the Ebro, it was surrounded by a brick wall ten to twelve feet high, into which were set a number of barracks and religious buildings. At the north-west were two of the five main gates into the city: the Sancho Gate, where the enceinte met the Ebro, and farther south the Portillo Gate, with the Portillo Church alongside. Continuing along the enceinte, there was the Cavalry Barracks backing on to the wall, near the bullring and the Misericordia hospital and workhouse; and on the southern wall three other gates, the Carmen Gate, the Santa Engracia Gate with the Santa Engracia Convent backing on to the wall, and the Quemada Gate. As the enceinte extended north to meet the Ebro again, it ran past the San Augustin Convent. A tributary of the Ebro, the River Huerba (or Huerva), covered the south and east of the enceinte, before turning south before the Carmen Gate. The city's 'outworks' included the Aljaferia Castle, an old brick structure just beyond the Portillo Gate; the Augustinian convent, nearer the Portillo Gate; and the suburb across the river, named after the San Lazaro convent, joined to the city by a stone bridge across the Ebro. The real strength of the city lay in its interior; solidly constructed buildings each a potential miniature fortress and, with the exception of the one main thoroughfare, 'El Coso', the streets were sufficiently narrow to be barricaded effectively. A serious weakness, however, was the flat-topped hill of Monte Terrero to the south, separated from the city by olive groves, an ideal artillery position overlooking the city, yet with no serious defensive works upon it, Palafox having had no time to construct anything save two batteries, and to loophole the buildings of the Aragon Canal establishment which were upon the hill.

Lefebvre-Desnouëttes believed that a rapid attack would be successful, and Palafox seems to have been of the same opinion, for when the French appeared outside the city on 15 June, he left with a small escort, ostensibly to raise reinforcements. Napier was duly critical of this conduct: 'It was a strange proceeding, and ill timed, that the chief should thus fly out at one gate while the enemy were pressing in at another, when the streets were filled with clamour, the dismayed garrison making little or no resistance, and all things in confusion.'[3] If in hindsight Palafox was guilty of misjudgement, if he believed the city were indefensible, his leaving may be seen as the act of a pragmatist, in that the loss of Saragossa did not mean the end of resistance in Aragon, which was his principal concern. In Palafox's absence, command of the garrison devolved upon Don Vincente Bustamente, whose somewhat despondent attitude was overborne by the popular determination to resist; and it appears that Palafox's departure was not known to the defenders in general until after the attack, so had no effect upon their morale.

Lefebvre-Desnouëttes assembled his forces in the meadows between the Portillo and Carmen gates, an area known as the Eras del Rey (by which name the action was known to the Spanish), and sent one column to storm both the above-mentioned gates, and a second against the Santa Engracia Gate. Covered by an artillery bombardment at short range, the Carmen Gate was forced by the French 70th Line, the wall of the Cavalry Barracks was scaled and the Portillo Gate penetrated; the Spanish battery covering the Santa Engracia Gate was overrun, and Lefebvre-Desnouëttes' Polish lancers charged through it and debouched inside the town walls.

Under normal circumstances, the penetration of so many places of a city's defensive perimeter would have been the signal for an honourable surrender by the garrison; but what the French encountered in Saragossa was a new style of defence: a spontaneous effort by the entire population to resist. Encouraged by their civic leaders and priests (who forsook the Sixth Commandment and even took up arms themselves), the citizens began to assail the French from roofs, barricaded alleyways and buildings whose barred windows and strong doors turned them into fortresses. Unsupported, the Polish lancers charged on too far, and were mostly shot down from the various strong-points; once repelled, the other French columns returned to the assault, and again the Spanish rallied and drove them off. Three times was the Cavalry Barracks taken and recaptured, until after nine hours' ferocious and often hand-to-hand combat, during which the French were assailed with such a shower of balls and stones from the roofs and barricades as to resemble a hailstorm (in Belmas' words),[4] the French called off the attack. Their losses were about 700 men, and six guns which had been firing upon the Portillo Gate but which Spanish fire had made it impossible to remove; Spanish losses were about 300.

Encouraged by the news of the French repulse, Palafox sent Lazan to take command of the city and to announce that he would march to its relief at the first opportunity. For this, he gathered two battalions of insurgents raised in south-west Aragon (the Ferdinand VII and 2nd Aragon Regiments), various deserters and levies, parties of bandits and smugglers and a company of 80 armed Capuchin monks; which represented, in microcosm, the type of forces deployed by the Spanish patriots in opposition to the French in the succeeding years. Lefebvre-Desnouëttes had withdrawn some distance from the city, made calls for its surrender, but otherwise awaited reinforcement; but on learning that Palafox was marching to the city's relief, took the hazardous step of dividing his small force, using part to demonstrate before Saragossa to keep the garrison occupied, and sent the Polish Colonel Chlopiski to intercept Palafox. The latter had probably less than 4,000 men, but Chlopiski even fewer, only the 1st Regiment of the Vistula Legion (Poles), a battalion of the French 15th Line, about 100 cavalry and one fieldpiece.[5] Nevertheless, he fell upon Palafox at Epila on the night of 23/24 June and routed the Spaniards; Palafox sent the levies back to south-west Aragon and by means of a circuitous march regained Saragossa with about 1,000 of his most determined followers on 1 July. Other reinforcements had also reached the city: on 19 June, for example, 300 men of the Estremadura Regiment from the garrison of Barcelona, and 100 volunteers from Tarragona.

In Palafox's absence, the defences of Saragossa had been improved, gates stockaded, walls strengthened with earthen banks, and a continuous firing-step constructed; but the French also were considerably reinforced. In response to Lefebvre-Desnouëttes' appeal, from 26 June more troops arrived, commanded by General Jean-Antoine Verdier, who being senior took command of the whole French force. More troops arrived progressively, including 1,000 National Guardsmen from the regions of *Hautes-Pyrénées* and *Basses-Pyrénées*, and from Pamplona the siege-guns needed to make an impression upon the city walls; according to the engineer Belmas, the total French force numbered 15,556 men, not including staff.

On 28 July Verdier attacked Monte Torrero with four battalions, to use it as a site for his artillery. The Spanish defences were held by only about 500 men, and as the Saragossans were occupied in extinguishing fires begun by the accidental explosion of their main magazine, they received no help; even so, resistance was so feeble that the Spanish commander, Colonel Vincente Falco, was tried and shot for cowardice. In their flight back to Saragossa, the Spaniards abandoned four 4-pounders and a howitzer. That very evening, Verdier began to construct his breaching-batteries, and others were established opposite the gates recently attacked. On the night of 30 June a powerful bombardment opened, causing severe damage and driving many of the city's non-combatants into their cellars; the remainder assisted the soldiers in repairing the damaged walls and constructing barricades behind the gaps.

On 2 July Verdier attacked with six columns, against the gates and those sections of the wall sufficiently beaten down. Despite a temporary lodgement around the Quemada Gate, the French were unable to establish a secure foothold, and drew off, having suffered some 500 casualties. It was during this action that the most enduring story of the siege originated, concerning 'the Maid of Saragossa'. The Spanish defenders of the breastworks at the Portillo Gate, having suffered heavily, abandoned the position as a French charge approached; suddenly, a girl ran forward, snatched a portfire from the hands of a dying gunner (said by some to be her fiancé), and applied it to the touch-hole of a deserted 24-pounder. It discharged its round of canister into the advancing French, and as they wavered, emboldened by the girl's shouts of encouragement, the defenders returned to the barricade and the position was saved.

This one act of heroism became famous throughout Europe, and came to represent the struggle of the Spanish nation against French oppression. Its appeal was obvious: in an age when women were not usually expected to concern themselves with such matters, the idea of a young, attractive girl rushing to defend a vital post abandoned by her male comrades, with the concept of revenge in taking the portfire from the hand of her dying lover, proved an irresistible image. The girl's name is usually given as Agostina Zaragoza, the latter name representative of the spirit of the city; Belmas calls her 'Augustina d'Aragon' and other versions include 'Maria Agostina' and 'Augustina Sarzella'. Palafox – who confirmed the story that the dying gunner was her fiancé – claimed to have witnessed the exploit, and commissioned her as sub-lieutenant of artillery, with a pension for life. Far from being merely a symbolic appointment, Agostina took to wearing uniform and after the siege was still serving with the artillery. Her celebrity was unchallenged: Byron immortalised her in *Childe Harold's Pilgrimage*, Goya depicted her firing the cannon in an etching titled (appropriately) *Que valor!*, and Sir Robert Wilkie painted a more melodramatic version of her exploit. Certainly, she was well suited to represent an incarnation of Spanish resistance: she was young and attractive (if not quite as ravishing as Byron suggested: 'See her long looks that foil the painter's power,/Her fairy form, with more than female grace'); Sir John Carr, who met her in 1809, described her face as 'remarkable for its sweetness', with eyes 'naturally soft',[6] her appearance heightened by her smart uniform bearing, as Sir Charles Vaughan described, a shield upon the arm inscribed with the battle-honour 'Zaragoza'.

For all her celebrity, praise was not universal. Referring to the actions of many Saragossan women in aiding the defence of their city,

Napier stated: 'The current romantic tales, of women rallying the troops and leading them forward at the most dangerous periods of the siege, I have not touched upon, and may perhaps be allowed to doubt; yet it is not unlikely, that when suddenly environed with horrors, the delicate sensitiveness of women, driving them to a kind of phrenzy, might produce actions above the heroism of men, and in patient suffering their superior fortitude is manifest: wherefore I neither wholly believe, nor will deny, their exploits at Zaragoza; merely remarking that for a long time afterwards, Spain swarmed with heroines from that city, clothed in half uniforms, and loaded with weapons.'[7] Sir John Carr noted that in Cadiz (seat of the Spanish provisional government) there were many 'who coldly called this young heroine the Artillery-woman; and observed, that they should soon have nothing but battalions of women in the field, instead of attending to their domestic concerns, if every romantic female was rewarded and commissioned as Augustina [sic] had been. Base detractors! happy would it have been for your country, if many of your soldiers, and most of your chiefs, had acted with the undaunted intrepidity and unshaken patriotism of this young female!'[8]

Having seen his assault fail, Verdier began a regular siege, beginning his siege-trenches on 3 July and pushing them nearer to the walls, in preparation for a main attack on the south, and a secondary attack on the north-west. He detached a contingent across the Ebro on 11 July to interfere with the city's route for supplies and reinforcement via the San Lazaro suburb, but with his entire force only 12–13,000 strong, he was unable to cut off the city completely, so that supplies and assistance still continued to get in.

By 24 July Verdier had captured the Capuchin, Trinitarian and San José convents which lay outside the walls, and in the first three days of August bombarded the city with howitzers and mortars. This caused great devastation, including the destruction of the central hospital; but despite the intensity of the bombardment, the inhabitants of the city continued to leave the safety of their cellars to extinguish the fires and repair the defences. In this they were encouraged by Palafox, who on 30 July issued a proclamation which stated that for the third time he had rejected Verdier's call to surrender, and that though 100 guns might be ranged against the city, 'what are 100 guns to us, who are used to them, and who, like our ancestors the Numantines, are resolved to bury ourselves under the ashes and ruins of our city!'[9]

Such exhortations were needed to help Saragossa face its next great trial. At dawn on 4 August Verdier directed his siege-guns against the gates and walls, opening three breaches, and at 2 p.m. columns were launched against them. The first, comprising the 1st Vistula Legion and the élite companies of the 15th and 70th Line, with four battalions in reserve, aimed for the Santa Engracia convent; the second, composed of the 14th Line and the élite companies of the 44th, stormed a breach near the Santa Engracia Gate; and the third, comprising the 2nd Vistula Legion and élite companies of the 47th Line, with two battalions of the 1st *Légion de Réserve* and the remainder of the 47th in reserve, attacked a breach near the Carmen Gate. Against furious resistance all three columns penetrated the city, until about 1,000 yards of the city's perimeter lay in French hands. Verdier, who had turned over command to Lefebvre-Desnouëttes after suffering a wound in the thigh, sent a message to Palafox requesting capitulation; which, under the prevailing 'rules of war', Palafox would have had every right to concede, without impugning his honour. Instead he sent a short reply: 'Headquarters, Saragossa. War to the knife'.

Throughout the terrible afternoon of 4 August, the French pushed northwards through the maze of squares and alleys towards the Coso, the city's main thoroughfare; every street, every corner, virtually every building was contested. Some of the city's population gave up hope and began to flee over the bridge across the Ebro; the stream of fugitives included both Palafox and his brother the Marquis. In defence of the former, he left to bring up, in person, some 2–3,000 regulars from Catalonia and Valencia who were, he was told, only seven miles from the city; Lazan's motives were less arguable: he admitted that he thought the city lost, and wished to evade capture.

Finally, the French reached the Coso, effectively half-way through the city; but here exhaustion brought an end to their advance. The pause was sufficient to put new heart into the Spaniards; those who had crossed the Ebro were rounded up by their officers and herded back across the bridge, on which a loaded gun was placed to deter further flight. At dusk they counter-attacked, the first charge across the Coso being led by a monk, Fray Ignacio de Santaromana; every member of the attack was shot down. Amid hellish scenes of hand-to-hand combat in which no quarter was given, the French began to be pushed back; burning buildings created an atmosphere which the French engineer Belmas likened to a volcano, with ears assailed by explosions, the cries of the combatants and the screams of the wounded. When fighting subsided after nightfall, the French had lost some of the ground they had won; Belmas records their casualties as 462 dead and 1,505 wounded, more than one-fifth of the troops engaged; Spanish losses must have been about the same.

Both sides laboured through the night of 4/5 August, strengthening barricades, loop-holing houses, and facilitating communications by cutting doors through adjoining properties. When morning came it was probably the French who were more on the defensive, as the Spaniards must have been greatly heartened by their counter-attack of the previous day; but as if both sides were temporarily stunned by the recent carnage, only desultory firing occurred whenever an enemy showed himself amid the hasty fortifications or the destroyed buildings. Palafox joined the relief force and sent one battalion into the city, but otherwise held off upon learning that more reinforcements were en route, and of the defeat and surrender of General Pierre Dupont's French army at Baylen on 22 July; he hoped that Verdier might raise the siege when he, too, received this news. Ultimately this is what happened, though not before Verdier had resumed his bombardment of the city for some days; house-to-house fighting also continued, with all the brutality, if not on the same scale, as before. On 8 August Palafox attacked the French force on the north bank of the Ebro, to clear an unthreatened path for the reinforcement of the city; Verdier withdrew this contingent in the night, and on 14 August blew up his own strong-points, including all those he held within the city, and retired.

The end of the siege was a landmark in the war in Spain, proving that a largely untrained force of civilians could by sheer determination and industry successfully resist a professional army, and by so doing almost turn upside down the accepted conventions of war. French losses in the siege were at least 3,500 – about 22½ per cent of the entire besieging force, and some 54 pieces of artillery (many damaged) were abandoned when Verdier withdrew; the Saragossans must have lost equally as many casualties, and probably considerably more. The Spanish victory, and even more the reasons for it, must have had an incalculable effect upon the resistance being generated throughout the country, in raising morale and demonstrating that the seemingly impossible could be achieved. On 13 August Palafox issued a proclamation which stated that the whole of Europe admired the defence, that soldiers and civilians were equally deserving of praise for their heroism, and that all was due to their fidelity, love of country and religion, and the determination to prefer death to servitude and the abasement of the name of Spain. He added that the wives and sisters of the defenders, 'the sublime women of Saragossa, have by their courage surpassed anything ever recorded in

history'.[10] Excessive claims might have been expected in such a proclamation, but in this case it would be difficult to deny the accuracy of
Palafox's words.

In the event the city's respite was but temporary. As commander
of the forces in Aragon, Palafox collaborated with the army of General
Francisco Castaños, the victor of Baylen, in an attempt to drive the
French from Spain. It never had a real chance of success, as the Spanish
forces, mostly newly raised, were much inferior to the French and hand-
icapped by uninspired or inexperienced commanders; on 23 November
the Spanish were routed at Tudela, most losses falling upon the Army of
Aragon, the survivors of which sought refuge in Saragossa as Castaños
fell back on Madrid. Within days, the French corps of Marshals Moncey
and Ney appeared in front of Saragossa, but when Ney was ordered by
Napoleon to seek out Castaños, Moncey withdrew his own forces to
await sufficient reinforcement to enable the city to be captured.

Ney's withdrawal provided Saragossa with three weeks' invaluable
respite which must have intensified the inhabitants' belief in the divine
supervision of the city's patron saint, Our Lady of the Pillar, who had
been called upon for intercession during the first siege. Indeed, had Ney
and Moncey fallen upon Saragossa in the immediate aftermath of the
Tudela débâcle, it is likely that the city would have been captured. The
engineer who had worked with Palafox during the siege, Don Antonio
San Genis, had planned to turn the city into a modern fortress, but as all
work had to be paid for, progress had been slow. The Tudela defeat, however, galvanised the entire populace, and a great amount of work was
performed in the invaluable three weeks' breathing space. Using rubble
from the ruins inside the city, a new enceinte was constructed, joining
the Augustinian and Trinitarian convents which acted as bastions, with
a semi-circular battery between the two; a ditch 45 feet wide protected
the western side of the defences, and the Aljaferia Castle was connected
to the main defences by a covered way. A new wall was pushed south so
that the river Huerba formed a moat, with two new outworks, the 'Our
Lady of the Pillar' redoubt covering the Santa Engracia Gate, and by for-
tifying the San José convent similar cover was provided for the Quemada
Gate. The ruins of Santa Engracia were made into an artillery position, a
new 'Palafox Battery' was constructed north of San José, and the
defences of San Lazaro were greatly strengthened. Inside the city, houses
were properly loop-holed and regular barricades made, so that with
'every strong building turned into a separate fortification, there was no
weak point, because there could be none in a town which was all

fortress'.[11] Monte Terrero remained a weak point, as there was time only to construct one redoubt and some not very formidable earthworks. Nevertheless the transformation of the city within so short a time was a considerable achievement.

Crucial to this was the leadership of Palafox and the co-operation of the citizens. Palafox recognised the importance of carrying popular support with him, but suggestions that he followed whatever course he believed most popular with the city's leading demagogues, and that they imposed such a reign of terror that the populace was more afraid of them than of the French, is probably an exaggeration. Certainly, the more fanatical of the civilian leaders combined effective dictatorship with religious zeal into a force that was difficult to control, and which was resented by some of the military; but nevertheless there was an unmistakable sense of purpose among all inhabitants of the city, civilian and military alike. The British delegation which visited in October – General Charles Doyle and the diplomat Sir Charles Vaughan – found a form of democracy peculiar for Spain, in which grandees, priests, artisans, farmers and labourers mixed together without prejudice, the great and good showing respect for the poor and humble, and vice versa, a mutual feeling of comradeship presumably born of the tribulations of the first siege, and held together by the force of Palafox's personality.

Palafox gathered huge quantities of food and munitions in the city, and with British supplies arranged by Doyle, there was actually a surplus of firearms. Heavy artillery was in short supply (there were only 60 guns of more than 12-pounder weight, and eight mortars), but of troops there were more than enough, even considering that Monte Terrero would require a garrison of 6,000, and San Lazaro and the San José fort 3,000 men each. Following the defeat at Tudela, thousands of soldiers had sought refuge in Saragossa, so that with reinforcements from Murcia and Valencia, Palafox's army at the beginning of the siege numbered at least 32,000 infantry, 2,000 cavalry and perhaps as many as 10,000 irregulars, most of whom were integrated into the organised regiments during the siege. On New Year's Day 1809, the 'regular' part of the garrison was computed at 30,524 infantry (including the sick; 19,912 under arms), 2,000 cavalry, 1,800 artillery and 800 engineers (mostly workers from the Aragon Canal), with about 2,400 volunteers and 4,100 men from broken regiments who were mostly assigned to artillery and engineering duties. In fact, Palafox probably kept too many men within the city; had a strong force been sent into the country to threaten French communications, far fewer French troops would have been able to concentrate against Saragossa. As it was, only the local peasantry was available to molest French lines of communication. Presumably Palafox's decision not to detach such a harassing force was evidence of his limited strategical appreciation, but perhaps also a reflection upon what had occurred recently when Spanish forces *had* met the French in the open field. Palafox must also have counted on the winter rains interrupting the French operations, flooding their trenches and bringing sickness into their camps; he could hardly have foreseen that the coming winter would be exceptionally dry.

As it happened, the French corps of Marshal Bon Adrien Moncey was already severely depleted by sickness, and probably not a little discouraged by the fact that many of its troops had already endured the horrors of the first siege; but the reinforcement, the corps of Marshal Adolphe Mortier, was in splendid condition. Even deducting Moncey's sick, the combined force arrayed against Saragossa was formidable: 41,671 infantry, 3,409 cavalry and 4,310 artillery and engineers, of whom 5,300 infantry and 700 cavalry were detached to cover communications. They arrived before Saragossa on 20 December, and on the following morning launched a major assault against the two weakest parts of the defences. For the loss of 20 killed and 50 wounded, the whole of Monte Torrero was captured, giving the French a dominating position over the city; the defenders, mostly Valencian troops of General Philippe de Saint-March (or 'Saint-Marc'), behaved badly, and he withdrew them into the main defences. An attack on San Lazaro across the Ebro went rather differently. Entrusted to Gazan's division of Mortier's corps, it was delayed until after the Monte Torrero operation, so that Spanish attention was not divided. Three battalions each of the 21st *Léger* and 100th Line made considerable inroads into the defences, capturing the 'Archbishop's Tower' and a house near the Jesus Convent; thereupon the defenders of the San Lazaro Convent bolted across the river, to be stopped by Palafox in person, who organised a counter-attack which evicted the French from their gains.

Next morning Moncey sent an envoy to Palafox suggesting that he surrender, to preserve the city from 'inevitable total ruin', and in light of the fact that Madrid had fallen. The reply was uncompromising: that those whose only concern was to die with honour couldn't care less about the tactical position, that the fate of Madrid had nothing to do with Saragossa, and that Palafox trusted that the wisdom for which Moncey was known, and which had earned him the name '*Bon*' (the Good), would not allow the French army to be slaughtered, so perhaps

Moncey would care to surrender instead? Moncey immediately began a regular siege, aiming initially at the outlying forts of the Pillar and San José, with a diversionary attack against the Aljaferia Castle. Works were also begun on the far bank of the Ebro to blockade the city from relief, but not to make another attack. As the trenches were opened and pushed nearer to their targets, the Spaniards replied with artillery, but made no large-scale sally against the besiegers, perhaps evidence of lack of tactical awareness on the part of Palafox, and timidity on that of his subordinates.

On 29 December Moncey was recalled to Madrid by Napoleon, his own troops being placed under the command of General Andoche Junot; on 2 January Mortier was ordered to open direct communication with Madrid, so marched away with his strongest infantry division (Suchet's), leaving Junot with fewer than 25,000 men, of whom 8,000 were operating the blockade of San Lazaro. With his forces so stretched, Junot's entire operation could have been disrupted or even overthrown by a determined sally by the Spanish, who had ample troops for such an enterprise without jeopardising the security of the city, but they remained content to stay behind their defences. Nevertheless minor sallies were made, such as one by 1,200 infantry and 300 cavalry on 31 December, which caused the French only about thirty casualties. On 6 January copies of a proclamation by Palafox were thrown into the French trenches, urging the 'foreigners' in the French army (Italians, Poles, Germans, Dutch, etc. – it was written in six languages) to abandon such a disgraceful war; Baron Lejeune, who was serving in the siege as an engineer officer, albeit in an unofficial capacity, noted that the French troops who read it just laughed! On the same day a different kind of sally was made from Saragossa: a Spanish priest bearing a crucifix advanced to within fifty paces of the French trenches and began to preach at them, saying that they were fighting in a bad cause and should follow the path to salvation instead. After a time the French began to fire over his head and he decamped.

On 10 January the main French bombardment opened on the San José and Pillar forts, inflicting terrible damage on the former, and probably hundreds of casualties. By nightfall Palafox had to withdraw its artillery to save the guns from damage or capture, but reinforced the garrison and made a nocturnal foray with 300 men, which was repelled by the fire of two French 4-pounders sited in the advance workings; the French lost two killed and five wounded, yet Lejeune stated that 60 dead Spaniards were left behind in the trenches. By the next afternoon a breach had been battered in the wall of San José, and at 3 p.m. General Grandjean, commander of the 1st Division of the French III Corps, made an assault with 600 men (the seven *voltigeur* companies of the 14th and 44th Line), while the engineer Captain Daguenet led a small party to a plank bridge at the rear. Part of the garrison escaped before the French broke in, others (according to Lejeune) were killed when the discharge of their own firearms brought down a damaged ceiling upon them, and others surrendered. For the loss of only eight dead and 30 wounded, the French had thus seized a vital post under the very walls of Saragossa; and then proceeded to reduce the second. By 15 January a breach had been opened in the Pillar redoubt, which was stormed that night by part of the 1st Regiment of the Vistula Legion and a small party of miners, under the command of the engineer Colonel Rogniat. Most of the defenders escaped before the attackers broke in; the French lost one man dead and two wounded, and now commanded the entire southern stretch of the enceinte.

As the siege progressed, conditions became progressively more unpleasant for both besiegers and besieged. At the start, all the French suffered was a lack of salt, compelling them to season their soup with gunpowder (even this deficiency was remedied when a geologist among the French officers discovered a convenient salt mine); but as time wore on supplies became interrupted, rations were cut and sickness increased. For the besieged the quality of life deteriorated more rapidly. Although rations were plentiful (fresh meat and vegetables excepted), some of the troops were ill clad and unable to keep warm, while the civilian population led a troglodytic existence, emerging from their cellars only at night to help repair the damaged defences. With so many packed into airless and insanitary cellars, disease spread so rapidly that by mid-January many of the regular troops were incapacitated by sickness. As the work of repair and fortification continued, the garrison lost its skilful engineer, Saint-Genis, who was killed at the Palafox battery while directing its fire on the French siege-works.[12] Napier paid him a memorable tribute, stating that he 'died not only with the honour of a soldier, but the glory of a patriot. Falling in the noblest cause, his blood stained the ramparts which he himself had raised for the protection of his native place.'[13]

The city was not entirely cut off; messages occasionally got in by boat along the Ebro, including those from Lazan, who had escaped by this route and was promising to bring relief; and Lejeune recorded an unsuccessful attempt by Doyle to send in further munitions. This conduit also allowed Palafox to issue an entirely bogus proclamation on 16

January, announcing victories over the French which had never occurred, but which served to raise morale.

The bombardment continued as the trenches pushed closer to the walls, but still Palafox declined to launch a serious counter-attack. A sally on 23 January succeeded in overrunning a section of the French forward trench and spiking the guns in a second-line battery, but even this was carried out by no more than 200 men, most of whom never returned to the city. By this time the French had a new commander. When Junot learned that Marshal Jean Lannes was returning from sick-leave to supersede him, he flew into a rage (perhaps evidence of the later mental instability which was to afflict him), and ordered an immediate attack to gain the glory of victory for himself. Fortunately the engineer commandant, General comte Lacoste, was able to dissuade him, the siege not having progressed far enough to permit an assault. Lannes arrived on 22 January to find the situation deteriorating, with illness among the besiegers and increasing guerrilla threats to their communications. Lannes protected his position by recalling Mortier closer, and intensifying the bombardment until three breaches were opened, two at the Palafox battery and one at Santa Engracia. Accordingly, Lannes informed Palafox of the imminence of assault, declaring that humanity forced him to request Saragossa's surrender, before the city was reduced to ashes. Palafox replied that Lannes would need ten times the number of troops before capitulation would be considered.

On 27 January two columns of *voltigeurs* under General Habert assailed the Palafox battery, and the 1st Regiment of the Vistula Legion under Colonel Chlopiski, Santa Engracia. One of Habert's columns was able only to make a lodgement, but the others seized their objectives, and a quarter of a mile of Saragossa's enceinte fell into French hands. Under normal conditions, this would surely have been the signal for the surrender of the garrison; but this was not a normal siege, and French success heralded only a period of terrible street-fighting. The fortitude exhibited by the citizens and garrison of Saragossa was exemplified by the Carmelite monk Santiago Sas, who claimed to have killed seventeen attackers on the day of the assault, and was seen with his robes tucked up to bare his arms and legs, covered from head to foot in the blood of those he had killed, running sword in hand among the defenders, urging them to follow his example. At the same time, recorded Lejeune, the redoubtable Agostina re-appeared in command of a company of women formed by the Countess Bureta, one of Saragossa's leading noblewomen, 'of heroic disposition, who is said to have displayed the greatest intelligence and the noblest character during both sieges'.[14] By assisting the combatants and in caring for the sick and injured, she contributed as much to the defence as anyone; and it is satisfying to record that she survived the siege, and afterwards married the head of Saragossa's last *junta*, Don Pedro Maria Ric.

In the final stage of the battle for Saragossa, Lannes decided to minimise his casualties by taking the city building by building, block by block, by means of mining, exploding charges of gunpowder under the Spanish-held defences, and by using the ruins of each captured building as a base for attacking the next, a slow but inexorable process. For their part the Spaniards determined to contest every foot, and despite the veneration with which ecclesiastical property was regarded in Spain, no compromise was made and religious establishments were contested just as savagely – perhaps even more so – than secular buildings, providing a dreadful contrast between the essential sanctity of religious buildings and the slaughter which occurred in them. This was remarked upon by Lejeune who, twice wounded on the day of the assault on the breaches, paused by a pietà, around which bodies were littered and which was splashed with blood. In his weakened condition, the smoke and dust swirling around the sculpture seemed to Lejeune to form a halo, and the figure of the Madonna seemed to move, as if requesting divine intervention to cause the carnage to stop. For a moment he thought he was witnessing a miracle, until brought to his senses by a draught of wine given him by General Valazé, chief of the engineer staff; but had such an event been possible, supplication for an end to the agony of Saragossa would not have been inappropriate.

Another desperate fight in a sanctified setting occurred on 1 February when the French blew a gap in the wall of the church of the San Augustin Convent, north of the Palafox battery. They stormed inside and took the high altar, but were faced with a barricade of benches across the nave, the defenders disputing every foot, and firing down from the organ-loft and even from the roof. Not until nightfall did the French finally gain possession of the ruin. It was in one of these fights that the ubiquitous Marcellin Marbot was shot leading an attack, by a flat, serrated-edged slug fired from a blunderbuss, calculated to do much more damage than a conventional musket-ball. Entering near the heart and being extracted next to the spine, this bizarre object was sent by Lannes to Napoleon to exemplify the extraordinary efforts being made by the defenders. Having examined it, Napoleon sent it to Marbot's mother as a souvenir!

Because of their determination not to quit even hopeless positions, the Spaniards' casualties were enormous, and even aroused the sympathy of the French. On 1 February Lejeune accompanied the chief engineer, General Lacoste, to the Santa Engracia area; as they walked, Lacoste spoke of his desire to retire to be with his new wife, with whom he had spent just five days before being ordered on service. Supervising the blowing up of some houses, Lacoste took such pity on the brave Spanish defenders that he ordered mortars to bombard them, in the hope that they would quit before the charges went up. Eventually the charge was fired and the buildings collapsed, two companies of the 1st Regiment of the Vistula Legion rushing forward to occupy the rubble; Lacoste and his aide were looking on when both were shot through the forehead by Spaniards who had not left the area. The aide was killed on the spot; poor Lacoste died shortly afterwards, the poignancy of his death subsumed by the carnage around him.[15] Napier again gave an appropriate verdict: 'a young man, intrepid, skilful, and endowed with genius [who] perished like a brave soldier'.[16]

With Rogniat appointed in Lacoste's place, the house-to-house fighting continued. Rogniat ordered his sappers to use reduced charges so as to leave parts of buildings standing to provide cover for the attackers; the Spaniards responded by coating the walls with tar and setting them alight (most buildings containing insufficient woodwork to make a respectable blaze), further to delay the French until the fires had been extinguished. The shortage of wood led to barricades being constructed from books, the ecclesiastical establishments losing priceless libraries for this purpose and for fuelling camp-fires. Also much in demand were ancient parchments which formed drier bedding than straw, and oil paintings, the varnished canvas being used as waterproof covers for the huts in which the besiegers sheltered.

Some of the fighting took place underground when the Spanish tried to disrupt French mining activity with countermines. Lacking trained miners they had little success, though fierce actions occurred when they did break into French galleries. On one occasion the French sprang a mine when they detected the approach of Spanish miners; the explosion entombed them alive, whereupon the French, showing rare humanity in so vicious a struggle, tried to dig them out, but managed to save only three. Not all the mining was totally destructive in its results; in their digging the miners found several hoards of ancient coins, so that the antiquary Captain Véron-Reville of the 8th Company of Miners acquired a valuable collection as a result of his excavations.

93

More significant was the subterranean existence of the city's population, the epidemic fevers being compounded by the miasma of putrefaction from the many unburied bodies lying in the streets. The thick fog which arose from the Ebro every morning mingled with the smoke from burning buildings and acrid gun-smoke, producing a pestilential air which choked the combatants of both sides. At least the French had some relief from the contagion by the regular rotation of units between firing-line and siege-camps, but for the besieged there was no escape, so that by the beginning of February the garrison was recorded as having less than 8,500 men under arms, having lost about 10,000 dead and the remainder sick. Palafox himself fell ill, but continued to direct the defence from his bed. So desperate was the plight of the besieged that almost all the troops who were fit to fight were deployed to oppose the French; the northern part of the city was held by a skeleton garrison and the western wall was guarded by the sick, some of whom actually died of their illness at their posts. French morale was also suffering, Belmas recording murmuring to the effect that they would all be buried under the rubble of the city before the fanatics were overcome.

To attempt something different, Lannes determined to open a new front on the far bank of the Ebro, so the bombardment of the San Lazaro suburb was intensified. One of its strong-points, the Jesus Convent, was stormed successfully on 8 February, but operations were then temporarily suspended as half of Gazan's division had to be withdrawn to face an attempted relief-force under Lazan and another of the Palafox brothers, Francisco, which approached to within twenty miles of the city but retired in the face of the French brigade. Meanwhile street-fighting continued inexorably at bayonet-point. Equal horrors were experienced behind the besieged garrison's firing-line, for the most fanatical of the defenders set up gallows to hang any who were regarded as insufficiently zealous. Something like a reign of terror circulated in the city, much to the disgust of Palafox, but ill as he was, he could not oppose the excesses of his colleagues who, in addition to slaying their own countrymen, were at least helping to maintain the resistance. It is sad to record that among those most guilty of the execution of their fellows were not only the peasant leaders, but a number of monks and other religious personalities.

On 10 February the French at last pushed their front line on to the Coso, the city's main thoroughfare, and captured the convent of San Francisco, which lay between the Coso and Santa Engracia, by means of a mine driven underneath it. Hearing the Spanish counter-mining, the

French hastened to explode 3,000 pounds of gunpowder; the result was devastating. Unaware of the imminence of the French attack, the Spanish had made no attempt to evacuate San Francisco, which housed their main equipment manufactory; so that in addition to blowing up the defenders of the position – the grenadier company of the 1st Valencia Regiment and 300 irregulars, about 400 civilian workers, mainly women, were also killed. The explosion provided yet another level of horror for those involved in the fighting, for human remains were flung high into the air, and scattered in terrible profusion not only around San Francisco itself but on to the streets and roof-tops for hundreds of yards around; describing a scene truly hellish, Lejeune recorded how blood from these rent bodies filled the guttering of a nearby building and poured out of gargoyles in a hideous torrent on to the fighters below. Small wonder that he remarked that even with his experience of combat, never in any war can there have been a more dreadful scene than that which greeted those who moved in to occupy the rubble of San Francisco.

If the French had hoped that this cataclysmic explosion would have stunned the Spaniards, such hopes were confounded immediately; even before the dust had settled a Spanish force dashed into the ruins to contest them foot by foot, and a party of irregulars, led by the French émigré Colonel de Fleury, seized the belfry, which still stood. De Fleury, commander of the Swiss Regiment of Aragon which had been destroyed in an earlier attack on San Lazaro, held out in the tower until next day, when he and his companions were overcome at bayonet-point. Those who fought inside the ruins of San Francisco discovered yet more horrors: the explosion had broken open old tombs and scattered the contents wide. Lejeune was particularly appalled by the shrivelled corpse of a bishop, dressed in his full vestments, which pointed its arms at the French as if condemning them for what they had done. Perhaps it is not surprising that, once the ruins were secured, the French soused themselves from wineskins discovered in the place, and having emptied the contents, blew up the skins and played football, surely an attempt to introduce some normality into a place which must have resembled nothing so much as a glimpse of hell.

The capture of the bell tower gave the French a position from which to overlook the Spanish-held part of the city. What they saw must have raised their morale, for the damage sustained was clearly visible, as were heaps of unburied bodies lying unattended in the streets; Lejeune remarked that the whole city resembled nothing but an open cemetery. Only the monks and the women seemed to retain any energy; from the

95

listless way they moved, the others seemed completely fought-out. The gallows also attracted much attention.

At least the rotation of troops allowed the attackers some respite, to withdraw to their camps outside the walls, where the mild winter had given way to an early spring, the scent of flowers and even the ripening of wild strawberries seeming to presage not only the end of winter, but an end to the horrors of the siege. Lannes himself adverted to this when, touring the French camp, he encountered a group of Poles (religiously more devout than many of the French) who were gazing with reverence upon a looted painting, a Murillo depicting Christ and Saint Peter walking on the water. Lannes likened the painting to their own situation, quoting Matthew 14:31: 'O thou of little faith, wherefore didst thou doubt?'; if only the troops trusted him, said Lannes, he would soon lead them to victory. This produced the first smiles and cheers evident in the French camp for days.

On 18 February Lannes took a major step towards the success he had promised, by storming San Lazaro on the far bank of the Ebro. After a bombardment opened breaches, three columns assailed them and drove on to seize the end of the bridge across the river. Some of the defenders managed to cross to the city (the commander of the garrison, the Baron de Versage, was killed by a roundshot as he crossed the bridge), others leaped into the river, but the main body of the garrison was captured as it tried to break out to the west. With the Saragossans preoccupied by this action, French attacks in the city made considerable progress, capturing the south-west corner of the city and the university; and with the fall of San Lazaro, the French were now able to bombard Saragossa from the east.

The operations of this day were decisive. Already surrender was being spoken of in the city without attracting the condemnation and the noose as before, and even Palafox had realised the inevitable. Too ill to continue, he resigned the military command to the *émigré* General Philippe de Saint-March, while sending an overture to Lannes (and thereby ensuring that it would be his successor who would bear any opprobrium arising from the surrender!). Lannes demanded unconditional surrender, and Palafox turned over the civil administration of the city, and the responsibility for negotiating, to a 33-strong *junta*, of whom eight were churchmen. (As a foreigner, Saint-March could not speak for the inhabitants of Saragossa, who still resented his conduct of the defence of Monte Terrero.) Some members of the *junta*, evidently including all the clergymen and even Saint-March, wanted to fight on;

but more realistic counsels prevailed, and Lannes sent his ADC (oddly, also named Saint-Marc) to open negotiations. As these began, in a palace near the Portillo Gate, some French engineers, who in the chaos of wrecked buildings had never received the order to suspend hostilities, let off a mine; suspecting treachery, a mob rushed the palace but Saint-Marc was saved by some Spanish officers who, with drawn swords, declared they would defend him to the death rather than have their honour violated by the mob's murder of the envoy. When the crowd had been quietened – Lannes sent another envoy to explain that the springing of the mine had been accidental – a deputation from the *junta* left the city to arrange terms of surrender. Lannes agreed that the civilians would be unmolested, provided they surrendered their weapons, but that any troops unwilling to swear allegiance to Joseph Bonaparte would be marched off as prisoners of war. With reluctance, especially on the part of the clergy, this was agreed, but part of the garrison stood to arms during the following night to suppress any mutiny by those who still pleaded to resist to the very end.

At about noon on 21 February the Saragossa garrison marched out of the Portillo Gate to lay down their weapons. The numbers were stated variously, between 8,000 and 13,000; Belmas put the number at 8,200, with the sick who were too ill to move raising the number to 12,000; but it was their appearance which made the greatest impression upon the French. Lejeune declared that he had never seen a sadder or more touching sight than those who marched out to pile their arms, 'all frightfully emaciated', many with scarcely the strength to carry their muskets, all wracked with disease, unshaven, tattered, filthy and reeking of powder-smoke; but although 'mere living spectres', 'their whole bearing still radiated forth an indescribable dignity and pride ... when the moment came for the gallant troops to pile their arms and deliver up their flags to us, many of them gave violent expression to their despair. Their eyes gleamed with rage, and their savage looks seemed to say that they had counted our troops, and deeply regretted having yielded to such a small number of enemies'.[17] They shuffled off towards imprisonment in France, many succumbing en route to the fevers which had finally compelled them to surrender.

The French who occupied Saragossa were appalled to find that the city resembled a charnel-house, the inhabitants like ghosts living among the 6,000 unburied bodies which lay in the streets; Lejeune observed that the sharp spring air had so dried the corpses that not only were they neither repulsive in appearance nor a source of contagion, but were so light that they might have been pasteboard cut-outs. Despite the terms of surrender granted by Lannes, there was some looting by the French, and some clergymen, regarded as being the most inveterate of their opponents, were maltreated. Notably, Palafox's chaplain, the Italian professor of theology and philosophy at the university, Basilio Boggiero, and the ferocious Santiago Sas, were both done to death. Few other reprisals were taken, for the sights and sounds of the city seemed to have stunned the victors. Belmas described it as 'a horror to behold', fires burning, ruined buildings laced with bodies and pieces of bodies, the injured and dying staggering about and expiring where they fell, and where the civilians gathered for shelter nothing could be heard but cries of hunger, suffering and despair.[18]

The same words, 'a horror to behold', were used by Lannes himself in his report of the conclusion of the operations. Inconceivably, he remarked, the city authorities had estimated that some 54,000 people had died during the siege, about 20,000 of them soldiers. Of a population numbering some 55,000 when the investment began, only some 15,000 starving, disease-ridden civilians were left, although some thousands had quit the city after the surrender in an attempt to escape the pestilence which, in about a month following the surrender, Lannes estimated might have claimed another 10,000 victims. French losses are difficult to estimate; Belmas recorded the casualties as including 3,000 infantrymen, but makes no mention of other arms-of-service or of those who died or were incapacitated by typhus and similar fevers. In all their losses may have been as high as 10,000.[19] In the city, it was weeks before the dead were buried, months before the taint of sickness left the air, and even five years later it was still one-third in ruins.

If the French generally treated the poor survivors with benevolence during the years of French occupation, they were less well-disposed towards Palafox; indeed, on Napoleon's instructions he was treated less like a prisoner of war and more like a traitor, and imprisoned in the fortress of Vincennes until December 1813. Like Palafox, Agostina fell victim to the fever and, although recognised by the French, was believed to be dying and was left in a hospital. Recovering unexpectedly, she evaded her guards and rejoined the Spanish royalist forces. At Cadiz she encountered General Doyle, who read her a letter written to him by his friend Palafox, during his journey to France as a prisoner, which gives a hint of the conditions under which he was held: dated Pamplona, 13 March, it pleaded: 'My dearest Doyle – my friend – my brother – for God's sake send by the bearer, or by letter on Bayonne, some money ... This is the only comfort I can now receive from your good heart. My dearest friend, they have robbed me to the very shirt, *Adieu – adieu – adieu!*' 'The face of Augustina, which ... is remarkable for its sweetness, assumed a mingled expression of commiseration for her hero, and revenge against his enemies. Her eyes, naturally soft, flashed with peculiar fire and animation; tears rolled down her cheeks; and, clasping her hands as the last word "*adieu*" was repeated, she exclaimed, "Oh, those base invaders of my country, those oppressors of its best patriots! Should the fate of war place any of them within my power, I will instantly deliver up their throats to the knife"'.[20]

Palafox survived his imprisonment and in June 1814 was confirmed as Captain-General of Aragon; but he was deprived of his offices and forced to retire into private life when he supported the liberal constitution against the king, whose continuing rule was only made possible by a French invasion in 1823, ironically in support of the same sovereign whom Napoleon had deposed. Palafox was accorded the title of Duke of Saragossa by Queen Maria Christina, and from 1836 was again Captain-General of Aragon, supporting the infant Queen Isabella II when the Carlist Wars began. He died in Madrid on 15 February 1847, almost thirty-eight years to the day, but for a week, since the capitulation of Saragossa. The other great character associated with the siege, Agostina, was laid to rest in the Portillo Church where a memorial to the heroes of the siege was erected.

Various theories were advanced to explain why the people of Saragossa made such a determined resistance, quite unprecedented during the Napoleonic Wars and against all the accepted 'rules' or expectations of warfare. Some explanations were less than generous, concentrating upon the compulsion exerted by fanatics and upon the powers of religion, which to contemporary British eyes was often equated with dread and superstition. Few British writers exhibited much sympathy with the religion they encountered in the Peninsula, especially when it involved the veneration of, and belief in the intercessionary powers of saints. A typical anecdote concerned the statue of the Virgin of the Pillar: 'When the French were driven out of Saragossa, the Spaniards said it was the statue of the Virgin which stood at their gates that performed the exploit. An Irish monk, who has lived here [Corunna] for 20 years, and who told us the story, said: "a fig for their saints – the English have two saints, St. Powder and St. Ball, and when they want to enter a place they use very little ceremony."'[21] Contemporary British comments should be tempered with a knowledge of such sentiments.

William Napier was perhaps the least charitable, stating of the Spanish that 'There is not upon the face of the earth a people so attractive in the friendly intercourse of society ... As companions, they are incomparably the most agreeable of mankind, but danger and disappointment attend the man who, confiding in their promises and energy, ventures upon a difficult enterprise.'[22] He accounted for the defence of Saragossa by 'the system of terror which was established by the Spanish leaders ... The slightest word or even gesture of discontent, was punished with instant death. A stern band of priests and plebeian-leaders, in whose hands Palafox was a tool, ruled with such furious energy, that resistance to the enemy was less dangerous than disobedience to their orders: suspicion was the warrant of death, and this system once begun, ceased not until the town was taken in the second siege.'[23] The spirit of Saragossa, he wrote, was neither common to the whole nation, nor 'the effect of unalloyed virtue. It was not patriotism, nor was it courage, nor skill, nor fortitude, nor a system of terror, but all these combined under peculiar circumstance, that upheld the defence'.[24] Napier admitted that 'the Spaniard is patient under privations, firm in bodily suffering, prone to sudden passion, vindictive, bloody, remembering insult longer than injury, and cruel in his revenge',[25] and after centuries of oppression by 'civil and religious despotism',[26] was peculiarly susceptible to the influence of religious fanaticism. He suggested that the religious establishment, fearing a decline of their influence under the more enlightened French government, 'found no difficulty in persuading an ignorant and bigoted people, that the aggressive stranger was also the enemy of religion and accursed of God; processions, miracles, prophecies, distribution of reliques, and the appointment of saints to the command of the armies, fanaticised the mass of the patriots. In every part of the peninsula the clergy were distinguished for their active zeal; monks and friars were invariably either leaders in the tumults, or at the side of those who were, instigating them to barbarous actions.'[27] Even Lejeune concurred, remarking that threats of divine and physical immolation so inspired the weakest to act 'much against their will'.[28]

Whatever the truth in these assessments, they are perhaps insufficient to explain the fortitude with which the defence of Saragossa was conducted. The additional element of natural bravery and ingrained loyalty to a cause was certainly accepted by some who witnessed the struggle of the Spanish people at first hand. Sir John Colborne explained why, in his opinion, even with these traits of character the Spanish armies enjoyed so little success: 'The privations and misery endured by a large mass of the people of Spain from their patriotism and hatred to their oppressors, were seldom equalled. With a brave, hardy, active, abstemious peasantry, fond of glory, it may appear extraordinary that the struggle of the Spaniards was prolonged for six years without any decided success, but the Central Junta and the presumption and obstinacy of most of the men placed at the head of the armies rendered their perseverance and courage useless.'[29] Dynamic leadership was another factor: Palafox may have been undistinguished as a strategist, but he was able to inspire both military and civilians into co-operation for the common cause; without him, probably neither section of the defenders would have held out as long as they did, and certainly neither could have done so alone.

For whatever reasons or combination of factors, the defence of Saragossa remains one of the most extraordinary stories of fortitude in the face of unimaginable horror, and against a reliable, professional army with a legacy of success. Saragossa was a Spanish defeat, but it served to inspire the Spanish nation to continue the fight, and perhaps began the process by which the French army, while continuing to do its duty, became progressively more disillusioned with the war in Spain. What for them had begun as another step on the virtually uninterrupted path to victory, became a trial which caused a fatal sapping of resources, leading to a resigned cynicism articulated in the popular expression, 'This war means death for the men, ruin for the officers, and a fortune for the generals'. In the final analysis, Napier's comment surely rings true: 'When the other events of the Spanish war shall be lost in the obscurity of time, or only traced by disconnected fragments, the story of Zaragoza, like some ancient triumphal pillar standing amidst the ruins, will tell a tale of past glory ...'[30]

NOTES

1. *Twenty-Five Years in the Rifle Brigade*, W. Surtees, London, 1833, pp. 77, 92.
2. *History of the War in the Peninsula*, W. F. P. Napier, London, 1832-40, I, p. 72.
3. Ibid., I, p. 65.
4. *Journaux des Sièges faits ou soutenus par les français dans la Péninsule, de 1807 à 1814*, J. Belmas, Paris, 1836, II, p.23.
5. Sir Charles Oman (*History of the Peninsular War*, Oxford, 1903, II, p. 151) states that Chlopiski had four guns; Belmas that there was just *'une pièce de 4'*, i.e., one 4-pounder.
6. *Gentleman's Magazine*, December, 1811, p. 549.
7. Napier, *op. cit.*, I, pp. 70–1.
8. *Gentleman's Magazine*, December, 1811, p. 549.
9. Belmas, *op. cit.*, II, pp. 95–6.
10. Ibid., p. 111.

11. Napier, *op. cit.*, II, p. 23.
12. The date of his death is reported variously: Oman accepts 13 January, Belmas 26 January, Napier 29 January, Lejeune 1 February.
13. Napier, *op. cit.*, II, p. 37.
14. Ibid., p. 24.
15. Lejeune (*Memoirs of Baron Lejeune*, trans. and ed. Mrs. A. Bell, London, 1897) mistakenly calls this area San Augustin; Belmas specifies that it was to the right of Santa Engracia.
16. Napier, *op. cit.*, II, p. 37.
17. Lejeune, *op. cit.*, I, pp. 201–2.
18. Belmas, *op. cit.*, II, pp. 323–5.
19. This figure is accepted by Oman (*op. cit.*, II, p. 140), where there are estimates of the numbers of sick among the French units.
20. *Gentleman's Magazine*, December, 1811, p. 549.
21. *The Public Ledger*, 22 November 1808.
22. Napier, *op. cit.*, I, p. 43.
23. Ibid., pp. 71–2.
24. Ibid., II, p. 48.
25. Ibid., I, p. 38.
26. Ibid.
27. Ibid., I, p. 39
28. Lejeune, *op. cit.*, I, p. 120.
29. *The Life of John Colborne, Field Marshal Lord Seaton*, G. C. Moore Smith, London, 1903, p. 135.
30. Napier, *op. cit.*, II, p. 48.

— 5 —

The Bridgehead
ASPERN-ESSLING
21–22 May 1809

An essential factor concerning any offensive operation is the ability to reinforce, supply and, if necessary, evacuate the troops in the front line. This ability can be compromised by the enemy, but natural hazards are also of crucial importance, most obviously command of the sea and the weather in amphibious operations. Few of these were undertaken during the Napoleonic Wars in the face of serious opposition, but the difficulties are demonstrated perhaps most clearly in the disastrous British expedition to Ostend in 1798, when heavy seas prevented the escape of the landing-force and resulted in its capture. Although often forming a strategic target or line of defence, rivers presented less of an obstacle, but an opposed crossing could involve similarities with a landing upon an enemy's coast. With the restricted room for manoeuvre at a bridgehead, the attackers might be forced to adopt a defensive posture against counter-attacks, the fighting being the more severe in the knowledge that withdrawal could at best be fraught with danger, and at worst virtually impossible. It was under such circumstances during the Austrian campaign of 1809 that Napoleon suffered the first major reverse of his career.

The principal campaign of the war against Austria was waged along the Danube, against an Austrian army re-formed and rejuvenated by the Archduke Charles, the foremost Imperial commander of his generation. After the Austrians gained an early surprise, Napoleon re-established the initiative and attempted to trap the Archduke's army on the southern bank of the Danube. However, the Austrians succeeded in crossing the river at Ratisbon (Regensburg), which put the great watercourse between Napoleon and themselves. Napoleon's strategic aim was always to defeat the enemy's field army rather than to occupy territory for its own sake, so his capture of Vienna on 13 May 1809 was of little consequence to the state of the war as long as the Archduke Charles maintained such a huge army to the north of the capital and the Danube.

Napoleon's dilemma was stark: if he delayed until his own forces were fully concentrated, the Archduke's army would also be reinforced and would present an even greater danger; but to act immediately and cross the Danube with all his army might give the Austrians the oppor-

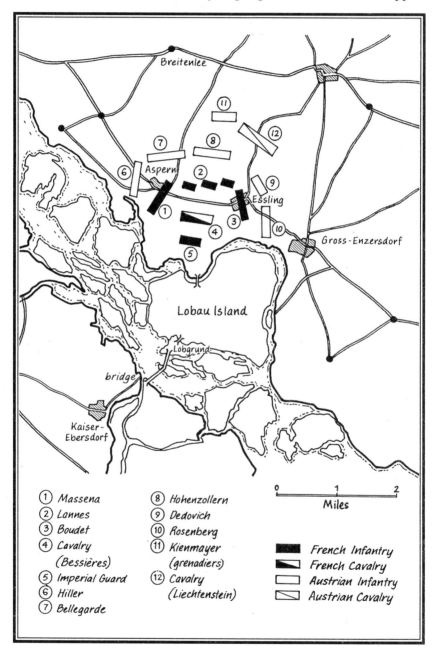

1. Massena
2. Lannes
3. Boudet
4. Cavalry (Bessières)
5. Imperial Guard
6. Hiller
7. Bellegarde
8. Hohenzollern
9. Dedovich
10. Rosenberg
11. Kienmayer (grenadiers)
12. Cavalry (Liechtenstein)

French Infantry
French Cavalry
Austrian Infantry
Austrian Cavalry

tunity of themselves crossing to the southern bank, severing Napoleon's communications. His decision was a compromise: to leave sufficient forces to protect his rear, and to cross the Danube to establish a bridge-head from which to operate against Charles, a plan which owed some-thing to the fact that Napoleon was unaware of how near the main Austrian army was, probably believing that he was faced only with that part of the Austrian army commanded by General Johann Hiller and the evacuated garrison of Vienna. His most immediate problem, however, was just how to cross the Danube, for the retiring Vienna garrison had cut the four bridges immediately north of the city, and the presence of Austrian forces in the vicinity of the northern bank precluded any attempt to force a crossing there. Bridging the river by pontoons or sim-ilar constructions would be fraught with hazard, not just from the Aus-trians but by the Danube's proclivity for sudden and violent rushes of the late spring flood-waters (in the event, the river rose some fourteen feet during the operation); but ignoring or at least being untroubled by the warnings he received, Napoleon sought a crossing-place.

Three locations were suggested. One, some ten miles east of Vienna, was discounted by virtue of its steep banks; another, at Nuss-dorf to the north of Vienna, was attempted briefly by Marshal Jean Lannes who ferried a small detachment across the river, but they were forced to surrender by the Austrians covering the destroyed bridges. (While observing this action Lannes tripped over a rope and fell into the Danube. Napoleon helped pull him out, and the incident perhaps helped convince them that a crossing at this point was impossible). The remaining alternative was to bridge the river about four miles east of Vienna, at the town of Kaiser-Ebersdorf, where the Danube was wider and the current slower, and where was the largest of the many islands in this part of the river. Lobau island, more than five miles in circum-ference, though some 825 yards from the south bank of the Danube, was large enough to be used as a base for crossing to the northern bank, 125 yards beyond. On the northern bank was a slight salient or semi-peninsula with a village at each end, Aspern in the west and Essling in the east, which were capable of being transformed into a defensible bridgehead, to resist counter-attacks while reinforcements were pushed over the river via Lobau island. It was a reasonable position provided that the line of communications across the Danube could be main-tained, and that only limited numbers of Austrian troops could be thrown at the bridgehead; but neither of these conditions worked in favour of the French, and the whole concept of the operation may demonstrate a level of carelessness into which Napoleon sometimes descended from this period of his career.

Napoleon's engineers and pontoneers began to prepare material for the crossing, involving a bridge to the small islet of Schneidergrund, another to the larger islet of Lobgrund, and yet another span from there over the twenty feet of water to Lobau itself. The total required some 68 pontoons and nine rafts; some of the material was improvised (for example, chests filled with roundshot served as anchors). On the evening of 18 May 1809 the first French troops crossed from the south bank to Lobgrund, elements of General Molitor's division of Masséna's IV Corps being rowed across and driving away the small Austrian garrison. Under cover of darkness the bridging began, and during the following day Molitor took possession of the partially wooded Lobau island, establishing six guns to cover the crossing-point at Mühlau, where the bridge from Lobau to the north bank would be fixed.

By midday on 20 May the bridge from the south bank to Lobau was completed, and immediately the troops who had been marshalled around Kaiser-Ebersdorf began to cross, the remainder of Masséna's corps in support of Molitor, including artillery and General Antoine Lasalle's light cavalry division. Napoleon himself crossed to Lobau and ordered the construction of the final bridge from there to the promontory on the north bank, the 125-yard gap being filled by fifteen Austrian pontoons and three trestles. The bridge was constructed under fire from Austrian troops on the north bank, but a small party of *voltigeurs* was thrown across the river and the Austrians retired. A breastwork was constructed at the Lobau end of the bridge, under cover of which the pontoons were launched, and by about 6 p.m. the bridge was operational. Immediately the troops began to cross from Lobau, led by Molitor's division, which fanned out to occupy the villages of Aspern and Essling, followed by Lasalle's light cavalry. Progress was not easy, however, the bridges being narrow and unsteady; the hazardous nature of the position being confirmed at about 5 p.m. when a large boat filled with stones, floated down the Danube by the Austrians, smashed the bridge between Schneidergrund and Lobgrund, marooning all the troops who had crossed to Lobau, and splitting in half Marulaz's light cavalry division as it was crossing. The bridge was repaired during the night and was operational again by morning.

Despite having a considerable force of light cavalry to reconnoitre, Napoleon still had no clear knowledge of the proximity of the Austrian army. He spent the night on Lobau, but asked that observation to be kept from the church tower at Aspern. About midnight or later a report was received that camp-fires were visible to the left of the French bridgehead, but in insufficient numbers to suggest that the whole Austrian army was bearing down upon them; but that, in fact, was what was happening. Of this the French troops spending the night on Lobau had no inkling, spending part of a beautiful, moonlit night by singing around their camp-fires with all the gaiety that might have been found during manoeuvres in peacetime.

Using the villages of Aspern and Essling as bastions on an enceinte, Napoleon was able to arrange a defensive perimeter to protect the bridgehead. Initially the first units had pushed east of Essling to the village of Gross-Enzersdorf, but as this would have been too exposed, they pulled back into Essling itself. The larger of the villages, Aspern, consisted of sturdy brick houses, a church and walled cemetery, with a watercourse and earth banks between the village and the Danube. Essling was only about half the size of Aspern, but included a natural strong-point in a large, three-storeyed granary, and walled and ditched gardens. Both villages had been occupied on the night of the 20th, but unaware of the proximity of the Austrians, no attempt had been made to entrench the positions. Conversely, the Archduke Charles was well-informed of the French crossing of the Danube, and determined to drive them from their bridgehead.

By 4 a.m. on 21 May Napoleon was up and canvassing the opinion of his Marshals as to the likelihood of a major Austrian offensive. Jean-Baptiste Bessières, commanding the cavalry reserve, relying on the inaccurate information supplied by his scouts, concurred with Lannes in believing that only the Austrian rearguard was in the vicinity; Masséna thought that the whole Austrian army might be near, but with the bridgehead established, it would have been unduly timid to have pulled back without certain information that a serious attack was about to be mounted. Having been split between Aspern and Essling overnight, Molitor's division was now united in Aspern, with the newly arrived divisions of Legrand and Boudet (both from Masséna's IV Corps) posted to Aspern and Essling respectively. The area between the two villages, along a slightly banked east–west road, was occupied by Bessières' cavalry. Although he was officially commander of II Corps (still in the neighbourhood of Vienna), Lannes was given temporary control of Boudet's division and charged with the defence of Essling, the most vulnerable part of the French position; it was entirely appropriate that he be given such a command, for Jean Lannes was perhaps Napoleon's closest friend and one of the most capable of his subordinates.

Following the repair of the bridge, the remainder of Marulaz's cavalry was able to cross, together with General Espagne's division of heavy cavalry, bringing Napoleon's force in the bridgehead to about 24,000 men and 40 guns. That so many of these were cavalry would seem to confirm that he believed his task would be to pursue a retreating enemy rearguard, whereas they were already bearing down upon him; and to compound his problems, the warm weather had melted the snow at the head-waters of the Danube, greatly increasing the flow of water which carried a number of waterborne missiles launched by the Austrians, including logs, fireships and floating mills (boats anchored in the river which used the force of water in the manner of conventional water-mills). Consequently, at about midday the bridge was broken again between Schneidergrund and Lobgrund, severing the route for rein-forcements until repairs had been effected by about mid-afternoon; until then the troops in the bridgehead would have to fight unaided, and even if Napoleon had considered withdrawing to Lobau, the ferocity of the Austrian attack soon precluded that option.

The Archduke Charles planned an attack in five columns; two from General Rosenberg's IV Corps towards and to the east of Essling, and three upon Aspern (from right to left, General Hiller's VI Corps, General Bellegarde's I Corps and General Hohenzollern's II Corps); deployment was organised in columns rather than by corps. A reserve of grenadier divisions under General Kienmayer was held back on the first day of the battle. General Liechtenstein's cavalry covered the gap between the two villages; in all, about 100,000 Austrians were involved, with about 292 guns. As these columns converged in a great crescent around the French bridgehead, the attack opened at about 1 p.m. on 21 May against Aspern, a preliminary bombardment setting fire to both villages. Shining through the smoke which rose from Aspern, the sun appeared as a blood-red disc and cast a curious crimson light over the field; Baron Lejeune, with his painter's eye, noted it especially and remarked that its red light, so suggestive of blood, would have alarmed the superstitious.

Against Aspern, the first, somewhat tentative attack by General Nordmann's vanguard of Hiller's corps was repelled even though Molitor had only one battalion in the village. As the Austrian pressure increased, Masséna brought up the remainder of the division. After three attacks were repelled, the Archduke, realising the strategic importance of the village from where the bridge to Lobau could be attacked, determined to make the heaviest assault possible at about 4.30 p.m., involving some twelve battalions from I Corps and four from VI Corps, with a brigade from II Corps in reserve. He led the attack in person, and Molitor's exhausted men began to give ground, losing the churchyard and cemetery. A most desperate, hand-to-hand combat ensued as the Austrian artillery poured in their bombardment, striking down friend and foe alike. With the troops half-blinded by the smoke from the burning buildings, Aspern changed hands six times: 'the parties engaged each other in every street, in every house, and in every barn ... every single wall was an impediment to the assailants, and a rampart for the attacked; the steeple, lofty trees, the garrets and the cellars, were to be conquered before either of the parties could stile [*sic*] himself master of the place, and yet the possession was ever of short duration; for no sooner had the Austrians taken a street or a house, than the enemy gained another, forcing them to abandon the former'.[1]

To relieve the pressure on Aspern, action was taken by Bessières' cavalry in the centre against the Austrian II Corps, and reinforcement in the form of Legrand's division, which hitherto had been held in reserve, was sent to Aspern to protect its right flank and to prevent the Austrians from outflanking the village. The first unit into the village was the 26th *Léger*, followed by the 18th Line and 3rd Baden Regiment (the latter one of the units supplied to Napoleon's army by the allied Confederation of the Rhine); these eight battalions enabled Molitor's shattered units to withdraw to reorganise. The murderous fighting continued until at about 6.30 p.m. the Austrians finally forced out Legrand's men; realising the desperate nature of the position, Napoleon ordered its recapture at all costs. The troops in the vicinity were at last aided by reinforcements, the repair of the bridge having enabled most of the remaining division of Masséna's corps, that of General Carra Saint-Cyr, to be pushed into the line at Aspern; it included a French brigade and one composed of the Hesse-Darmstadt *Leib-Garde* and *Leib-Regiment*. Their counter-attack re-established a foothold in the village, and as fighting declined in the late evening, both sides remained in possession of part of the village. That the French had been able to hold even some of Aspern against such odds was testimony to the determination which had infused the defenders; and also, perhaps, to the unco-ordinated manner in which the Austrian attacks had been launched, which had not made best use of their overwhelming numerical superiority. The presence and conduct of Masséna had proved a great inspiration to his men in addition; having had all his horses killed by Austrian fire, on one occasion he marched at the head of a counter-attack, and for much of the battle stood beneath the elm trees on the village green beside the church, indifferent to the clatter of Austrian shot on the church roof, and to the branches falling on his head as they were stripped from the trees by Austrian artillery fire!

In the central position of the French 'front', the space between the two villages was occupied by Bessières' cavalry and the opposing Austrian cavalry reserve under General Liechtenstein. The French delivered some artillery fire from Essling upon those Austrian troops in range, but ceased when the French cavalry carried out limited advances to oppose the Austrians in their front and to attempt to relieve the pressure on Aspern. Initially the French force consisted only of the light cavalry of IV Corps and the first reinforcement, Espagne's 3rd Heavy (cuirassier) Division, but once the bridges were re-opened, a further augmentation arrived in the shape of General Saint-Sulpice's 2nd Heavy (cuirassier) Division and part of General Nansouty's 1st Heavy Division, General Saint-Germain's cuirassier brigade; but as the remaining cuirassiers and carabiniers attempted to follow, the bridge gave way again. A number of French charges were made, but numbers were insufficient (and the Austrians too steady) for any decisive result, though they did distract some Austrian attention from the desperate battles being waged on the flanks.

As a consequence of their circuitous approach-march, it was not until about 6 p.m. that the first Austrian troops fell upon Boudet's division at Essling. With the great stone granary acting as a bastion, the French repelled the attacks by the Austrians' fourth column, and seconded their defence by cavalry attacks delivered from the centre of the French line. Having already been in action, Espagne's cuirassiers were again used, led by their redoubtable general, Jean Louis Espagne (or 'd'Espagne'). Earlier in the day the corner of his cocked hat had been shot through; he merely turned the undamaged corner to the front and carried on as if unconcerned. At this juncture, according to Marcellin de Marbot who was one of Lannes' ADCs, the two Marshals concerned with this sector of the line came into conflict. Because of the especial trust Napoleon reposed in Lannes, and because of his seniority, Bessières had been put under his command; this was the cause of much resentment on Bessières' part, as the two disliked each other intensely. Requiring the cavalry to charge in support of the defence of Essling, Lannes sent two ADCs to Bessières, *ordering* him to charge; but each ADC, afraid of speaking harshly to a superior, only implied that Lannes had *suggested* a charge. As each returned to report how the message had been delivered,

Lannes grew increasingly angry and instructed Marbot to *order* Bessières to charge *home*, reinforcing the point by jabbing a finger into Marbot's ribs in imitation of sword-thrusts.

Bessières duly ordered the charge. As usual, the gallant Espagne led his own division (already one of his brigadiers, General Fouler, and one of his regimental commanders, Colonel d'Haugeranville of the 6th Cuirassiers, had fallen), and in charging a battery of Austrian artillery he was mortally wounded when it fired. Espagne's loss was felt grievously; his body was borne away for burial on Lobau. The cavalry enjoyed little success; as they approached the Austrian infantry, the latter closed up into their 'mass' formation, a large and solid phalanx, and drove back the French with musketry. Other French charges were made in the centre of the line, which though not decisive at least prevented any Austrian attempt to drive into the centre of Napoleon's position, separate Aspern from Essling and break through to the bridge from Lobau.

At about 8 p.m. the Austrians' fifth column completed its long approach-march and reached its place in the attack on Essling; it made some progress in the outskirts of the village, and at about 9.30 p.m. the fourth column renewed its attack, but was again halted by fire from the granary. As elsewhere, the Austrian failure to co-ordinate their attacks tended to negate their great numerical superiority, and Lannes was able to hold his position until at about 11 p.m. General Rosenberg pulled his columns out of the firing-line and fighting around Essling subsided.

Both sides must have had some cause for satisfaction at the results of the day's fighting. Although the Archduke had not driven his enemies into the Danube, his forces were in place for a renewed attack in the morning, and he must have been confident of success if only because of the great disparity in numbers. Napoleon, conversely, must have experienced some relief that, by the desperate efforts of his army, he was still on the north bank of the Danube instead of in the river. The good fortune he had experienced as a result of the Austrian lack of co-ordination of their attacks, arising partly from the long marches they had had to make, he could not expect to be repeated on the morrow, for the whole Austrian army was poised to strike. To counter such an attack Napoleon needed reinforcement and re-supply, but such were dependent entirely upon the rickety bridge to Lobau, and upon the debris which was carried down the ever-rising Danube.

From about 10 p.m. the bridge was repaired, permitting the bridgehead to be reinforced. The fresh troops included the élite Old and Young Guard divisions of Dorsenne and Curial respectively (the former

111

Napoleon's most experienced corps, though scarcely 2,800 strong), and three of the four divisions of Lannes' II Corps, that of General Saint-Hilaire and the two divisions of 'combined grenadiers' of detachments drawn from many units, commanded by Generals Tharreau and Claparède, together under the direction of that much-scarred and indomitable general, Nicolas Oudinot. As the fourth of Lannes' divisions, that of General Demont, was about to follow, the bridge broke again, and he was unable to cross until later in the morning. Nevertheless this was a crucial reinforcement which gave Napoleon the opportunity to take the offensive on the morrow; and he ordered Marshal Davout to assemble his III Corps on the south bank of the river, to prepare to cross in support. Conversely, the Archduke appears to have issued no orders for an immediate renewal of the assault at dawn, but did order fireships and floating mills to be sent against the bridges.

The French bivouacked for the night in the positions where they had fought, and 'though anxiety chilled the hopes, it no way daunted the courage of the French. Stretched amidst the dead bodies of their comrades, they resolved to combat to the last man on the morrow, for their beloved Emperor and the glory of their country. Sleep soon closed the eyes of the soldiers; the sentinels of either host were within a few yards of each other; Napoleon lay down in his cloak on the sand of the Danube, within half a mile of the Austrian batteries.'[2] Lannes left Essling to join Napoleon, but decided upon a detour to Aspern, to speak to Masséna; Marbot, who as ADC accompanied him, remarked that their route was clearly visible in the moonlight and by the fires still burning at Aspern. At Masséna's bivouac Bessières was encountered, still seething with anger at the tone of Lannes' message. After some harsh words, only Masséna's stepping between them prevented the two Marshals from drawing swords. Lannes then went on his way to join Napoleon, to whom he recounted the story; Bessières was then summoned immediately to receive a reprimand, his discomfiture increased by the fact that Napoleon did not invite him to share his supper. Marbot claimed that he was glad to escape from so embarrassing a scene, even though he had to stay awake all night, guiding reinforcements across the bridges.

Some of these troops came up with the greatest hurry. The grenadiers and *chasseurs* of the Old Guard were pushed on with such speed that they were unable to pause even to don their bearskin caps (a sign that action was expected: they marched in forage caps). The dress caps were carried in cases upon their knapsacks, and as they marched each man unpacked the cap of the man in front so as not to interrupt

112

their march for even a moment; the undress caps were thrown into the Danube as they passed!

With his forces at the bridgehead now increased to about 50,000 infantry, 12,000 cavalry and 144 guns, Napoleon intended to launch an offensive in the central position between the two villages; where Lannes commanded the three divisions of his own corps, Tharreau, Claparède and Saint-Hilaire, respectively from left to right, with Bessières' cavalry behind them, its commander suitably chastened. Boudet's division was left to hold Essling, Legrand and Carra Saint-Cyr in Aspern, with the remnants of Molitor's ravaged battalions in reserve, possibly reduced to an effective strength of about one-quarter of their original numbers. The Guard was placed as a general reserve.

Lejeune reported that the Austrian artillery opened first on the morning of 22 May, as early as 3 a.m., but it was the French who obtained the early advantage as Masséna evicted the Austrians from Aspern, even from the church and cemetery, which they had fortified during the night, so that by about 7 a.m. the village was again wholly in French hands. As Lejeune remarked about the previous day's conflict in the village, 'The history of our wars relates no more thrilling incident than this long and obstinate struggle.'[3] Irresolute Austrian leadership also probably played a part towards the French success: one of Bellegarde's divisional commanders, General Wacquant, appears to have fallen back without orders. A renewed Austrian attempt was made upon Essling by the fourth and fifth columns of Generals Dedovich and Rosenberg respectively, the latter in overall command. They made some progress, but aided by elements of the Young Guard, Boudet's men held the position, so that with both flanks temporarily secure Napoleon could contemplate his break-out from the bridgehead. Probably he intended that Davout should support the manoeuvre, but renewed breaks in the bridges meant that his corps would take no part in the battle. Nevertheless Napoleon was sufficiently confident to order the attack from the centre of his position, perhaps believing that Davout would still arrive.

When the early morning mist lifted to reveal the massing of Lannes' troops, Archduke Charles realised the danger and rode to take command in the centre in person, leaving Hiller and Bellegarde with orders to take Aspern at all costs. At about 7 a.m. Lannes' corps began to advance in echelon, Saint-Hilaire leading on the right, and Oudinot following in the centre and left with the divisions of Claparède and Tharreau. They marched into a sustained bombardment, but the Austrians in the front wavered and Charles brought up his reserve grenadier divisions to cover the centre. Bessières' cavalry also advanced, the light cavalry on the left having little success, but the heavy cavalry on the right caused Liechtenstein's cavalry to fall back, and Hohenzollern's third column began to buckle. Marbot described how Austrian officers and sergeants could be seen belabouring their men with their canes in an attempt to make them stand, but it was a different gesture which supposedly rallied the crumbling Austrian ranks. One of the units of General Brady's division of Hohenzollern's column was Infantry Regiment No. 15 (Zach) (Austrian regiments bore both a number and the name of their current *Inhaber* or colonel-in-chief); and pressed by cavalry and bombarded by artillery, Regiment Zach began to break. The Archduke Charles was said to have ridden up and snatched one of their flags, waving it to rally the unit, which re-formed and went forward. Whether or not he did actually grab the flag – he always made light of the incident – his personal intervention at this critical moment probably saved his army.

As the Austrian centre held firm, in the face of heavy fire which had virtually silenced the supporting French artillery, it became obvious that Lannes' attack could not succeed, even though some participants claimed that it was called back when on the point of victory. In fact, they were stalled under very heavy fire; indeed, it was remarked that their reverse was due in no small measure to their advancing in columns, not attempting to deploy into line, limiting the number of muskets which could reply to the Austrians assailing them on three sides, with the position becoming worse the longer the fight went on. The most distinguished victim of the Austrian fire was General Louis Saint-Hilaire, whose left foot was smashed by a grapeshot, a wound which was to prove mortal. Marbot was hit in the thigh by the same discharge and had the unhappy task of bearing news of Saint-Hilaire's fate to Napoleon and Lannes, who were in discussion; both were considerably affected by the news of this popular and capable comrade, 'the pride of the army, as remarkable for his wit as for his military talents'.[4]

It is likely that Napoleon realised that his attack in the centre had failed even before he received news that the bridge had broken again, and that thus he could expect no further reinforcement. The Austrians had made great efforts to damage the bridges, and equal exertions by the French to keep them open, by repairing breaks as they occurred and even by intercepting floating missiles against the bridge connecting Lobau to the north bank, for example, the Austrians had sailed a large boat, but the slower current on that arm of the Danube enabled some of

Molitor's men to swim from shore and bring the boat into the bank before it struck the bridge. Finally, however, an enormous breach was made by a burning mill, which prevented any hope of repair for the remainder of the day, leaving Napoleon marooned on the north bank with the corps of Masséna and Lannes. Even had the failure of Lannes' attack not been evident, this would surely have signalled an end to Napoleon's thoughts of offensive action; and so he ordered Lannes to break off his attack and return to his original position.

The collapse of the bridge not only deprived Napoleon of the reinforcements which might have proved decisive; it also seriously affected the fighting ability of the troops already across the Danube. Lejeune hints of its effect on morale, by noting that staff officers apprised of the breaking of the bridge spoke of it in whispers, lest the news spread to the troops, and even Lejeune admitted to being 'greatly dejected'.[5] Secondly, the interruption of communications deprived the army of its re-supply of ammunition, of which stocks were already running so low that French gunners were ordered only to fire when they were sure of the shot taking effect. Lejeune was sent to the bridge to see if it might be possible to transport some supplies over the Danube by boat, a process which could never supply an adequate quantity, although the munitions which Davout was able to ferry to the fighting did enable the French to maintain some kind of opposing fire.

As Lannes' corps fell back, the Austrians were able to re-organise their centre, with the two grenadier divisions relieving Hohenzollern's battered column in the front line. All this time there had also been renewed fighting on the flanks. The Austrians' first and second columns assailed Aspern again, and another desperate fight occurred among the rubble until the defenders were pushed out by an artillery barrage which set fire to whatever was not already burned. Attack and counter-attack disputed possession of the village; the French gained ground, then an assault by the Austrian Regiments nos. 31 and 51 from General Vincent's division of the first column regained the church and cemetery only to be forced out again by French reinforcements, Young Guard battalions from the reserve. Finally, a renewed Austrian push swept into the village and beat off the final French attack shortly after 1 p.m.; and with no reserves remaining and their men utterly fought-out after a day's almost uninterrupted and savage combat, the French finally gave up the village for lost. Few locations during the period can have been contested for so long and with such vigour and bitterness as Aspern; but in the end the Austrians were just too strong for even the most gallant defence.

With his centre stabilised, Archduke Charles ordered a renewed assault upon Essling, at about 11 a.m. At first Rosenberg's attacks were beaten off, but reinforced by grenadiers from the centre, a renewed push partially succeeded, although the huge granary still held out, with Boudet inside. Napoleon sent in a counter-attack of four Young Guard battalions, led by General Georges Mouton, whose conduct in this and subsequent operations led to his being ennobled as comte de Lobau. This proved insufficient to recapture and hold the village, so General Jean Rapp was sent with two more Young Guard battalions to disengage the troops struggling in Essling and to cover their withdrawal. Evidently Rapp had no liking for this task, and instead persuaded Mouton to join him in a renewed counter-attack which eventually re-took the village and repelled a renewed Austrian assault. The Archduke thereupon called his troops back to prevent further casualties, the grenadiers in particular having suffered appallingly. Napoleon actually commended Rapp for his act of disobedience, saying that the safety of the army depended upon the holding of Essling.

Attention again switched to the centre, where to relieve pressure on Lannes' men Napoleon sent in his cavalry once again; again the Austrian infantry held firm and the cavalry retired into the now shrinking French bridgehead. Limited charges, in a defensive role, to stabilise the line, was not the ideal use for cavalry, but the exertions of Napoleon's horsemen were courageous and significant in the extreme. With the Austrian offensive in the centre having thus been stalled, and with the French left wing preventing him from breaking out of Aspern into the bridgehead, the Archduke limited his operations to a great bombardment along the front of the French line, which because of their inferiority in numbers and shortage of ammunition the French could not match. One of the greatest ordeals in the warfare of the period must have been to stand immobile under fire, as described by Jean-Roch Coignet, at the time a sergeant in the Old Guard. He had already had one narrow escape when, feeling an urgent call of nature and knowing that he was not allowed to retire to attend to it, he had run out into the no man's land between the armies. He was about his business when an Austrian roundshot ricocheted about a yard from him, hurling a hail of stones over him, and thinking his position a little too desperate, he ran back to his unit with musket in one hand and trousers in the other, and black and blue in that portion of his anatomy which had been exposed when the shot hit the ground. Returning safely, if bruised and embarrassed, he was greeted by the offer of a swig of rum from his major's flask, and remarked to his captain that he had come back in such a state because the Austrians' lavatory paper was too hard to use! The remainder of his experiences that day were not so fortunate in their outcome or humorous in content.

Coignet recalled that no words could describe the agony – no other word was appropriate – of standing in rank, under bombardment, awaiting death without even firing a shot in reply. Whole files were carried away as the Austrian shot ploughed through the ranks, knocking the bearskin caps twenty feet into the air, and all Coignet could do was to call out a constant litany of 'Close up! Close up!' as the gaps in the ranks were filled. Two guns nearby made some reply until all their gunners were down; General Dorsenne, commander of the 2nd (Old Guard) Division of the Imperial Guard, sent forward a dozen grenadiers to replace them. They too fell, and the gun-carriages were splintered and scattered like so much firewood. Both Dorsenne's horses were killed under him, so he remained at the head of his men on foot; then with dismay they saw him fall as a shell exploded beside him. He stood up, covered in dirt, and called, 'Your general is not hurt. You may depend upon him, he will know how to die at his post!'[6] The file next to Coignet was hit, and he saw his right arm all bloody. He thought he had lost it until his lieutenant seized his arm and the awful mess fell off, revealing his sleeve undamaged: it had merely been numbed when hit by the remains of one of his comrades. As Coignet had no feeling in the arm, the officer told him to drop his musket and draw his sabre with his left hand; but finding the hilt to have been carried off by a cannon shot, he decided to use his musket one-handed instead. As the bombardment and the carnage continued, some of the battered units of Lannes' corps began to waver; but the Guard stood firm and the shaken troops re-formed behind them.

By now it was obvious that Napoleon's position was desperate; deprived of reinforcements and ammunition, his only realistic option was to abandon the bridgehead and retire to Lobau, to await the re-establishment of the bridge. Even disengagement was fraught with hazard, however, and before it was accomplished the French army suffered one of its greatest losses. So heavy was the fire around the Old Guard that they cried out to Napoleon, threatening to lay down their arms if he did not retire out of danger; so he returned to Lobau and left the task of withdrawal in the hands of the capable Lannes. The Marshal had very few of his staff left, only two ADCs (one of whom, Marbot, was wounded but unwilling to leave), and was walking with his friends at the rear of the front line as the Austrian bombardment began to slacken, perhaps in response to the French fire having almost ceased entirely for want of ammunition. Lannes was conversing with old General Pouzet when a ball struck the latter on the head and laid him dead at Lannes' feet. Pouzet had been a sergeant in the regular army of the *ancien régime* and Lannes' first instructor, and it was to Pouzet that Lannes believed he owed much of his success; and thus the death of such a dear friend came as an unbearable blow. Lannes wandered away distractedly some hundred yards and sat alone upon the bank of a ditch, staring blankly at the movement of the troops. Some moments later four soldiers came by carrying a body; as they paused to rest the cloak in which it was wrapped fell open to reveal poor Pouzet. Lannes jumped up with the cry 'Is this terrible sight going to follow me everywhere?',[7] then walked away to sit on another bank, legs crossed and with a hand over his eyes. As he sat in sorrowful meditation, a ricocheting 3-pound roundshot bounced nearby and struck his crossed legs, smashing one kneecap and lacerating the sinews at the rear of the other. As Marbot limped over to him Lannes exclaimed, 'it's nothing much; give me your hand to help me up',[8] but the injury was too severe. Marbot commandeered some infantrymen to carry the Marshal to safety, but without a stretcher lifting him caused great agony, whereupon a sergeant ran to procure a cloak to use as a litter. It was that in which Pouzet was being carried; Lannes recognised that it was soaked with his friend's blood and refused to use it, so Marbot sent the other surviving ADC, Lieutenant Le Coulteux, to get some branches with which to make a stretcher.

Lannes was carried to an aid-post near the fortified bridgehead, where there was such a scene of horror that Lejeune recalled it with the words 'Oh, my God!' Amid the piles of dead and wounded, the surgeons advanced conflicting theories about the best treatment for Lannes; that of Larrey prevailed, and in less than two minutes the leg with the worst damage was amputated. Hearing that his friend was severely stricken, Napoleon hurried up and knelt in tears beside Lannes' stretcher, embracing the Marshal (which smeared blood on Napoleon's waistcoat), and declared that he *would* live. 'I trust I may,' replied Lannes, 'if I can still be of use to France and to your Majesty.'[9]

On the French left flank, the fighting died down once the Austrians were secure in their possession of Aspern. This gave Hiller, commanding in that sector, the opportunity to re-organise for a major drive to roll up the French line from west to east. He was bringing up additional troops and artillery when General Baron Wimpffen, chief of staff, arrived with orders not to pursue the action. Hiller protested and a heated argument ensued until Wimpffen asserted his authority; as it was clear that the French were abandoning their bridgehead, the Archduke had decided that enough had been achieved and that it was prudent to disengage while his forces were in the ascendancy, rather than risk the chance of a reverse in pressing on for an outright victory. The decision not to pursue enabled Napoleon to extricate his army from the north bank of the Danube, and although some Austrian plans were made to attack Lobau, preparations were never realistic and no attempt was made. Probably it was believed that Napoleon's reverse had been so severe that he would be forced to negotiate.

The withdrawal was unhurried, Masséna still commanding on the left flank, and now Bessières on the right. The demeanour of the latter was especially impressive; after posting skirmishers to fire at the Austrian artillery in place of the French batteries, whose ammunition was virtually exhausted, Bessières strolled up and down behind the line, hands behind his back, exuding calmness and confidence. The withdrawal to Lobau was not entirely orderly, the small bridge being broken and repaired more than once, and in the later stages of the battle the walking wounded, stragglers and riderless horses created a press at the bridgehead which was the cause of much confusion. The guard posted there, and the engineers and pontoneers whose task was to keep the bridge operational, forcibly prevented many of the wounded from blocking the bridge, so that many pushed down to the shore of the Danube and even plunged into the water in an attempt to climb on to the bridge from the side. Some of the wounded on the river bank were unable to clamber back and were swept away by the rising river. Only when Napoleon retired from the bridgehead was there any order in the crowd, as the wounded shuffled together to allow him unimpeded access to the bridge. Evidently he found their cries of 'Vive l'Empereur!' very affecting; Lejeune recalled that he fixed his eyes on the ground in front of him lest he show emotion, and only recovered his composure when the injured were allowed to file across the bridge after him.

At about 10 p.m. the chief of staff, Marshal Berthier, ordered Lejeune to prepare a boat to carry Napoleon from Lobau to the south bank of the Danube. It was pitch black, the period of the new moon, so Lejeune had the greatest difficulty finding his way across the island to the site of the still-demolished bridge, frequently falling over wounded whose cries of anguish were partially drowned by the howl of a rising wind in the island's trees. Having filled the best boat with fifteen experienced oarsmen, pilots and a few good swimmers (in case it should be upset and Napoleon had to be rescued), Lejeune tried to grope his way back to headquarters, hands outstretched to prevent his walking into a tree in the blackness; instead he bumped straight into Napoleon, who was making his way to the boat. Napoleon consulted his watch; it chimed eleven and he remarked that it was time to retreat. By the light of a flickering torch, using his sabretache as a writing-desk, Lejeune wrote the order for withdrawal for Masséna and Bessières; Berthier signed it, and then Napoleon was gone, his oarsmen pulling the boat out into the Danube. The torch was blown out by the wind almost immediately, and the boat disappeared into the gloom; not until late in the following day, when he heard of its safe arrival on the far bank, did Lejeune shake off the fear that it had been swamped and Napoleon drowned.

Bearing the order, Lejeune again stumbled across Lobau to the little bridge, commandeered a captured horse and set off to find Masséna and Bessières. He made for Aspern, visible by the glow from its ashes, unaware that it had fallen; a sentry's challenge, 'Wer da?' ('Who goes there?') told him that he had ridden into Hiller's Austrian right wing. 'Stabsofficier', he answered ('Staff officer'); an Austrian officer came forward and, presumably deceived by the shabraque on the captured horse Lejeune was riding, asked him the time. 'Mitternacht', replied Lejeune, then rode for his life as someone recognised his uniform, and sent a volley of shots after him. Riding into the French lines, he was greeted by a volley from the French sentries as well, until he encountered an officer he knew (General Claude Legrand, commander of Masséna's 1st Division, who swore at Lejeune for disturbing his sentries; his ill-humour may have arisen in part from the fact that his hat had been spoiled when a cannon-ball passed through it!). Trying to locate Masséna, Lejeune approached a man lying wrapped in his cloak, quite alone; 'Don't ride over my legs!', said the man: it was Masséna. Having transmitted the order, Lejeune rode off to find Bessières, an easier task as he was with his cavalry, and the two Marshals organised the withdrawal to Lobau. (It is interesting to reflect that a better-aimed musket-ball from an Austrian in Essling might have delayed the French withdrawal so long that once the Archduke had learned of the fate of the main bridge, he might have attacked on the morrow and destroyed most of the French army on the north bank of the Danube.)

But for a small detachment of light infantry left to cover the bridge, the whole French army had passed on to Lobau by 3.30 a.m. on 23 May, when the little bridge was dismantled; Masséna was virtually the last man over. When two boats brought off the light infantry guard about half an hour later, the bridgehead was emptied and that stage of the campaign concluded.

Although the fighting had ended, the privations of the troops now marooned on Lobau were far from over. 'Never was an army assembled under more disastrous circumstances than the French on that memorable night ... Above twenty thousand brave men were there, weltering in their blood, or murmuring in their last moments a prayer for their mothers, their children, their country. Gloom had seized on every mind, despair had penetrated the bravest hearts ...'[10] The trees and bushes on the island provided shelter, but they had no other comforts, no rations and not even drinkable water. The only food available was horse-meat – Coignet recalled that even the officers had nothing left but saddles and bridles, and that the Austrian prisoners were given the heads and entrails of horses that had been eaten – and as Larrey and his colleagues continued to operate on the wounded, the whole island resounded with shrieks and groans which led Coignet to remark that it was impossible to describe the privations suffered by the exhausted men on Lobau. The injured Lannes remained on Lobau, the risk of a boat journey being considered too great; even for him there was no fresh water to drink, for the flooding of the Danube produced a thick and muddy torrent. Not until Marbot improvised a filter from one of the Marshal's shirts, which strained out most of the mud, was the injured man able to assuage his thirst; as he said himself, they were like sailors who died of thirst while surrounded by water.

On the following day, 23 May, Napoleon sent a boat to collect Lannes and remove him to Kaiser-Ebersdorf for treatment; at first he appeared to be making good progress, but he succumbed to gangrene on 30 May. Napoleon was desolate; sitting by his body, he kept repeating 'What a loss for France and for me!'[11] Not until 25 May was the bridge to Lobau re-established, allowing the troops to return to the safety of the south bank of the Danube. The wounded were moved first, some 10,000 who had been fed on horsemeat and nettles, cooked in cuirasses at Larrey's insistence, and then the remainder, excepting Masséna's IV Corps which remained to fortify Lobau in preparation for Napoleon's second attempt to cross the river. This occurred some six weeks later, and the campaign was ended by his defeat of the Archduke at Wagram on 5–6 July. For this renewed advance, two strong bridges were built from the south bank to Schneidergrund, three to Lobgrund; upstream a line of piles was driven into the river bed to intercept any floating missiles, and boats were maintained on the river for the same purpose. It was sad that the near-defeat of the French at Aspern-Essling and the enormous casualties caused by that battle were necessary before it was appreciated that adequate measures were required to secure the river-crossing.

It is difficult to estimate precisely the number of casualties caused by this terrible battle. The Austrians reported their losses as 87 officers and 4,199 other ranks dead, twelve generals, 663 officers and 15,651 other ranks wounded, and one general officer, eight other officers and 829 men prisoners, which figures are probably accurate. (Other published statistics record 16,314 wounded and 836 prisoners, the difference being the wounded and captured general officers, who may or may not have been included in the original officer casualty figures; in addition, 1,903 were reported missing, though not in the first accounts). Napoleon published a gross under-estimation of his own casualties, admitting only 1,100 dead and 3,000 wounded. The actual French loss was probably about 7,000 dead (which the Austrians claimed to have buried on the battlefield, though they also reported that many were lost in the river) and perhaps 16,000 wounded; the Austrian estimates of more than 5,000 wounded in their hands, and 29,773 being treated in Vienna, plus 2,300 prisoners, would seem to be too great. The trophies taken by the Austrians were not so many as to signal a major victory (three guns, 17,000 muskets, 3,000 cuirasses, a pair of colours and seven ammunition wagons were claimed), but it was clearly the most serious reverse suffered by Napoleon in recent years. Aided by the Austrian failure to exploit their success, he soon recovered by means of his great victory at Wagram; but for a brief time his omnipotence on the battlefield was challenged, and it certainly provided him with a more realistic view of the ability of Austrian military prowess, which he did not underestimate again, refusing to gamble a second time on crossing the Danube in so hazardous a fashion.

French participants of the battle were inclined to regard the Aspern-Essling bridgehead as a victory spoiled by the vagaries of the Danube. Less doubtful is the view, for example expressed by Lejeune, that it reflected much glory on French arms; that 'by dint of marvellous courage and perseverance'[12] a force numerically inferior, compressed into so small a compass that wide-ranging manoeuvre was impossible, had resisted so powerful an enemy for two days, latterly devoid of support and with ammunition in short supply. The Austrian view was somewhat different: 'a conflict of two days, which will ever be memorable in the annals of the world, and in the history of war. It was the most obstinate and bloody that has occurred since the commencement of the French Revolution. It was decisive for the glory of Austrian arms, for the preservation of the Monarchy, and for the correction of public opinion ... For the first time, Napoleon has sustained a defeat in Germany. From this moment he was reduced to the rank of bold and successful Generals, who, after a long series of destructive achievements, experience the vicissitudes of fortune. The charm of his invincibility is dissolved. No longer the spoiled child of fortune, by posterity he will be characterised as the sport of the fickle goddess. New hopes begin to animate the oppressed nations...'[13] Some of these remarks were invalidated by the subsequent victory of Wagram, but 'obstinate and bloody' the battle certainly was.

Perhaps the most lasting impression of Aspern-Essling should not be one of a plan undone by taking insufficient consideration of the state of a river and the difficulty of maintaining a line of communication over a single bridge, but rather one of the dogged heroism of the French army which clung to a defensive line longer than could ever have been expected. The conduct of many of the French commanders was undoubtedly inspirational – as a tribute to his exertions, Masséna was awarded the title 'Prince of Essling' (the whole battle was usually referred to by the French under that name, which is why he received the title of a village at which he was not personally engaged) – but probably the most significant factor was the character of the troops involved. The Austrian account claimed that 'Napoleon rode through his ranks, and according to the report of the prisoners, made them acquainted with the destruction of his bridge, but added, that he had himself ordered it to be broken down, because in this case there was no alternative but victory or death.'[14] This hardly accords with Lejeune's recollection that the collapse of the bridge was something to be concealed from the French army, and from this it is likely that the French troops in general did not realise that they were marooned on the north bank, so this knowledge can hardly have been a cause of spurring them to greater efforts. Rather, it was more likely that the inherent discipline and morale of Napoleon's army was the reason it fought so long and so hard, against a sterling enemy whose valour was proven by the manner in which their infantry held firm against repeated French cavalry charges, and by the desperate fighting over possession of Aspern and Essling. The French army continued to fight well throughout the Napoleonic Wars, but the attritional drain of casualties among those who marched so willingly behind Napoleon meant that many of his most devoted followers died before their time, like all those who met their end in the burning ruins of the two villages on the bank of the Danube. Had they been aware of it, it might have been small compensation that episodes like the defence of the granary at Essling have passed into legend.

NOTES

1. *Relation of the Operation and Battles of the Austrian and French Armies in the Year 1809*, W. Müller, London, 1810, pp. 27–8. Substantially the same translation appeared in *The Gentleman's Magazine*, July, 1809, p. 664, quoting *The London Gazette* of 11 July 1809.
2. *History of Europe, from the Commencement of the French Revolution to the Restoration of the Bourbons*, Sir Archibald Alison, Bt., Edinburgh and London, 1860, IX, p. 48.
3. *Memoirs of Baron Lejeune*, trans. Mrs. A. Bell, London, 1897, I, pp. 273–4.
4. Ibid., I, p. 181.
5. Ibid., I, p. 280.
6. *The Note-Books of Captain Coignet, Soldier of the Empire,* intr. Hon. Sir John Fortescue, London, 1929, p. 178.
7. *Memoirs of Baron de Marbot*, trans. A. J. Butler, London, 1913, I, p. 346.
8. Ibid.
9. Ibid., I, p. 347.
10. Alison, *op. cit.*, IX, p. 59.
11. Marbot, *op. cit.*, I, p. 352.
12. Lejeune, *op. cit.*, I, p. 298.
13. *The Gentleman's Magazine*, July 1809, pp. 664–5, quoting *The London Gazette*, 11 July 1809; substantially the same text appeared in Müller, *op. cit.*, pp. 34, 42.
14. *The Gentleman's Magazine*, July 1809, p. 665; Müller, *op. cit.*, p. 38.

Hearts of Oak
CERRO DEL PUERCO, BARROSA
5 March 1811

S tories of units standing firm or advancing under fire, closing the gaps in their ranks and carrying on undaunted, are the very essence of military mythology. The maintenance of discipline under fire defied that most basic of human reactions, the urge for self-preservation; but for every such story there is the reverse case, of units which when pressured beyond toleration gave in to their innate reactions and abandoned the fight. It is fortunate that some did, or battles would have been even greater fields of butchery than they were. Much emphasis was placed at the time upon the 'character' of the soldiers of various nations, and without debating the validity of such beliefs, it is certainly true that whatever 'character' existed was most evident under circumstances of the greatest trial. Never was this demonstrated more forcibly than when a unit broke under pressure, but then re-formed and spontaneously re-entered the fight. This appears to have been recognised by the Duke of Wellington, according to an entry in Sir Walter Scott's journal (27 April 1828): 'I heard the Duke say today that the best troops would run now and then. He thought nothing of men running, provided they came back again.'[1] One such remarkable incident occurred during the Battle of Barrosa.

From the spring of 1809 most British operations in the Iberian peninsula were conducted under the inspirational supervision of Sir Arthur Wellesley, later Duke of Wellington, but among the exceptions were those in southern Spain. Cadiz, the centre of the Spanish royalist government after the appropriation of the throne by Joseph Bonaparte, was thus an obvious target for French attack; and to disrupt the French blockade of the city a British contingent was dispatched to support the Spanish forces. Its commander was Sir Thomas Graham of Balgowan, one of the most unusual military commanders of the era. Born in 1748, he was known primarily as a landowner and great sportsman (he made the top score in the first cricket match in Scotland for which a full score survives), and was a Whig MP of early middle age when he experienced the fury of the French Revolution at first hand, when the coffin of his wife – 'the beautiful Mrs. Graham' immortalised by Gainsborough – was despoiled by French republicans as it was being conveyed home from the Riviera, where she had died. This engendered in Graham a deep loathing of the French régime, and though devoid of military training he devoted all his energies to its destruction, raising a regiment (90th Perthshire Volunteers) and serving in a number of voluntary capacities until given regular employment, including in 1810 command of the British division at Cadiz.

This division represented only about one-third of the Allied field force which had to oppose Marshal Claude Victor's French army; the remaining two-thirds were Spanish, under General Manuel La Peña, who commanded in chief, with Graham under his orders. This was not a felicitous arrangement for La Peña was an uninspired commander (commonly known as 'Donna Manuela', implying that he was as incompetent as an old woman, who had achieved and retained his command from family and political influence), and his Spanish troops were not the most resolute of allies with which the British division had to co-operate.

An attempt was made to disrupt the French blockade of Cadiz by landing an expedition some 40 miles along the coast, where the Allies held the port of Tarifa, and marching from there in the direction of Cadiz, compelling the French to divert part of the army blockading Cadiz. The British contingent of the expedition sailed from Cadiz to Tarifa with Graham, and picked up more troops there; it comprised two infantry brigades and several other units. Dilkes' brigade, about 1,350 of all ranks, was composed of the 2nd Battalion 1st Foot Guards, two companies each of the 2nd Battalion 2nd (Coldstream) Guards and 2nd Battalion 95th Rifles, and three companies of the 2nd Battalion 3rd (Scots) Guards; Wheatley's brigade of just under 1,700 of all ranks consisted of the 2nd Battalions of the 67th and 87th Foot, plus eight companies of the 1/28th picked up from Tarifa. Additional forces included two squadrons of the 2nd Hussars of the King's German Legion, the flank companies of the Portuguese 20th Line, and two composite battalions created for Graham by General Campbell, commander of the British garrison at Gibraltar. These, often known as 'flank battalions' from their being composed of the flank companies (i.e., grenadiers and light infantry) of a number of regiments, consisted of Barnard's Battalion (four companies of the 3rd Battalion 95th Rifles plus the two flank companies of the 47th Foot) and Browne's Battalion (two flank companies from each of the 1/9th and 2/82nd, from Gibraltar, and 1/28th Foot, from Tarifa).

The latter battalion, less than 540 men strong, was commanded by the lieutenant-governor of Tarifa. Lieutenant-Colonel John Frederick Browne[2] of the 28th, alias 'Mad John Browne', was one of the 'characters' of the British army, 'most wild and eccentric',[3] a major in his regiment but lieutenant-colonel by brevet rank. He had joined the 28th in 1781, commanded their grenadiers in Egypt (where at the landing at Aboukir he had charged and captured a battery), and led the battalion in the Corunna campaign. A thorough, experienced professional, while very popular and respected by his men, he showed no obvious signs of an extensive education; Sir George Bell, who knew him in the Peninsula, claimed that the longest speech he ever made to his men was 'There they come, boys; if you don't kill them, they'll kill you; fire away!', and that 'He never had but one book, and that was the Army List.'[4] (He once admitted that the only books he had ever read were the Bible and the Articles of War). As is the way with eccentrics, he attracted stories which have become exaggerated in the telling, such as his habit at Tarifa of using his crook-ended stick to lift the veil of every Spanish lady he encountered, until the ladies of the city began to reveal their faces voluntarily to escape the attentions of the stick. (Having seen their faces, Browne would merely raise his hat and pass on.)

By the end of February 1811 La Peña's Spanish troops had arrived to join Graham at Tarifa. La Peña commanded three divisions, two Spanish (under General Manuel Lardizabel and the Prince of Anglona) and Graham's British, to which La Peña added two Spanish battalions by way of reinforcement; he also had four cavalry squadrons commanded by Colonel Samuel Whittingham, a British officer in Spanish service. With these forces La Peña began to march in the direction of Cadiz, to menace the French besiegers of that city in their rear; to oppose him, Marshal Victor had a field army about 10,000 strong, thus numerically inferior, but because of the irresolution of the Spanish commander and his troops, it was possible for the French to achieve 'local superiority' on parts of the battlefield.

La Peña began his march along the coast in a somewhat disorganised manner and virtually walked into a trap. Finding the road to Cadiz blocked by a French division on 5 March 1811, although his troops had been under arms for fourteen hours and had marched as many miles in the dark, La Peña announced that he would attack immediately with part of his army, while the remainder guarded against any French attack on flanks and rear. As the French division duly fell back upon La Peña's advance, Victor's other two divisions prepared to fall

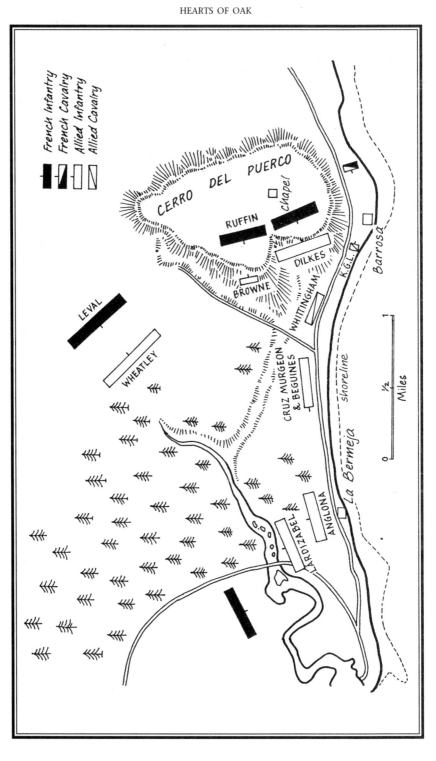

Above: Charge of the 15th Light Dragoons at Villers-en-Cauchies, 24 April 1794. (Illustration after P. Sumner).

Right: The Emperor Francis II, later Francis I of Austria, whose life it was claimed was saved by the charge of the 15th Light Dragoons and Sentkeresky's hussars at Villers-en-Cauchies.

Left: Louis Charles Antoine Desaix, 1768–1800, saviour of the French army and of Napoleon's reputation at Marengo. (Engraving by R. G. Tietze after J. Guerin).

Right: Desaix commemorated by a medallion which laments his death in the battle of '25 Prairial, An 8', the date of Marengo in the French republican calendar. The obverse inscription uses the two adjectives universally acknowledged as the most appropriate for Desaix: *brave* and *juste*.

Below: Napoleon (wearing the grey greatcoat, centre) attempts to stem the retreat of the French army at Marengo. (Print after F. de Myrbach).

Right: Joachim Murat, 1767–1815, the most flamboyant cavalry leader of the age, who mounted the great charge at Eylau to save Napoleon's position. (Engraving by H. Wolf after Gérard).

Below: Eylau: Marbot attempts to save the 'Eagle' of the 14th Line, a scene which accords with Marbot's version of events. (Print after L. Royer).

Left: 'The Maid of Saragossa': Agostina in her military uniform. (Mezzotint by H. Meyer).

Below: Street-fighting in Saragossa: a scene which epitomises the vehemence of the Spanish defence, as priests lead the fight against the French attackers. (Print after J. Girardet).

Above: 'The Defence of Saragossa': a romanticized version of the story of Agostina, as painted by Sir David Wilkie in 1828. (Engraving by W. M. Lizars after Wilkie).

Right: The victor of Aspern-Essling: the Archduke Charles, 1771–1847, one of the most able of Napoleon's opponents. (Engraving by T. W. Harland after Kellerhoven).

Left: Jean Lannes, 1769–1809, Napoleon's most trusted and arguably most able subordinate, who commanded the great attempted break-out at Aspern-Essling. (Engraving by G. Kruell after J. B. P. Guerin).

Below: French infantry engaged in desperate street-fighting during the defence of Essling. (Print after F. de Myrbach).

Above: Kienmayer's Austrian grenadiers attempt – unsuccessfully – to storm the granary at Essling. (Print after F. de Myrbach).

Right: Napoleon visits Lannes soon after the Marshal's leg has been amputated; the surgeon Baron Larrey stands behind Lannes' pillow, having just dressed the wound. (Print after E. Boutigny).

Left: Sir Thomas Graham, 1st Baron Lynedoch of Blagowan, 1748–1843, the victor of Barrosa. (Print after Sir Thomas Lawrence).

Right: William Carr Beresford, 1st Viscount and Marshal of Portugal, 1768–1854, the victor of Albuera. (Engraving after Sir William Beechey).

Above: Sir William Inglis, commander of the 57th at Albuera, whose exhortation 'Die hard, 57th, die hard!' inspired not only his own men but following generations of his regiment.

Above right: Sir John Colborne, later 1st Baron Seaton, 1778–1863, as commanding officer of the 52nd (Oxfordshire) Light Infantry, which he led with great distinction at Waterloo;

the brigade he commanded at Albuera was very much less fortunate.

Below: British infantrymen attempt to defend the Colours of their regiment at Albuera, after Colborne's brigade was ridden down by the lancers of the Vistula Legion. (Print after W. B. Wollen).

Above: Marshal Beresford defends himself against a Polish lancer at Albuera; to the left, a British Colour is about to be captured, while at the right an ensign prepares to conceal his flag beneath his body. (Engraving by T. Sutherland after William Heath).

Left: Lieutenant-Colonel Charles Macleod of the 43rd (Monmouthshire) Light Infantry, 1784–1812, commander of the leading elements of the Light Division in the storm of the breaches of Badajoz, 'an ornament to his profession' whose death was lamented universally.

Above: The storming of the breaches, Badajoz: a contemporary print which exaggerates the progress made by the stormers, for they never reached to within hand-to-hand combat with the enemy.

Above: The storming of Badajoz: the *chevaux-de-frise* blocking the breaches are illuminated by the flash of an exploding mine. (Engraving by T. W. Terry & D. J. Pound).

Left: The chaos and slaughter of the storming of a breach are shown in this depiction of San Sebastian; the scene at Badajoz was similar, but even worse. (Print by T. Sutherland after William Heath).

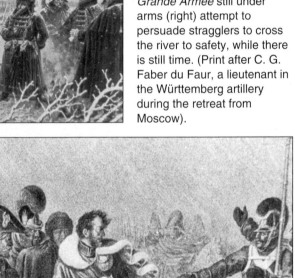

Centre left: On the road to the Berezina, Napoleon (centre right) elicits information from captured Russian peasants. The officer in the plumed cap, second right, is Murat. (Print after V. Verestchagin).

Below: On the east bank of the Berezina, members of the *Grande Armée* still under arms (right) attempt to persuade stragglers to cross the river to safety, while there is still time. (Print after C. G. Faber du Faur, a lieutenant in the Württemberg artillery during the retreat from Moscow).

Above: Panic among the crowds of fugitives on the east bank of the Berezina as Russian artillery shells drop among them. (Print after C. G. Faber du Faur).

Below: Crossing the Berezina: chaos as fugitives are pushed into the river in the scramble to reach safety. (Print after F. de Myrbach).

Above: Crossing the Berezina: fugitives fight each other in the rush to escape the crush at the eastern end of the bridges. (Print after J. Belten).

Below: The Berezina: a cuirassier guides his wife and child to safety, having crossed the river. (Print after Raffet).

Right: Hougoumont: a view from the base of the ridge of Mont St. Jean, showing the ruins of the North Gate, around which some of the most desperate fighting occurred after the French broke in. (Engraving after Whitehead).

Right: The ruins of the interior of Hougoumont. The building with the dormer window is the gardener's house; the ruins of the château are in mid-ground.

Right: Hougoumont: a view from the garden executed later in the 19th century, the rural tranquility of the scene contrasting with its violent past.

Left: James Macdonell of Glengarry, 'the bravest man at Waterloo'; later General Sir James Macdonell, GCB, KCH, Colonel of the 79th Highlanders 1842–49, and of the 71st Highland Light Infantry 1849–57.

Left: Alexander George, 16th Lord Saltoun, 1785–1853, a noted defender of Hougoumont, in the later uniform of his 1st Foot Guards.

upon the Allies' rear. Here, near a coast guard tower at Barrosa, was a long, low ridge named the Cerro del Puerco ('Boar's Hill' or 'Hog's Back', from its supposed resemblance to a recumbent pig), upon which there was a ruined chapel (so called at the time; apparently it was originally a watch-tower). It was not the imposing hill suggested by some writers, but had gentle slopes and in places no very defined crest, which is why fighting could take place so easily on the slopes as well as on the plateau at the top.[5] On one side of the hill was the coast, on the other the plain of Chiclana from where the French would advance, and inland from the coast road along which the Allies marched was a thick pine wood. Troops on the Cerro del Puerco could therefore dominate the road, and either attack the Allies between the woods and the coast, or at least leave them no option but to retire on Cadiz, which would foil the entire purpose of the expedition.

Graham appreciated the significance of the Cerro del Puerco, but his advice that it should be held was disregarded by La Peña, who ordered the British division to leave it and close up to the Spaniards along the coast road; and detailed six battalions under Generals Cruz Murgeon and Beguines to hold the Cerro as a rearguard to cover the withdrawal of the British, when they were also to retire. Five of these battalions were Spanish; the sixth was 'Mad John' Browne's flank battalion. As the British division marched away (by a more inland route to avoid congestion along the coast road), about half an hour after noon, Victor's main body appeared: a division under General Ruffin approaching the Cerro del Puerco and one under General Leval menacing the retiring British force. Clearly, the British at least would have to fight.

The Spanish generals on the Cerro del Puerco had orders to retire once Graham's main body was safely away, but had not been told what to do if they themselves were attacked. Six battalions could surely have held the position against a similar force (Ruffin's division also comprised six battalions, some 2,500 infantry plus a strong force of artillery and some dragoons), but they decided to follow their orders, albeit prematurely, fall back upon the main body and abandon the important heights to the French. More reprehensible was the fact that Cruz Murgeon seems not to have informed Browne of his intentions, but simply begun to withdraw. Seeing this, Browne sent his adjutant, young Lieutenant Robert Blakeney of the 28th, to investigate. According the Blakeney, Cruz Murgeon claimed that he was only shifting his position, but it became obvious that they were retiring; and as he rode back to Browne he saw French cavalry moving towards the coast road, the vanguard of

129

Ruffin's column. Covering the Spaniards' retreat was Samuel Whittingham with five squadrons (the two from the King's German Legion and three Spanish), and he rode in person up the Cerro to find Browne railing against the Spanish generals, who had also arrived.

Riding up to Browne, Whittingham inquired, 'Colonel Browne, what do you intend to do?'; with his anger rising, and perhaps expecting more from a fellow-countryman, Browne replied, 'What do I intend to do, sir? I intend to fight the French.' Whittingham said he could do as he pleased, but the others were determined to retreat. 'Very well, sir,' said Browne. 'I shall stop where I am, for it shall never be said that John Frederick Browne ran away from the post which his general ordered him to defend.' Cruz Murgeon and Beguines stood silent during this exchange, with Blakeney translating for them, and then apparently returned to their retreating troops. Showing at least some concern for Browne's predicament, Whittingham tried again, and offered a squadron of cavalry to cover Browne's retreat, should he prefer to retire on Graham's main body. This Browne ignored completely, deliberately turned his back and stumped off to his battalion.[6] Accompanied by scowls from their British allies, the Spaniards continued their retreat, though some made it evident that they were most unhappy to leave. Even more dissatisfied were Whittingham's two German squadrons. In the coming fight, their commander, Major Augustus von dem Bussche, was to use one of his squadrons in limited attacks against the French advance-guard, and left it under Captain Werner von dem Bussche between Graham's force and the Cerro; the other squadron, which could have assisted Browne, Whittingham steadfastly refused to move. Augustus von dem Bussche begged to be allowed to do something, but like the Spanish cavalry was forced to remain inactive, until in the last stage of the battle Whittingham consented to allow them to harry the retiring French rearguard. The British never criticised the Germans for their inactivity, for the reputation of the German Legion was second to none in the Peninsular army; and when they were finally permitted to move, they were roundly cheered by the British troops whom they passed.

Consideration of the Germans' actions is to run ahead of the course of events upon the Cerro del Puerco. As Cruz Murgeon's Spaniards marched away, Browne was left upon the hill, alone but for his battalion. Although 514 rank and file are noted in the official statistics,[7] Blakeney recorded their strength as only 470, the balance perhaps detached as baggage-guards, as was usual. To improve his position, Browne ordered Lieutenant Sparks of the 30th Foot, who was serving in the role of acting engineer, to loop-hole the 'chapel' on the summit of the Cerro, and formed his battalion in an oblong around it. As the French approached, their cavalry lapped around the coastal side of the hill, threatening envelopment, while Ruffin's six battalions and artillery came within Browne's view. For all his determination not to quit his post, he was above all an experienced soldier, and realised that against such odds the position was untenable. Reluctantly, he formed his battalion in column and began to retire down the hill, where the uneven slopes were dotted with trees and shrubs which provided some cover. Browne dared not delay, for once the French artillery had occupied the Cerro they would be able to bombard him before he had retired beyond their range, and despite the menacing French cavalry he dare not form square for fear of presenting an even more vulnerable target. On reaching the bottom of the hill, the route to safety crossed a ravine on to flat ground with much less cover, terrain more suitable for cavalry, so Browne threw out skirmishers on his flanks, whose fire dissuaded the French cavalry from pressing on; until, on reaching the cover of the pine wood, he re-formed in line, the sight of which caused the cavalry to withdraw. Meanwhile, Ruffin's infantry and artillery occupied the Cerro.

Learning of the French approach, Graham realised that it would be impracticable to continue to withdraw through the woods to join La Peña around the village of La Bermeja on the coast road, and threatened disaster if the whole Allied force were attacked without room to manoeuvre, between the woods and the shore. To prevent Leval's approaching division from linking up with Ruffin, Graham decided that immediate action was necessary, to attempt to defeat the French in detail, by using Wheatley's brigade to oppose Leval and sending Dilkes to the Cerro, to take on Ruffin. Briefly there was consternation that the French had marched down the coast road to threaten Graham's rear, for Cruz Murgeon's Spaniards, marching away from the Cerro, were mistaken for Frenchmen; but Captain Felix Calvert, an officer on Graham's staff, glimpsed red uniforms through the trees, exclaimed that it must be Browne's battalion, and went to confirm the fact.

Although Graham's plan was formulated, he had one difficulty: as his division had been marching through the woods when the French appeared, they would need considerable time to deploy and move into open ground to meet the French; in the meantime, the French had to be delayed. Against the most immediate threat, from Leval's division, Graham had a ready solution: the four rifle companies of Barnard's flank

131

battalion, and the 20th Portuguese, were thrown out of the wood in a skirmish-screen to delay Leval until Wheatley's brigade could form up and advance out of the woodland. Dilkes' brigade, plus a wing of the 67th from Wheatley's, was to advance to the Cerro to engage Ruffin; but Graham had no troops with him who could similarly buy time until Dilkes could deploy from the woods. Instead, Graham followed Calvert and rode over to meet John Browne, where he had formed his battalion on the fringe of the woodland (Napier stated that this was in response to a request for orders from Browne).[8]

Graham was surprised, and probably angry, to find that the Cerro del Puerco had been occupied by the French without opposition. He was brusque: 'Browne, did I not give you orders to defend Barrosa Hill?' 'Yes, sir,' said Browne, 'but you would not have me fight the whole French army with four hundred and seventy men?' Graham was unimpressed: 'Had you not five Spanish battalions, together with artillery and cavalry?' 'Oh!' replied Browne, 'they all ran away long before the enemy came within cannon-shot.' Graham considered for a moment. 'It is a bad business, Browne; you must turn round immediately and attack.' 'Very well,' replied Browne. 'Am I to attack in extended order as flankers, or as a close battalion?' 'In open order,' said Graham, before returning to his troops in the woods.[9] He must have reflected that while a line of skirmishers could hold Leval in check until Wheatley had deployed, something more was needed to occupy Ruffin, considering that Dilkes' brigade had farther to march before they could come into action; so he rode back to Browne to order a hopeless, if not potentially suicidal, manoeuvre. 'I must show something more serious than skirmishing,' said Graham. 'Close the men into a compact battalion'. 'That I will, with pleasure,' replied 'Mad John', 'for it is more in my way than light bobbing',[10] a remark which might have been expected from the grenadier officer Browne had once been. He ordered his buglers to sound the call to re-form the line from skirmish order; and, presumably realising what fate awaited the battalion if they attacked in that formation, sent an officer after Graham to inquire whether he was to advance as soon as his line was re-formed, and if he were to go straight ahead or to the right. The reply came: an immediate attack, straight ahead.

Browne rode to the front of his battalion, swept off his hat and declared in a voice so loud that all could hear: 'Gentlemen, I am happy to be the bearer of good news. General Graham has done you the honour of being the first to attack those fellows. Now follow me, you rascals!';[11] and, pointing towards the enemy, led the advance singing his favourite song, David Garrick's exhortation to British seamen, *Heart of Oak:*

> 'Come, cheer up my lads! 'tis to glory we steer,
>> To add something more to this wonderful year;
> To honour we call you, not press you like slaves,
>> For who are so free as the sons of the waves?
> Heart of oak are our ships,
>> Heart of oak are our men:
> We always are ready;
>> Steady, boys, steady;
> We'll fight and we'll conquer again and again.'

Despite the brave words, there was never any chance of more than one outcome of this attack, which must have been one of the most hopeless endeavours of the period. Giving orders to attack with the bayonet and not to fire (so as not to impede even for a moment the pace of the advance), Browne led his battalion in line back across the ravine and on to the lower slopes of the Cerro where, despite the light cover, it became fully visible to the French on the crest. An artillery battery had been planted close to the chapel, and three battalions faced the advancing British: the 2/9th *Léger*, 1/96th Line and one of two battalions of the 24th Line (Ruffin's remaining two battalions were grenadiers assembled from all the units in his own and Leval's division). Observing that only one battalion was approaching, the French held their fire to maximise the effect of the first volley, which when it came was devastating. Three battalions and eight guns (firing canister) opened fire simultaneously, and almost 200 of Browne's men, and half the officers, went down (this was Blakeney's estimate; the true casualty figures suggest that the losses were not quite so devastating, possibly because some lightly wounded men were not reported as casualties).

So many gaps were cut in the battalion that it resembled a skirmish line, and it closed in towards its centre as it continued to stumble uphill; but during this movement another fifty men and more officers fell as the French musketry became continuous. All the 28th's officers were hit, save Browne: Captains the Hon. Edward Mullens and Joseph Bradley, commanders respectively of the grenadier and light companies, and all their subalterns. Blakeney was struck by grapeshot under the hip, but having passed through an orange, a loaf of bread and a roast fowl in his haversack, the impact was deadened. He scrambled to his feet when he saw his great friend, Lieutenant Joseph Bennett of the light company, fall in the act of cheering on his men; Blakeney ran to him to find that he had been shot through the head. Amid this maelstrom of artillery-fire and musketry, no amount of coaxing, even by John Browne, could persuade the survivors to form line again. They scattered, but did not run away; no troops in the world could have withstood the hail of death which came down from the crest of the Cerro, and most men would have obeyed the natural instinct for self-preservation, and made off. Not so Browne's men; although they would no longer stand in line to be shot at, they took cover behind trees, bushes or folds in the ground, and began to fire at the Frenchmen on the crest above them (half of the battalion were light infantrymen, so these were the tactics for which they had been trained). Visible on the slopes of the Cerro were now only the dead and wounded, and two officers, Browne upon his horse and Blakeney. Observing the carnage around him, and Dilkes' brigade emerging from the woods, Browne said, 'I shall go and join the Guards; will you come?'[12] Blakeney replied that his wound prevented his moving quickly, and as long as three men of the battalion were still resisting, he would not leave. Browne rode off and left Blakeney standing amid the dead and dying, with the remnant of the battalion in cover around him, attempting to do what damage they could with their irregular musketry.

As a consequence of the confusion in the dense woodland, Dilkes' brigade did not make its way to the Cerro complete, two companies of Coldstream Guards by mistake having joined Wheatley, while a wing of the 67th from Wheatley's brigade followed Dilkes. They rushed out of the woods with such speed that they appeared not to be in order, and were preceded by two companies of the 2/95th Rifles. Instead of following Browne's route, Dilkes directed his men to the right (where Browne had suggested to Graham that he might attack), where there was more cover, with folds in the terrain creating 'dead ground' immune from French artillery-fire. Nevertheless they suffered some casualties as the French on the Cerro, now directed by Victor in person, switched their fire from Browne's men and on to the new target. As Blakeney was watching all this, Felix Calvert galloped up to tell him that some members of his battalion were farther down the Cerro, firing at longer range, and suggested that Blakeney go and bring them up; Blakeney indicated his wound and suggested that as Calvert was mounted, *he* should do it. Calvert smiled and rode off, not to the rear but presumably towards Dilkes.

Partially protected by the nature of the ground and its standing cover, Dilkes' brigade was nearing the crest of the Cerro before it began to lose heavily. Napier seems to have caught their mood, noting that they 'never stopt even to reform the regiments, came up, with very little order indeed, but in a fierce mood, when the whole run up towards the summit; there was no slackness on any side, and at the very edge of their ascent their gallant opponents met them'.[13] These were the two battalions of the French 24th which, seeing the disordered state of Dilkes' men, charged in column to sweep them off the hill. It was a somewhat unequal contest; the British desperately tired after a long day's march and a two-mile dash towards the Cerro, and in haphazard formation, whereas the French were comparatively fresh and with the advantage of charging downhill, in formation. But ragged though it was, Dilkes' brigade stood firm and opened such a fire on the French column that shot its head to pieces. Halted in its tracks, the column remained in a confused mass, exchanging musketry with the British.[14] Marshal Victor then ordered forward the two grenadier battalions, under General Chaudron Rousseau, to support the attack – Victor was seen waving them on with his white-plumed hat – and they also came to a halt in front of the British line. A reinforcement at this stage could have swung the course of the action, and Victor still had his two right-flank battalions, the 2/9th *Léger* and 1/96th, which he now ordered to support their comrades who were on the point of giving way.

At this juncture, Browne's flank battalion again came into the equation, despite apparently having been destroyed while buying time for Dilkes' brigade to come up. As much of the French fire was switched to the new target, movement on Browne's part of the Cerro became less suicidal, which enabled Blakeney to assemble some eight or ten men – principally grenadiers of the 9th and light infantrymen of his own 28th – from their individual hiding-places. Blakeney suggested that they charge a howitzer which was firing immediately in their front, and when they agreed, he picked up a discarded musket. Seeing this, Drummer Adams of the 28th's grenadiers remarked that he would do likewise were it not for the fact that he would have to pay for his drum if he lost it. Blakeney told him that *he* would pay for the drum, so Adams cheerfully flung it away and grabbed a musket. Blakeney recorded that 'I have always thought Adams the bravest man, or rather boy, whom I ever met – not for seizing a musket and gallantly charging, for in the excitement that was natural enough; but that he should stand calmly calculating the price of a drum when hundreds of balls were passing close to his body is scarcely credible; but so it was.'[15]

Blakeney's little band dashed forward and reached the howitzer as it was being reloaded; two of the gunners were bayoneted and the rest made off on mule-back. So that there should be no doubt about who had captured the gun, Blakeney found a piece of chalky earth and wrote on it '28th Regiment'. When he looked around, he was surprised to see that more than a hundred men of the flank battalion had joined him, emerging from hollows and from behind bushes and trees, and as he led them further up the hill, more joined at every step. These survivors now engaged the French troops to their front, the battalions which Victor intended to use as a reinforcement for the wavering mass opposed to Dilkes' men; and though few in numbers, the men of Browne's battalion were sufficient to deflect the French from their intended purpose. This was the critical moment; deprived of support, there came a loud murmuring sound from the French ranks as the whole mass gave way and fled, followed by the British, whose cheer began in the centre and spread to the flanks as they charged to complete the rout, encouraged and now commanded by Graham in person, who had had a horse shot from under him on the hill. Despite the efforts of Marshal Victor, which drew plaudits even from his enemies, the whole of Ruffin's division tumbled back off the Cerro, leaving two guns in the hands of the British. General Rousseau, commander of the grenadiers, was found grievously wounded in the thigh; he died during the night and was laid to rest on the shore by a burial-detail under Quarter-Master Surtees of the 95th. In his pocket was found a leave of absence which would have enabled him to return home to France on the grounds of ill health, but the gallant officer had delayed his departure, knowing that action was imminent.

On the crest of the hill, the hobbling Blakeney – the only officer of the flank battalion still on his feet – met John Browne, who had charged up the Cerro with the Guards. The colonel shook Blakeney's hand and declared that he would never forget what had occurred, and then resumed command of the two hundred-odd bloody and exhausted men who had fought their way back up the Cerro behind Blakeney. In his account of the action, Blakeney took care to state that no criticism should be levelled at Browne for having left his battalion, for when he rode off to join the Guards, there was no battalion to command: the rest having taken cover, there were not ten men in sight, and only four or five near the two officers.

Elsewhere on the field, similar discomfiture befell Leval's division as had overtaken Ruffin; Graham's skirmishers had held up the French (though at heavy cost) until Wheatley's brigade emerged from the woods and drove them away. In their retreat, Leval's men fell in with Ruffin's, and despite their disorganisation Victor rallied enough men to cover his withdrawal until they were upset by the charge of a squadron of King's German Legion hussars, which had broken out of Whittingham's stranglehold and pursued the French dragoons from around the Cerro into Victor's infantry, so the whole mass retired in disorder. There was no pursuit; Graham's men were in the last stages of exhaustion, and La Peña declined to use any of his Spanish troops despite the protests of some of his subordinates. (In fairness to them, Graham acknowledged in his dispatch that when battle was joined, the two Spanish regiments attached to his division – Ciudad Real and 4th Walloon Guards – did attempt to support the British, but appear not to have arrived in time to participate.) Even worse, La Peña decided to give up the expedition and retire into Cadiz, so that the French blockade was not, after all, interrupted, which gave Victor the excuse to declare that Barrosa had been a French victory, an implication not unknown in some modern writings. The consequence of La Peña's inaction was almost immediate: on the following morning Graham formally gave notice that he no longer consented to serve under Spanish command, using his discretionary powers granted him by the British government. La Peña implied that only Graham's refusal to co-operate on the following day had led to the abandonment of the expedition, but the British had no doubts that Graham was correct, as Wellington wrote to him on 25 March:

'I beg to congratulate you, and the brave troops under your command ... I have no doubt whatever that their success would have had the effect of raising the siege of Cadiz, if the Spanish corps had made any effort to assist them; and I am equally certain ... that if you had not decided with the utmost promptitude to attack the enemy, and if your attack had not been a most vigorous one, the whole allied army would have been lost. You have to regret that such a victory should not have been followed by all the consequences which might reasonably be expected from it, but you may console yourself with the reflection that you did your utmost, and, at all events, saved the allied army; and that the failure in the extent of the benefit to be derived from your exertions is to be attributed to those who would have derived most advantage from them. The conduct of the Spaniards throughout this expedition is precisely the same as I have ever observed it to be. They march the troops day and night, without provisions or rest, and abusing every body who proposes a moment's delay to afford either to the famished and fatigued soldiers. They reach the enemy in such a state as to be unable to make any exertion, or execute any plan, even if any plan had been formed; and then when the moment of action arrives, they are totally incapable of movement, and they stand by to see their allies destroyed, and afterwards abuse them because they do not continue, unsupported, exertions to which human nature is not equal.'[16]

The lack of success of the expedition did not prevent La Peña from receiving a decoration from his country's council of regency, but when the truth of what had happened became apparent he was removed from command. Such was Graham's resentment that he declined the offer of a Spanish title, and as he could not be left at Cadiz to co-operate with allies about whom he had been so critical, he was sent to serve directly under Wellington.

British casualties at Barrosa were severe; the returns showed 1,238 out of 5,217, or a loss of some 23.7 per cent. For Browne's flank battalion, the return showed 238 casualties out of a nominal 536, or 44.4 per cent; or if Blakeney's estimate of 470 rank and file actually in the firing-line is accurate, when the officers are considered the casualty-rate becomes about 50 per cent. The available statistics appear not to be absolutely precise; those recorded by Oman state that eleven officers were wounded, whereas the casualty-return of Lieutenant-Colonel John Macdonald, deputy adjutant-general, notes thirteen, the discrepancy presumably caused by the fact that three lieutenants of the 9th's flank company are recorded as wounded, but only one named.[17] These statistics do not include the fact that two of the wounded officers died of their injuries: Lieutenant John Light of the 28th's grenadiers, and Blakeney's friend Bennett, who never regained consciousness and died on the morning of 7 March. The officers of their battalion erected a marble slab in the chapel of Government House, Gibraltar, in their memory. It must have been small consolation to the survivors that the losses of the French engaged against the British at Barrosa were even greater, some 2,062, about 28.5 per cent; and even less consolation that despite this carnage, the profits from the battle were in the long term virtually nil.

'Mad John' Browne continued to serve in the army, joining the 56th Foot for a time (where he continued to exercise his individual style of command: in the Netherlands he captured some guns after asking his men if they could see the rascals ahead, and 'Let's take a run at them!'),[18] but returned to the 28th as regimental lieutenant-colonel in 1819 and retired in 1827. Blakeney also soldiered on, feeling that his promotion was not as rapid as it might have been had Browne not delayed in recommending him to those in authority. Thomas Graham, who despite undergoing the rigours of campaigning comparatively late in life – he fought his last battle at the age of 66 – lived to the age of 95, loaded with honours (he was promoted to full general in 1821), and deservedly raised to the peerage as Baron Lynedoch of Balgowan. Sadly, little recognition was accorded to the men of Browne's battalion for their exploits on the Cerro del Puerco.

It is difficult to account for the behaviour of Browne's battalion unless some consideration is taken of what must have been the innate character of the individuals involved, as would have been accepted at the time. As Blakeney admitted, the initial attack had not the slightest chance of success, and although the first returns state that only 25 men were killed outright, the storm of shot into which they advanced would have defeated any troops, let alone a body so outnumbered and probably nearing exhaustion (Blakeney calculated that by the end of the action, the men had been under arms for 24 hours, sixteen of which had been spent in marching). If the battalion's dispersal was only to be expected, the subsequent events were the more remarkable. It was perhaps significant enough that having broken, the men (without orders) took cover and began to fire, even if (as Felix Calvert observed) some had fled a considerable distance; but what was most unusual was that these exhausted and perhaps partly demoralised men should spontaneously and without orders follow a wounded officer back up the slope once the enemy's fire had slackened sufficiently for this not to mean almost certain death or injury. If Blakeney's calculation of numbers is accurate, when casualties are deducted, it would appear that about 85 per cent of the survivors followed him in their final charge. Folds in the terrain prevented any sight of the fight on the adjoining slope, so it was not a case of seconding an attack which could be seen in progress, for Dilkes' brigade was entirely hidden from their view, which makes the renewed charge of the remnant of the flank battalion all the more heroic.

Generals' dispatches routinely made mention of the gallant conduct of their troops, so that such comments became almost commonplace. But Graham's Barrosa dispatch – in which Browne's name appeared first in the paragraph of officers whose service he 'earnestly recommended' – contained the following:

'No expressions of mine could do justice to the conduct of the troops throughout. Nothing less than the almost unparalleled exertions of every officer, the invincible bravery of every soldier, and the most determined devotion to the honour of His Majesty's arms in all, could have achieved this brilliant success, against such a formidable enemy so posted.'[19] In the case of Browne's battalion in particular, this must have been no more than the literal truth.

NOTES

1. Quoted in *The Life of Wellington*, Sir Herbert Maxwell, London, 1899, II, p. 139.
2. His name is sometimes spelled 'Brown' in the *Army List*.
3. *Twenty-Five Years in the Rifle Brigade*, W. Surtees, London, 1833, p. 110.
4. *Rough Notes of an Old Soldier*, Sir George Bell, London, 1867, I, p. 137.
5. Comments on the terrain appear in *History and Campaigns of the Rifle Brigade*, Colonel W. Verner, London, 1919, II, pp. 214–15, contrasting the gentle slopes of the Cerro with the steep hill sometimes described. Verner states that Oman's 'remarkable' map (*History of the Peninsular War*, Oxford, 1911, IV, p. 124) was taken from a 'luckless Spanish map' which was 'extraordinarily incorrect', as proven by Verner's survey, photographs of which he published in *The Rifle Brigade Chronicle* of 1911. Early published maps appear in *History of the War in the Peninsula*, W. F. P. Napier, London, 1832–40, III, p. 446, and a considerably different one in *History of the King's German Legion*, N. L. Beamish, London, 1832, I, p. 314, the latter showing a lower ridge without a defined crest. Comments and illustrations concerning the modern appearance of the area can be found in *Fields of Fire: Battlefields of the Peninsular War*, I. Fletcher and A. Cook, Staplehurst, 1994, pp. 109–10.
6. Dialogue from *A Boy in the Peninsular War*, R. Blakeney, ed. J. Sturgis, London, 1899, pp. 184–5.
7. See Oman, *op. cit.*, IV, p. 612.
8. Napier, *op. cit.*, III, p. 443.
9. Blakeney, *op. cit.*, pp. 186–7.
10. Ibid., p. 187. 'Light bobs' was the universal nickname for light infantry.
11. Ibid., p. 188.
12. Ibid., p. 190.
13. Napier, *op. cit.*, III, p. 444.
14. Verner, *op. cit.*, p. 215.
15. Blakeney, *op. cit.*, p. 192.
16. Wellington to Graham, 25 March 1811; *Dispatches of Field Marshal the Duke of Wellington*, ed. J. Gurwood, London, 1834–8, VII, pp. 385–6.
17. Oman, *op. cit.*, IV, p. 612; *London Gazette*, 25 March 1811.
18. *Old Stick-Leg: Extracts from the Diaries of Major Thomas Austin*, ed. H. H. Austin, London, 1926, p. 26.
19. Graham's dispatch, 6 March 1811; *London Gazette*, 25 March 1811.

— 7 —

Dying Hard
ALBUERA
16 May 1811

I n late April 1915 the 3rd Battalion Middlesex Regiment, part of the 28th Division of the British Expeditionary Force, was thrust into a gap in the line at Ypres, where it had been broken by a German gas attack. Two companies were wiped out in this operation, and the battalion's commanding officer, Lieutenant-Colonel Eric Stephenson, was killed. His last recorded exhortation to his men was 'Die hard, boys, die hard!', a regimental rallying-call which had originated almost 104 years earlier, and which in the intervening period had become legendary both in the regiment and the army in general. Its use demonstrates the significance of regimental tradition and esprit de corps, which has been developed more fully in the British Army than in many others.

'Red Albuera' (to quote the regimental song of the Middlesex Regiment)[1] was a rare example of a major battle fought by the British during the Peninsular War without the inestimable benefit of Wellington's guiding hand. The fact that it was so sanguinary a contest, one of the most costly battles of the entire Napoleonic Wars, is perhaps as great a testimony to Wellington's absence as it is to the determination of the troops on both sides who disputed a small amount of territory for hours on end.

During the Peninsular War, great significance attached to possession of the border fortresses which protected the principal routes to and from Portugal and Spain: Almeida (Portuguese) and Ciudad Rodrigo (Spanish) in the north, and Elvas (Portuguese) and Badajoz (Spanish) in the south. The distances between them precluded any one commander from overseeing simultaneous operations in person, and when in the spring of 1811, following the retreat of Marshal Masséna's French army from Portugal, the Allied (Anglo-Portuguese) forces invested Almeida, Wellington was in personal command of this northern sphere of operations. The French attempt to relieve the beleaguered garrison was halted by Wellington's victory at Fuentes de Oñoro (3–5 May), which turned back the immediate French threat in that region.

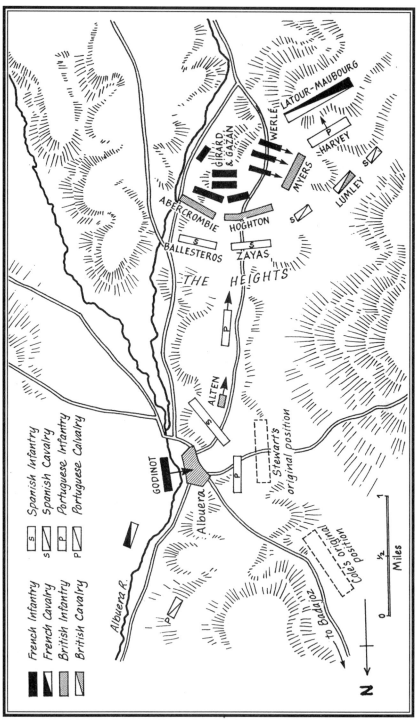

To the south, the Allies laid siege to Badajoz. Although the general direction of the campaign was decided by Wellington, in operational command was William Carr Beresford, Marshal of the Portuguese army. A natural son of the 1st Marquis of Waterford, he had served in the British Army from 1785 and was installed as commander of the Portuguese army on 9 March 1809, as the beginning of a process of re-organisation (including the integration of a number of British officers and the imposition of British methods and discipline) which transformed the Portuguese forces. Much of the credit for the Portuguese becoming so vital and valuable a part of Wellington's army was due to Beresford's administrative talents, and his qualities were acknowledged by Wellington when asked who might be his preferred successor. He described Beresford as 'the ablest man I have yet seen with the army ... if it was a question of handling troops, some of you fellows might do as well, nay, better than he; but what we want now is some one to feed our troops, and I know no one fitter for the purpose than Beresford.'[2] He was not an inspired field commander, however, and although he was criticised somewhat unfairly by the first great historian of the Peninsular War, William Napier, it is a fact worthy of consideration when assessing the carnage of Albuera.

Conversely, the commander of the French force intent on relieving Badajoz was Marshal Jean de Dieu (called Nicolas) Soult, one of the most able and popular of Napoleon's subordinates. The army he was able to deploy at Albuera numbered more than 24,000, all reliable French troops (with the exception of some 200 Spanish Bonapartist *chasseurs*). Against them, on 13 May Beresford drew out his army from around the siege-lines of Badajoz, and to meet Soult in the open field established a position some fifteen miles away, around the village of Albuera. Beresford's command was numerically superior, but included only some 10,400 British troops, the remainder being 10,200 Portuguese and 14,600 Spaniards, the latter under the command of General Joachim Blake, an officer of Irish descent, some 12,000 being members of his own army and the remainder from the army of Captain-General Xavier Castaños. The nucleus of the entire force were the four brigades of British infantry, numbering some 7,640 men; three of the brigades belonged to William Stewart's 2nd Division (those commanded by John Colborne, Alexander Abercrombie and Daniel Hoghton); the fourth, plus a detachment of three additional companies, comprised part of Galbraith Lowry Cole's 4th Division. There was also an independent brigade of King's German Legion light infantry, some 1,100 strong. These and the Portuguese were thoroughly reliable, but the British in particular had no great opinion of the Spaniards, whose morale was believed to be shaky and their leadership poor.

The position adopted by Beresford to bar Soult's path was around the village of Albuera, where a bridge crossed the river of the same name (which was fordable along much of its length). The position was not especially strong, but was the best available to Beresford, who assembled his forces in a line lying approximately north–south, behind (i.e., to the west of) the river, on undulating ground, bare of vegetation, which descended to the river. Rising ground to the south of the line (i.e., Beresford's right flank) formed the so-called 'heights' of Albuera, though that term is somewhat misleading in that there was no great prominence or ravines as sometimes suggested. On the slopes to the east of the river, where Soult first deployed his army, a dense covering of olive-groves concealed their movements; though from the south, where Soult launched his main attack, while the defenders of 'the heights' had a reasonable view of French dispositions, undulations in the terrain prevented the French from observing manoeuvres in the rear of Beresford's position.

Beresford deployed his forces along and behind the river, expecting that Soult would attack down the high road which ran east–west through Albuera village. William Stewart's division held the centre, posted east of the village which itself was garrisoned by the two K.G.L. light battalions. On his left flank Beresford deployed most of his Portuguese infantry (Hamilton's division and Collins' independent brigade, in all ten line battalions and one of *Caçadores* (light infantry), with a small force of Portuguese cavalry on the extreme left. Beresford's right flank was occupied by Blake's Spaniards, posted there in the belief that the higher ground would be the least likely to be attacked; Blake's army had only come up on the night of 15 May and not until shortly before the battle began did they sort out their dispositions. A small force of British and Spanish cavalry occupied the extreme right flank. At the rear of the main position was Beresford's reserve under Lowry Cole, a single brigade of his 4th Division (the rest not having arrived in time for the battle) and Harvey's Portuguese brigade, composed of four line battalions and one of the Loyal Lusitanian Legion, Portuguese troops in British pay. Lowry Cole's troops were late leaving the siege-lines of Badajoz and after a march of about 4½ hours only arrived at 6.30 a.m. on the morning of the battle but had an opportunity to rest before they had to fight to save the day.

Soult's plan was based on the misconception that Blake had not yet joined Beresford, the slight fold behind 'the heights' hiding their presence from view, Beresford having adopted Wellington's tactic of posting his troops on the reverse slope of a ridge to conceal them from the enemy. Consequently Soult chose to concentrate his attack on Beresford's right flank in the hope of driving behind Beresford's army and interposing his troops behind the Anglo-Portuguese and the Spaniards whom he believed were still marching up. Ironically, in attacking where he did, it was against Blake's force that he was initially engaged.

On the morning of 16 May Soult began the action by using the six battalions of Godinot's brigade to demonstrate against Beresford's centre, around Albuera village, to keep as much as possible of the Allied army occupied. This brigade of fewer than 4,000 men, plus about 800 men from Briche's cavalry brigade, attracted the attention of much of the Portuguese contingent, the German Legion and some Spaniards for most of the battle, which served to equalise the numbers involved in the main combat, Soult's attack on 'the heights'. With the remainder of his army, and under cover of the olive groves, Soult swung round the Allies' right flank. The appearance there of French cavalry alerted Beresford to the danger, and he rode over to confer with Blake, ordering him to swing round half his Spaniards to form a new line at right-angles to the existing position, to hold the heights against flank attack, while he (Beresford) dealt with the French advance against Albuera village. He also ordered William Stewart's three brigades to prepare to support Blake if necessary.

Necessary it certainly was, as the French attack was led by General Girard's 1st Division advancing in column, apparently not even attempting to deploy into line before contact, but intent in driving through whatever defenders were present on the heights. Girard's nine battalions were followed by the ten of General Gazan's division, and in reserve were the nine battalions of Werlé's division, and a composite unit of grenadiers just over 1,000 strong.[3] Against this strong force, Blake had originally moved only four battalions from the division of General Zayas, two from Regiment 'Irlanda' (originally Irish mercenaries in Spanish service) and the 2nd and 4th Spanish Guards; and although, once the extent of the danger was obvious, Blake began to hurry up more units, for a time the greater part of the French army was bearing down upon only these four battalions.

Beresford ordered Stewart's division from its position behind Albuera village to march to the support of Blake on the heights, transferring some of the Portuguese from the left flank to fill the gap in the centre; and ordered Lowry Cole's men, who after their march had now finished their breakfast, to move south to act as a reserve for the troops on the heights. It was as well that he did, for only the sight of these three British and five Portuguese battalions prevented a massed attack by almost the whole of Soult's cavalry, which under General Marie Charles Latour-Maubourg was concentrated on the left of the French attack against the heights. They were faced by only small numbers of Spanish and British cavalry, which could have been swamped had Latour-Maubourg moved against them, for the Spanish cavalry was of little reliability, and General the Hon. William Lumley's British contingent numbered only some 750 men.

Zayas' four battalions and one battery bore the entire weight of Girard's attack, for the first supporting troops, Ballesteros' Spanish division, deployed to the left of Zayas, against which the French merely threw out skirmishers to keep them occupied. Zayas' men confounded the critical British opinion of them by standing firm and exchanging fire with the French, who by virtue of advancing uphill discovered that their rear formations could also target the Spaniards by firing over the heads of the leading ranks, thus bringing against them a greater weight of musketry than would have been expected. Even under these conditions, and under bombardment from the French artillery which accompanied the attack, the four Spanish battalions held on so long that Girard's assault came to a halt, and as the two sides blasted each other to pieces the Spanish line began to shrink as the gaps caused by casualties were filled by the men closing in towards their centre.

At this juncture the first British troops arrived on 'the heights'. Beresford claimed that he intended to deploy the whole of Stewart's division into line before advancing to support Zayas, but he was busy directing the Spanish reinforcements, and William Stewart, accompanying his leading brigade, saw an opportunity to deal a decisive blow against Girard's now static column. Stewart's leading brigade was commanded by Lieutenant-Colonel John Colborne, one of the best regimental officers in the army and later, as Lord Seaton, a distinguished field marshal; but he was comparatively new in his command and apparently unwilling to question the orders of his divisional commander. He later remarked that 'I had nothing to do with the arrangement, but merely obeyed the orders of General Stewart';[4] which orders led to one of the worst débâcles of the entire war.

Colborne's brigade was composed of four battalions: the 1/3rd (Buffs), 2/31st (Huntingdonshire Regiment), 2/48th (Northamptonshire

Regiment) and 2/66th (Berkshire Regiment). Stewart marched around Zayas' right flank to assail the unprotected left flank of Girard's column, hurrying his battalions forward in echelon (some actually through part of Zayas' line), led by the Buffs, followed by the 2/48th and 2/66th. Providentially, the 2/31st, by bringing up the rear of the brigade, was still marching forward as the others prepared to go into action. Beresford suggests that Colborne had been aware of the dangers of advancing thus, with a flank exposed, and says that he requested that he be allowed to form the Buffs into square or column, but that Stewart, in his urgency to relieve Zayas, refused. Stewart also brought up Captain Andrew Cleeves' battery of King's German Legion artillery, and four guns got into action as Colborne made his attack. Initially, it succeeded; the flank of Girard's column faced outwards and began to exchange fire with the British, but the weight of Colborne's musketry was such that the French began to waver as their casualties mounted, French officers being seen beating their men back in line with the flats of their swords. It seems that some limited bayonet charges were also delivered by the British; Ensign Edward Close of the 2/48th described how his battalion had charged after delivering only two or three volleys, and so early in the action that only the Buffs on their right and the grenadier company of the 2/66th had come up. They re-formed after these charges but the 48th had suffered so heavily that Close described their line as more like a cordon of skirmishers. At this moment, disaster struck.

The French cavalry had been hovering at the left of the attack on the heights, and upon seeing Girard's column under such pressure, Latour-Maubourg ordered his two nearest regiments, the 2nd Hussars and 1st Lancers of the Vistula Legion, to go to their support. Although less than 900 in number, they proved how devastating a cavalry attack could be, especially by troops armed with lances, upon infantry not formed in protective square. The morning had begun fair but had worsened progressively until a storm of rain and hail descended which, mingling with the gun-smoke, prevented Colborne's brigade from seeing the French cavalry until they were actually being overrun. It was less of a fight than a massacre, for three-quarters of the brigade was destroyed within five minutes. The first to fall were the Buffs, nearest to the point of the French attack; they appear to have faced about just before the cavalry fell upon them, but did not fire, perhaps because they were unsure if the cavalry were French or Spanish, and were ridden over. It is difficult to ascertain the casualties caused by the cavalry, for some parts of the brigade appear to have been hit quite badly by French artillery fire when engaging Girard; but the total loss for the battalion in the battle was more than 85 per cent: of 27 officers and 728 men, four officers and 212 were killed, fourteen and 234 wounded, two and 177 missing (mostly captured).[5] (Such statistics can be slightly deceptive in that the numbers of men present probably include baggage-guards not present in the firing-line, so that the reported casualties may represent an even higher percentage when compared with the consequently lower number of troops actually in the fight. However, it is recorded that the 23rd at least made all efforts to get the maximum number of men into action, by rushing up those who were not absolutely essential for guarding the baggage. Comparison of casualty-returns with muster-rolls shows that a considerable number of the wounded soon succumbed to their injuries, so that the number of fatalities was in fact considerably greater.)

A most furious fight developed around the Buffs' Colours. The Regimental Colour was carried by 16-year-old Ensign Edward Thomas; as the cavalry swept over the battalion, he held up the flag and tried to rally his company after its officer commanding, Captain William Stevens, was wounded. Thomas called out, 'Rally on me, men, I will be your pivot'; and when summoned to yield his precious burden he replied 'Only with my life!' He was cut down and the Colour was taken.[6] After the battle his body was buried by a sergeant and a private, the only survivors of the 63 men who had formed his company. The King's Colour was borne by Ensign Charles Walsh; its pike was broken by a roundshot, Walsh was wounded and about to be taken prisoner when Lieutenant Matthew Latham seized the Colour from him. Latham was immediately surrounded by French cavalry, one of whom dealt him a dreadful, disfiguring blow across the face; but he continued to defend himself with his sword until another massive sabre-blow severed his left arm. Dropping his sword, Latham seized what remained of the colour-pike with his right arm and continued to struggle until he was ridden down, trampled and speared by lancers endeavouring to capture the flag. With the last of his strength he tore the fabric from the pike and concealed it in the breast of his coat.

The 2/48th was the next to be ridden down. Of 29 officers and 423 other ranks, four officers and 44 other ranks were killed, ten and 86 wounded and nine and 190 reported as missing (presumably captured), a loss of almost 76 per cent. The Vistula Lancers appear to have behaved with unwarranted brutality, deliberately trampling and spearing the helpless. Major William Brooke of the 48th, captured after receiving a severe head wound, recorded that as he was being escorted to the rear by two French infantrymen, a lancer rode up, deliberately cut him down and tried to make his horse trample him. He was rescued by two more infantrymen and a dragoon who saw him safely to the rear of the French position; Brooke believed that the Poles were all drunk. Such conduct was not an isolated case; two officers of the 66th were reported to have been deliberately speared while lying disabled by earlier wounds. Edward Close of the 48th recalled that as he took to his heels to escape the rampaging horsemen, he was knocked over by another fugitive and while lying helpless was about to be speared by a lancer when a Spanish dragoon appeared and dealt the lancer such a blow with his sabre that he flew right over his horse's head. Close escaped and continued running until he encountered Lowry Cole's reserve.

The 2/66th appear to have been mauled in the infantry duel, even before they were the next to be ridden down by the cavalry. Lieutenant George Crompton, who was captured but freed by some Spanish cavalry who were hovering around the flank of the action, wrote that it was the first time – 'and God knows I hope the last – I saw the backs of English soldiers turned upon French'.[7] As he and Lieutenant John Clarke both recalled, after the initial break the battalion made an unsuccessful attempt to rally; Clarke stated that small groups of men ran to individual officers and tried to make a stand, but were ridden down. Both their Colours were lost, Crompton noting that a lieutenant seized a musket with which to defend them, but was shot through the heart.[8] Ensign James Hay was run through by a lance, but struggled to his feet to continue the fight; he was run through a second time and was found sitting on the field in the evening, remarking to those who sought to help him that there were many in a worse plight. He survived his injuries but died of a lung complaint some years later.

Having ridden over the Buffs and assailed the other two battalions from the rear, the French cavalry had almost run out of steam, so the 2/31st, farthest from the initial point of impact, had time to form square and drive off the horsemen without much difficulty. Cleeves' artillery battery, however, was overrun and severely hindered by the press of fugitives around them. Sergeants Hebecker and Bussman managed to limber-up the two guns farthest from the cavalry, but the horses of one team were wounded and fell, and the driver was shot off the lead horse of the other. One of the gunners, Corporal Henry Fincke, jumped from his own horse on to the empty saddle and drove the team at a gallop through the cavalry, his riding-horse galloping by his side and thus preventing any Frenchman from getting close enough to aim a cut at

Fincke. The other guns and Cleeves were captured but almost immediately recovered, less a single howitzer which the French took away. Wellington rewarded Fincke's bravery with a gift of 100 dollars.[9]

As the cavalry began to scatter, discouraged by the steady fire of the 31st, parties careered on along the rear of Zayas' battalions, chasing off that general and his staff and engaging Beresford and his aides in person; the Marshal himself, a very powerful man, parried a lance-thrust and wrested the lancer from his saddle. Having witnessed the disaster, General Lumley sent forward two squadrons of 4th Dragoons to assist; but they were intercepted by the cavalry which Latour-Maubourg had sent to cover the withdrawal of the lancers, and the British cavalry fell back having achieved little beyond having both their squadron commanders captured (Captains John Phillips and Carlisle Spedding), though the momentary confusion permitted a number of British prisoners to escape. The French cavalry had also suffered quite severely during their devastating charge: the 1st Vistula Lancers sustained 130 casualties and the 2nd Hussars 73.

With virtually the whole of Colborne's brigade swept away, the defence of 'the heights' again fell to Zayas' Spaniards, although by now the second of Stewart's brigades was coming up, that of Major-General Daniel Hoghton, consisting of the l/48th, 1/57th and 29th Foot, the former in the lead. They opened fire upon the scattered, retiring French cavalry, but in so doing shot many of Zayas' men in the back, and were only stopped after Beresford's military secretary, Major Robert Arbuthnot, risked his life by riding in front of the 29th. The firing was also taken up by the 57th (West Middlesex) Regiment, whose commanding officer, Lieutenant-Colonel William Inglis, had just had his horse shot from under him; he ran to the front of his battalion and commanded them to order arms, and the shooting stopped. Even after this incident, the Spanish troops held firm.

Girard now ordered up Gazan's division to replace his own badly mauled formation; but the space was so confined that the two divisions became entangled, Girard's men remaining in the firing-line alongside the newcomers, forming a powerful if not very cohesive body about 8,000 strong. The pause occasioned by the French re-deployment gave Beresford the opportunity to re-form his own front line along 'the heights', by moving Stewart's two surviving brigades to replace the Spaniards, who were at last withdrawn. The discipline displayed by the British at this juncture was highly impressive; Hoghton's brigade, which replaced Zayas', stood with ordered arms until the exhausted Spaniards had withdrawn, and not until their frontage was clear did Hoghton raise his hat, the signal for his brigade to commence firing. Zayas' four battalions had sustained 615 casualties in their hour's duel with the French, a casualty-rate of more than 30 per cent, one of the most outstanding performances by Spanish troops in the entire war. Abercrombie's brigade (2/28th, 2/34th and 2/39th Foot) moved to occupy the sloping ground to the left, to replace Ballesteros; but against them the French action was largely skirmishing, and the renewed main attack continued to fall upon the 'plateau' sector of 'the heights', now held by only the three battalions of Hoghton's brigade and the 2/31st which had survived the destruction of Colborne's command. These redcoats, less than 2,000 in number, took on virtually the whole of the French attack, a protracted and murderous musketry duel at close range, the French supplemented by the fire of some 40 pieces of artillery, a bombardment to which the Allies were almost unable to reply in kind. This fight was entirely unusual in the context of the warfare of the time, for such combat usually resulted in the withdrawal of one of the protagonists, or the advance of one side when it appeared their opponents were beginning to give way; but here, on a very restricted front, both sides stood their ground and pounded each other like the most stubborn of prize-fighters.

Moyle Sherer of the 34th wrote a graphic account of the action, from the moment his brigade was directed towards 'the heights':

'We formed in open column of companies at half-distance, and moved in rapid double quick to the scene of the action. I remember well, as we moved down in column, shot and shell flew over and through it in quick succession; we sustained little injury from either, but a captain of the twenty-ninth had been dreadfully lacerated by a ball, and lay directly in our path. We passed close to him, and he knew us all; and the heart-rending tone in which he called to us for water, or to kill him, I shall never forget.[10] He lay alone, and we were in motion, and could give him no succour; for on this trying day, such of the wounded as could not walk, lay unattended where they fell: all was hurry and struggle; every arm was wanted on the field. When we arrived near the discomfited and retiring Spaniards, and formed our line to advance through them towards the enemy, a very noble-looking young Spanish officer rode up to me, and begged me, with a sort of proud and brave anxiety, to explain to the English, that his countrymen were ordered to retire, but were not flying. Just as our line had entirely cleared the Spaniards, the smoky shroud of battle was, by the slackening of the fire, for one minute blown aside, and gave to our view the French grenadier caps, their arms, and the whole aspect of their frowning masses. It was a momentary, but a grand sight; a heavy atmosphere of smoke again enveloped us, and few objects could be discerned at all, none distinctly ... This murderous contest of musketry lasted long ... To describe my feelings throughout with fidelity, would be impossible: at intervals, a shriek or groan told that men were falling around me; but it was not always that the tumult of the contest suffered me to catch these sounds. A constant feeling to the centre of the line, and the gradual diminution of our front, more truly bespoke the havock of death. As we moved, though slowly, yet ever a little in advance, our own killed and wounded lay behind us; but we arrived among those of the enemy, and those of the Spaniards who had fallen in the first onset: we trod among the dead and dying, all reckless of them. But how shall I picture the *British soldier* going into action? He is neither heated by brandy, stimulated in the hope of plunder, nor inflamed by the deadly feelings of revenge; he does not even indulge in expressions of animosity against his foes; he moves forward, confident of victory, never dreams of the possibility of defeat, and braves death with all the accompanying horrors of laceration and torture, with the most cheerful intrepidity ...'[11]

Melodramatic though the last sentiments may appear, the fact is that both sides – Hoghton's brigade greatly outnumbered – fought it out almost toe-to-toe. It is difficult to calculate the French casualties at this stage of the action, for Girard's men had been engaged earlier, but it has been estimated that no less than 2,000 of their casualties occurred here. Hoghton's casualties are more obvious, for they all occurred here. Daniel Hoghton himself, the 41-year-old younger son of the late MP for Preston, Sir Henry Hoghton, Bt., of Hoghton Tower, was mortally wounded early in the action, and command of the brigade devolved temporarily upon William Inglis of the 57th. His battalion went into action with 31 officers and 616 other ranks, of whom 23 officers and 405 men were killed or wounded, a casualty-rate of more than 66 per cent. Inglis himself was grievously wounded by grapeshot which entered his left breast and lodged in his back, but he refused to be carried to the rear, lying in front of his battalion's Colours and calling upon his men with the immortal exhortation, 'Die hard, 57th, die hard!' The very Colours were riddled, the Regimental Colour receiving 21 bullet-holes and the King's Colour seventeen and a broken staff; Ensign James Jackson, who carried the latter, was wounded in three places and handed it to Ensign James Veitch; when Jackson returned from having his wounds dressed he found that Veitch, though himself wounded, refused to give up the precious burden. Emulating his commanding officer, Captain Ralph Fawcett refused to be carried away when wounded but lay by his company, calling on them to fire low and steadily; but unlike Inglis, who survived, Fawcett died of his injuries.

The 1/48th went into action with 33 officers and 464 other ranks; they lost sixteen and 258 respectively, plus six men missing, a casualty-rate of more than 56 per cent. Their young commanding officer, Lieutenant-Colonel George Duckworth, was the son of the distinguished admiral; he was hit in the left breast by a musket ball, but 'the same noble blood which runs in the veins of the father flowing equally warm in those of the son, he could not be induced to quit the field'. Shortly afterwards he was hit in the throat, 'when he expired without a groan'.[12] By melancholy coincidence, news of his death reached his home on the day before the funeral of his only son, aged four. (Unwillingness to quit the field when wounded was no prerogative of rank: Lieutenant George Beard of the 39th, in Abercrombie's brigade, was wounded in the wrist early in the action but declined his captain's advice to retire for treatment; remaining with his company, this 'brave young officer'[13] was killed by the bursting of a shell.)

The 29th numbered 31 officers and 476 other ranks; they lost seventeen and 308 respectively, plus eleven missing, a casualty-rate of more than 66 per cent, one of their officers recalling how in places whole sections went down until the battalion resembled a line of skirmishers. Their commanding officer, Lieutenant-Colonel Daniel White, was severely wounded; one of their Colour-bearers, Ensign Edward Furnace (or Furness) refused to go to the rear when severely wounded, and was hit again and killed. His replacement, Ensign Richard Vance, observing the regiment dying around him, tore the Colour from its pike lest it fall into French hands. After the battle he was found dead, with the flag concealed in the breast of his coat.

It is perhaps surprising that both sides permitted this unrelieved butchery to continue for so long, especially as both commanders had reserves in hand. Soult stated that he chose not to commit his once he realised that Blake's army *was* present, deciding to do no more than hold his position. Beresford held back Lowry Cole's division in the belief that it was preventing Latour-Maubourg's cavalry from attacking, so to support Hoghton he tried to bring up the infantry of Castaños' army, some 1,800 men of Carlos de España's brigade. They were unwilling to move; Beresford even seized one colonel by his epaulettes and attempted to drag him forward, but without success, and from the fact that the brigade suffered no fatalities and sustained only 33 men wounded it is clear that they failed quite spectacularly to emulate the heroism of their countrymen in Zayas' brigade. Instead, Beresford sent for two brigades of Hamilton's Portuguese infantry which was covering the French demonstration against Albuera village, but they took at least half an hour to begin to move, apparently because Beresford's messenger (Arbuthnot) had difficulty finding their commander, Major-General John Hamilton, who had unexpectedly moved forward ('as for old Hamilton, it never took much persuasion to get him, at any time, into the hottest of it').[14] In desperation Beresford called Major-General Charles von Alten's German Legion light infantry from Albuera village, to march towards 'the heights'. As they withdrew the French occupied the village; and within half an hour, the fight on 'the heights' being decided, von Alten was stopped in his march and sent back to recapture the village, which he did for the loss of about 10 per cent of his men.

What happened to decide the action was a source of much argument in subsequent years. It was claimed by some (notably William Napier, whose opinion of Beresford was low and whose subsequent conflict with him, in print, is well known) that the advance of Lowry Cole's troops, which saved the day for Beresford, was ordered by Lieutenant-Colonel Henry Hardinge, Deputy Quartermaster-General of the Portuguese army, and it was thus to him that the victory was due. What actually happened may be deduced from statements made by the main participants. Lowry Cole had been ordered by Beresford to retain his position, to prevent Latour-Maubourg's advance and to keep open a route of retreat should all go awry. Cole was acutely aware of his inaction and sent an ADC – a Swiss officer, Alexander de Roverea of the Sicilian Regiment – to Beresford to ask for orders. Roverea was caught up in the attack on Beresford's staff by the lancers, but received orders only after Beresford saw that Cole was already moving, when he was sent to order Spanish support for the advance. He was unable to complete this mission, being hit on the head by a lump of shell and knocked unconscious. When he came round he was evidently concussed, for he remounted and rode about wildly until a friend escorted him to medical assistance; after convalescence in Britain he made a full recovery.

Lowry Cole was thus deprived of communication with Beresford, and while he awaited Roverea's return, Henry Hardinge arrived. He had been with Hoghton's brigade for some time – the 57th was his old regiment – and had watched with growing dismay as the casualties mounted. With the battalion commanding officers all down, Hoghton dead and William Stewart twice wounded, Hardinge himself had helped direct the brigade's fire, ordering that some French skirmishers who had lapped around the right flank be driven off. He saw survivors calling to the wounded to empty their pouches, as ammunition was almost exhausted, and that the brigade was so 'crippled and exhausted' that it was 'in a military sense ... almost exterminated'.[15] Having seen Beresford's unavailing attempts to get Castaños' men to move, Hardinge realised that unless Hoghton's men were relieved quickly, the position would be lost. The only troops available to provide such succour were those of Lowry Cole, so Hardinge galloped off to consult their commander, arriving in such a lather that, contrary to good form, he spoke to Cole with his sword still drawn. Hardinge informed Cole of what was happening, which he was unable to see for himself because of the cloud of smoke which enveloped the fighting. Hardinge made it clear that he did not bring orders from Beresford but spoke only for himself; but Cole's ADC, Captain Thomas Wade of the 42nd (later severely wounded) recalled that not only Hardinge but 'every Staff Officer attached to Sir Lowry Cole'[16] including Assistant Adjutant-General Lieutenant-Colonel John Rooke, and Assistant Quartermaster-General Sir Charles Vere) urged that something be done. Hardinge recalled that he was urging Cole to move when Rooke rode up to confirm the desperate plight of the troops on 'the heights', and when Cole remarked that 'Hardinge is pressing me to attack the enemy's column', Rooke agreed. Cole was less inclined to admit that his manoeuvre was initiated by Hardinge, whom he claimed was not sufficiently experienced to be able to persuade him (Cole) to adopt a course of action which he had not already considered; but conceded that the entreaties from Hardinge and Rooke did influence his decision to advance towards 'the heights'. Perhaps the most accurate statement on what actually happened was the comment Cole made to Hardinge in later years: 'I fully admit that the merit of originating the movement rests with you, but the credit of having incurred the responsibility is mine'.[17] As soon as this was decided, Hardinge rode off to order Abercrombie's brigade to wheel and engage the French right flank, to exert extra pressure to that which would come from Cole.

Lowry Cole's command consisted of one British and one Portuguese brigade. The British formation was known as the Fusilier Brigade from its composition of the 1/ and 2/7th Royal Fuzileers (contemporary spelling) and 1/23rd Royal Welch Fuzileers, commanded by the 28-year-old Lieutenant-Colonel Sir William Myers, Bt., of the 7th. William Harvey's Portuguese brigade comprised two battalions each of the 11th and

155

23rd Portuguese Line, and the 1st Battalion Loyal Lusitanian Legion under Lieutenant-Colonel Edward Hawkshaw. Even with such good troops, an advance across open, rising ground, supported only by the rather mangled units of Allied cavalry, in the face of a large French cavalry force, was a very considerable risk; had the situation not been so desperate, Cole would surely never have contemplated it. As one officer recalled, it was 'a neck-or-nothing affair'.[18]

Cole advanced with his three fusilier battalions in echelon, the 1/7th on the left, 2/7th in the centre and 1/23rd on the right, with the Portuguese to their right. To secure the flanks from cavalry attack, the Loyal Lusitanian Legion marched in column on the left, and on the right a provisional battalion formed of the light companies of the component units, and apparently also three additional companies from the 2/27th, 1/40th and 97th which were also present. One of the 23rd's officers confirmed that the advance was made in columns, the units deploying into line before engaging.[19] Those involved realised the perilous nature of the advance and certainly regretted the absence of their trusted leader, for Wellington's presence would have given them confidence of success. John Cooper of the 7th recalled an exchange with Fusilier Horsefall as they marched towards 'the heights': Horsefall asked, '"Whore's ar Arthur?" I said, "I don't know, I don't see him." He rejoined, "Aw wish he wor here." So did I.'[20]

The sight of Cole's advance compelled Soult to commit his reserve: Werlé's nine battalions marched diagonally behind the struggling mass of Girard's and Gazan's men, and came up on the left of the fighting mass on 'the heights', in three columns. Captain John Humphrey Hill, commanding the 23rd's light company on Cole's extreme right flank, was able to discern that the French columns were nine companies deep.[21] The French seem to have made some attempt to deploy into line, but this was difficult under fire and seems to have failed; Edward Blakeney, commanding the 2/7th, remarked that he 'saw the French officers endeavouring to deploy their columns, but all to no purpose; for, as soon as a third of a company got out they immediately ran back, to be covered by the front of the column'.[22]

As Cole advanced, Latour-Maubourg sent four dragoon regiments against the Portuguese on the right of Cole's line; but untried troops though they were, they remained steady and drove off the French with musketry. Small parties of French cavalry were reported to have evaded the Spanish cavalry on the flank and taken prisoner some of the British wounded who were making their way to the rear, but with the Portuguese neutralising Latour-Maubourg's cavalry, the fusiliers were able to engage Werlé's troops without interference. On the other flank, the Lusitanian Legion suffered 171 casualties out of 572, mostly from artillery fire during the advance, a loss of almost 29 per cent.

Casualties among the fusiliers were very much greater. They advanced into an absolute storm of fire, so that their men went down like skittles (to use Cooper's homely simile), firing as they advanced, behaving 'most gloriously, never losing their ranks, and closing to their centre as casualties occurred ... the battalions never for an instant ceased advancing, although under artillery firing grape the whole time'.[23] Most of the British commanders were hit: Cole was wounded but refused to quit the field; Myers was mortally struck; Lieutenant-Colonel Henry Walton Ellis of the 23rd had the third and little fingers of his right hand shattered as he was holding his bridle (he survived to fall at Waterloo); Blakeney of the 2/7th was severely wounded; and the colour-pikes of the 7th were shattered. As the fusiliers advanced up the reverse slopes of 'the heights' the only orders heard were 'Close up!', 'Close in!', and 'Fire away!',[24] as each battalion took on one French column. For perhaps as long as twenty minutes the fusiliers and Werlé's men faced one another, blasting away with musketry; until the French suddenly broke. Napier's account is perhaps the most celebrated piece of military writing in English:

'... a fearful discharge of grape from all their artillery whistled through the British ranks. Myers was killed; Cole and the three colonels, Ellis, Blakeney, and Hawkshawe, fell wounded, and the fuzileer battalions, struck by the iron tempest, reeled, and staggered like sinking ships. Suddenly and sternly recovering, they closed on their terrible enemies, and then was seen with what a strength and majesty the British soldier fights. In vain did Soult, by voice and gesture, animate his Frenchmen; in vain did the hardiest veterans, extricating themselves from the crowded columns, sacrifice their lives to gain time for the mass to open out on such a fair field; in vain did the mass itself bear up, and fiercely striving, fire indiscriminately upon friends and foes, while the horsemen hovering on the flank threatened to charge the advancing line. Nothing could stop that astonishing infantry. No sudden burst of undisciplined valour, no nervous enthusiasm, weakened the stability of their order; their flashing eyes were bent on the dark columns in their front; their measured tread shook the ground; their dreadful volleys swept away the head of every formation; their deafening shouts overpowered the dissoneant cries that broke from all parts of the tumultuous crowd, as foot by foot and with a horrid carnage it was driven by the incessant vigour of the attack to the farthest edge of the hill. In vain did the French reserves, joining with the struggling multitude, endeavour to sustain the fight; their efforts only increased the irremediable confusion, and the mighty mass giving way like a loosened cliff, went headlong down the ascent. The rain flowed after in streams discoloured with blood, and fifteen hundred unwounded men, the remnant of six thousand unconquerable British soldiers, stood triumphant on the fatal hill!' [25]

This feat was regarded at the time as something quite exceptional; a week after the battle Hardinge stated that 'The Fusiliers exceeded anything that the usual word *gallantry* can convey',[26] while Cole called it 'an example of steadiness and heroic gallantry which history I believe cannot surpass'.[27] On its own, however, it was not entirely decisive, for at the same time, on Hardinge's instigation, Abercrombie's brigade wheeled and assailed the flank of Girard and Gazan's troops, which gave way at the same time as Werlé's, and the whole mass rolled back upon Soult's only remaining reserve, the two grenadier battalions, which themselves had suffered severely from artillery fire. Despite the destruction of his infantry as a cohesive force, Soult still had his 40 guns and cavalry, which inhibited any serious attempt at pursuit by Beresford's troops. The exhaustion of the Allied troops prevented any exploitation of the victory, even though the Portuguese brigades finally came into line (their casualties were not severe, though one of their brigadiers, Richard Collins, lost his leg to a cannon-ball. An expert linguist, artist and military historian, not even the removal of his thigh from gangrene prevented him from returning to the war with a cork leg.) The pitiful remnant of the 57th did attempt to pursue the French, but Beresford himself stopped them, calling that it would be a sin to let them go on, and accordingly the pursuit was halted by the battalion's adjutant, Lieutenant William Mann, the most senior officer surviving.

The losses of Werlé's brigade were estimated at between 1,450 and 2,000; among the dead was François-Jean Werlé himself, a companion of Soult's for many years, whose loss was a sad blow to the French commander. Although Werlé's brigade had lost more than a quarter of their number, Myers' fusiliers had suffered much more severely in percentage terms, to a considerable degree the result of the artillery fire into which they advanced. The 1/7th, from 27 officers and 687 other ranks, lost 65 dead and fifteen officers and 277 other ranks wounded, exactly 50 per cent casualties; the 2/7th, from 28 officers and 540 other ranks, lost two and 47 dead and thirteen and 287 wounded, a loss of more than 61 per cent; and the 1/23rd, from 41 officers and

692 other ranks, lost two and 74 dead, eleven and 246 wounded, and six men missing, a loss of almost 47 per cent. As a brigade, casualties totalled almost 52 per cent. (Percentage losses would appear greater if the rear-echelon baggage-guards were deducted; for example, instead of more than 2,000 in all, Cole believed that the fusilier brigade consisted of only 1,500 rank and file, which if accurate would put the brigade's casualties at about 67 per cent. None of the casualty statistics include men who were slightly wounded or who straggled away during the fight, so the number of men capable of effective resistance at the end of the action may have been considerably less than the casualty-figures imply; so that when Cooper claimed that his battalion went into action only 435 strong and had only about 80 men left at the end, or that the 57th was able to muster only 160 men, with No. 2 Company's rations being able to fit into a drummer's cap, such stories may be more accurate than the official returns might imply. These revised calculations make the achievement even more amazing.)

The ground occupied by Hoghton's men presented a sight more appalling than anything witnessed by even the most hardened campaigners; as Hardinge remarked, 'the carnage which marked the position of this celebrated brigade, exceeded on so small a space of ground anything ever witnessed on an open field of battle'.[28] Only two captains in the brigade were operational, one of whom succeeded to command of it: Gilbert Cimetière of the 48th who, ironically, was a French émigré. Moyle Sherer recalled that Hoghton's brigade 'went into action led by a major-general, and with its due proportion of field officers and captains. I saw it at three in the afternoon: a captain commanded the brigade; the 57th and 48th regiments were commanded by lieutenants; and the junior captain of the 29th was the senior effective officer of his corps'. Of them and the fusiliers he wrote: 'I have read the annals of modern warfare with some attention, and I know of little which can compare with, nothing which has surpassed, the enthusiastic and unyielding bravery, displayed by these corps on the field of Albuera.'[29] In his dispatch, Beresford commented: 'It is impossible by any description to do justice to the distinguished gallantry of the troops, but every individual most nobly did his duty, and which will be well proved by the great loss we have suffered, though repulsing the enemy; and it was observed, that our dead, particularly the 57th regiment, were lying, as they had fought, in ranks, and every wound was in the front.'[30] Those who walked over 'the heights' were universally appalled by the carnage on an area not much larger than a football pitch; not only did the dead carpet the ground, but literally lay in heaps, one pile seen by Cooper being more than three feet high.

The survivors spent a wretched night, bivouacked among the dead and wounded, drenched with rain and most without rations or wood for camp-fires. Exhausted as he was, Cooper found sleep impossible, though he curled up like a dog amid a tuft of rushes, on account of cold and hunger. Only when the sun rose next morning did he and his comrades cease to shiver, which their first issue of rations – a mouthful of rum – may have helped. After the battle, both the Buffs' lost Colours were recovered; the Regimental Colour was found and restored to the regiment by Sergeant William Gough of the 7th, and astonishingly Matthew Latham was found still alive, with the King's Colour in his coat. Originally, Charles Walsh was credited with saving this invaluable treasure, and was praised for it in the House of Commons; but when Walsh escaped from the French he confirmed the truth. Latham was accordingly promoted to captain (in February 1813) and presented by his regiment with a gold medal worth £100 which portrayed his act of heroism, and which he was permitted to wear in uniform. The Prince Regent defrayed the expenses of a leading surgeon who repaired Latham's facial injury, and on his retirement in 1820 he received a pension of £170 per annum.

Soult remained facing Beresford for some 36 hours, until news of Wellington's approach compelled him to withdraw. He admitted 2,800 casualties, but his losses were probably approaching 8,000; Beresford's total losses were almost 6,000, more than two-thirds of them British. Such was the decimation of Beresford's British infantry that even after the arrival of reinforcements he could never have contemplated using them in an attack on Soult's position. Indeed, there were not even enough troops left to move all the wounded, some having to lie where they fell for two days before they received attention. Some units had so few men left that two battalions of the 7th had to be amalgamated, and both of the 48th, and the other shattered units had to be amalgamated into a provisional battalion, the 3rd, 29th, 31st, 57th and 66th each contributing two companies.

Although Soult was unable to relieve Badajoz, that city did not fall to the Allies until the following year. Much discussion and acrimony centred upon the conduct of the respective generals; Soult reprimanded Godinot for not pressing the feint attack sufficiently to prevent the transfer of Beresford's reserve to 'the heights', but such criticism was probably unfair (he was reprimanded again the following year, which may have contributed to the fact that he shot himself). Soult's attack on 'the heights' might well have succeeded had he committed Werlé's brigade earlier, or conversely he might have broken off the action with much less damage to his army when he realised that Blake's army *was* present, instead of trying to switch from an offensive to defensive action when he realised the odds against him.

Beresford has been much criticised for his handling of the battle, especially by Napier, yet criticism is easily over-stated. Well though Zayas' brigade behaved, the other Spanish formations did not emulate them; Blake was slow to combat the threat to the Allied right flank, and William Stewart was surely unwisely impulsive in the manner in which he hurried his division forward, which were the causes of most of Beresford's troubles. Beresford, certainly, was shocked and appalled by the carnage, which was evident in his first report. Wellington recalled that 'He wrote me to the effect that he was delighted I was coming; that he could not stand the slaughter about him nor the vast responsibility. His letter was quite in a desponding tone. It was brought to me next day, I think, by General Arbuthnot[31] when I was at dinner at Elvas, and I said directly, "This won't do; write me down a victory." The dispatch was altered accordingly.'[32] In reply, Wellington immediately sent a note of support:

> 'My dear Beresford,
> I arrived here about two this day, and received your letter of the 17th ... Your loss, by all accounts, has been very large; but I hope that it will not prove so large as was first supposed. You could not be successful in such an action without a large loss, and we must make up our minds to affairs of this kind sometimes, or give up the game.'[33]

Despite such encouragement, on the following day Beresford wrote again to Wellington in a tone still very self-critical, saying that he could scarcely forgive himself for offering battle, and only agreed to because Blake was determined that the Spaniards would. On 21 May Wellington visited the field and found that 'We had a very good position, and I think should have gained a complete victory in it, without any material loss, if the Spaniards could have manoeuvred.'[34] He complimented the Spanish on their bravery but again criticised their lack of ability or willingness to manoeuvre, thus creating 'a necessity for using the British infantry in all parts of the field, and to have thrown upon us the great burden of the battle ... Our loss is very large; but we must expect loss whenever we engage the British troops with the Spaniards as allies.'[35] He admitted that 'The late action has made a terrible hole in our ranks; but I am working hard to set all to rights again';[36] yet 'adverting to the nature of the contest, and the manner in which they held their ground against all the efforts the whole French army could make against them, I think this action one of the most glorious and honorable to the character of the troops of any that has been fought during the war.'[37]

Moyle Sherer thought that Albuera exerted a more lasting effect than just frustrating Soult's attempt to relieve Badajoz: 'It added one to the many bright examples of British heroism; and, when Soult rode by the side of his Imperial master on the field of Waterloo, as the cheering of the English soldiery struck upon his ear, Albuera was not forgotten, and he could have whispered him, that they were men, who could only be defeated, by being utterly destroyed.'[38]

Albuera looms large in the life of the regiments engaged, whether it be the honorary membership of one another's messes enjoyed by officers and warrant officers of the Royal Fusiliers and Royal Welch Fusiliers (which arrangement has continued even after the Royal Fusiliers were absorbed into the Royal Regiment of Fusiliers in 1968), or the fact that 'ALBUHERA' [sic] was the one battle-honour displayed on the cap badge of the Middlesex Regiment, or the proud nickname 'Die Hards' used by that regiment. It should also be remembered that in order for so sanguinary and protracted action to take place, their opponents must have been equally determined, and it was the refusal of either side to yield their ground which led to the fearful slaughter on 'the heights', circumstances scarcely matched during any of the campaigns of the era. Hardinge himself made this point in a letter to Cole eight days after the action: 'Without considering the total numbers on each side, but merely the numbers in action at the point of contest, it must be admitted that our 6,000 British fought more desperately and bravely than anything that has yet taken place in the Peninsula, and the enemy in conduct dangerously rivalled them.'[39] None the less, the British were under the greatest disadvantage, of numbers and the greatly superior artillery fire with which they were bombarded, which makes their performance all the more creditable. That units could stand and sustain such horrendous casualties and still remain in action is scarcely credible; for example, deducting Abercrombie's brigade (which lost 'only' 24 per cent) and the divisional light troops (three companies of 5/60th), the remainder of Stewart's division suffered some 64 per cent casualties. An analysis of how this was possible must conclude that it must simply have been a matter of morale and regimental *esprit de corps* and a determination not to be defeated while any men were still on their feet. It is easy to understand how this conduct could have brought forth the following:

> 'In the same rank they fought – they died,
> Each by his Brother Soldier's side,
> With all their honour'd wounds before –
> Not Spartan Valour could do more!
> Thus when the Tempest rends the Wood,
> The Giant Oak fall where it stood!
> No eyes behold one Briton yield,
> Or turn his back, or quit the field;
> Oppress'd by numbers he must die,
> But never – never – never fly!'[40]

Perhaps more impressive still were the words of Soult: 'There is no beating these troops, in spite of their Generals; I always thought them bad soldiers, but now I am sure of it; for I turned their right, and penetrated their centre: they were completely beaten; the day was mine, and yet they did not know it, and would not run.'[41]

NOTES

1. 'The Jolly Die-Hards', written in the late 1860s or early 1870s by C. Moore, the bandmaster; quoted in *Songs and Music of the Redcoats*, L. Winstock, London, 1970, p. 230.
2. *The Wellington Memorial*, A. J. Griffiths, London, 1897, p. 308.
3. The disposition of the French in this attack has been the subject of debate; Sir Charles Oman found a document which implied that they had attacked in *ordre mixte*, i.e., partially in line and partially in column, which was quoted in his *History of the Peninsular War*, Oxford, 1911, IV, pp. 379–80; but initially at least it appears that Girard took the unusual step of not attempting to deploy from column of attack into line, as Beresford wrote of Girard's 'fatal imprudence' of attacking in column (in his criticisms of Napier's account); see also 'Column Versus Line', J. R. Arnold, in *Journal of the Society for Army Historical Research*, 1982, LX, p. 204.
4. *The Life of John Colborne, Field Marshal Lord Seaton*, G. C. Moore Smith, London, 1903, p. 161.
5. These and the other regimental statistics which follow are in accordance with Oman, IV, p. 631, derived from the return by Major-General Charles Stewart, Adjutant-General: see *London Gazette*, 3 June 1811.
6. This dialogue as quoted in *Historical Records of the Buffs*, Captain C. R. B. Knight, London, 1935, I, pp. 350–1.
7. Letter quoted in *JSAHR*, 1922, I, p. 130.

8. Presumably Lieutenant Lewis Shewbridge (see *London Gazette*, 3 June 1811).
9. Cleeves' own account is in *History of the King's German Legion*, N. L. Beamish, London, 1832, I, pp. 385–6.
10. This was presumably Captain John Humphrey, who died of his injuries.
11. *Recollections of the Peninsula*, M. Sherer, London, 1823, pp. 217–21.
12. *Gentleman's Magazine*, 1811, I, p. 679.
13. Ibid., 1811, II, p. 88.
14. 'Albuera' by 'An Old Soldier', in *United Service Journal*, 1840, III, p. 108
15. Hardinge's own account is in *USJ*, 1840, III, pp. 246–9.
16. *USJ*, 1840, II, p. 396.
17. Ibid., III, p. 248.
18. 'Old Soldier', in ibid., III, p. 107.
19. 'The Royal Welch Fusiliers at Albuera', M. Glover, in *JSAHR*, 1988, LXVI, pp. 150–1, quoting Lieutenant John Harrison.
20. *Rough Notes of Seven Campaigns*, J. S. Cooper, Carlisle, 1914, p. 68.
21. Hill's letter says that the depth was '9'; were this to mean nine ranks, the frontage of each column would have been approximately 180 to 220 men wide ('Albuera and Vittoria: Letters from Lieutenant-Colonel J. Hill', ed. C. D. Hall, in *JSAHR*, 1988, LXVI, p. 194); Oman (IV, p. 391) presumed that each of the three regiments of Werlé's brigade formed one column each, each regiment (and thus column) of three battalions, thus with a two-company frontage the depth would be nine companies. It would have been easier for Hill to have counted nine companies deep than had each column consisted of only nine ranks.
22. *USJ*, 1841, I, p. 539.
23. Blakeney, in ibid.
24. Cooper, *op. cit.*, p. 65.
25. *History of the War in the Peninsula*, W. F. P. Napier, London, 1831, III, pp . 540–1.
26. *USJ*, 1841, I, p. 541.
27. Ibid., p. 540.
28. Ibid., 1840, III, p. 247.
29. Sherer, *op. cit.*, p. 215.
30. *London Gazette*, 3 June 1811.
31. Arbuthnot rose to the rank of lieutenant-general but at the time was a lieutenant-colonel.
32. Griffiths, *op. cit.*, pp. 307–8.
33. *Dispatches of Field Marshal the Duke of Wellington*, ed. J. Gurwood, London, 1834–8, VII, p. 558.
34. Ibid., p. 565, to Sir Brent Spencer, 22 May 1811.
35. Ibid., p. 564, to C. Stuart, 20 May 1811.
36. Ibid., p. 569, to Lieutenant-Colonel Henry Torrens, 22 May 1811.
37. Ibid., p. 561, to Admiral the Hon. G. Berkeley, 20 May 1811.
38. Sherer, *op. cit.*, p. 216.
39. *USJ*, 1841, I, p. 541.
40. 'The Battle of Albuera, or, Beresford and Victory', W. T. Fitz-Gerald, in *Gentleman's Magazine*, June 1811, p. 566.
41. Quoted in 'British Arms, as they were, and as they are, compared with the Opinions of Foreigners", anon., in *USJ*, 1842, I, p. 150.

Forlorn Hope
THE BREACHES AT BADAJOZ
6 April 1812

S ieges and the assault of fortifications were not a common feature of Napoleonic warfare, the destruction of the enemy's field army generally taking precedence; but where the storm of defended places did take place, the results could be more sanguinary than any battle in the open field involving the same numbers of troops.

If defended fortresses could not be starved into surrender by means of a blockade, a regular siege would be commenced, involving the construction of concentric lines of trenches ('parallels') which were pushed ever closer to the outer defences (enceinte), and of batteries from which the besiegers' artillery could bombard the fortress. Such fire was directed towards the opening of one or more breaches in the fortress wall. Under the prevailing 'rules' of war, once a breach was deemed 'practicable' (capable of being stormed successfully), the commander of the fortress was regarded as being at the mercy of the besiegers, and could capitulate without impugning his honour or that of his garrison. This was a result of the contemporary courtesies of 'civilised' warfare, which held that lives should not be risked unnecessarily; and it was accepted equally that if a garrison refused to surrender in such circumstances, but forced the besiegers to suffer heavy losses in an assault, that garrison forfeited any consideration to quarter or humane treatment once the place was captured. In that case, not only could the garrison be put to the sword, but the fortress could be ransacked or destroyed, and any civilian inhabitants might expect to be caught up in the violence.

Even the most upright and honourable commanders accepted the necessity of so brutal a departure from the tenets of 'civilised' warfare; as Marshal Michel Ney wrote to the governor of Ciudad Rodrigo on 28 June 1810, a continued defence 'would force His Highness the Prince of Essling [Masséna] to treat you with all the rigour authorised by the laws of war ... you have to choose between an honourable capitulation and the terrible vengeance of a victorious army.'[1] (In this case, the governor, General Andrès Herrasti, agreed to surrender to spare the lives of his garrison and the attackers, and received all the 'honours of war'). Indeed, the maintenance of such dire threats against a garrison which resisted too long were even recommended as a way of reinstating 'civilised' warfare. The British engineer John Jones criticised Napoleon for insisting his subordinates defend their fortifications to the end: 'when ... the governor insists on the ceremony of storming the last entrenchment, as he thereby unnecessarily, and without an object, spills the blood of many brave men, his life and the lives of the garrison should be made the forfeit ... humanity towards the enemy in such a case, is cruelty to our own troops'; were such examples to be made, he wrote, 'the practice of not capitulating would soon drop, and towns would be given up when resistance ceased to have an object beyond a further effusion of human blood. The principle to be combated is not the obligation to resist behind the breach ... but the abominable doctrine that surrender is not to take place when resistance can no longer be made – a doctrine too inhuman for a Turk, and not to be tolerated in a Christian.'[2]

Such was the slaughter expected in the assault of a defended breach that while the main storming-parties would be detailed for duty in the usual way, the group which led the attack was often composed of volunteers who offered themselves for what was often the right to be killed first. The very name of such a contingent was chilling: 'forlorn hope', an Anglicisation of the Dutch *verloren hoop*, 'lost party'; the French equivalent, *les enfants perdus* ('the lost children') was equally descriptive of their expected fate.

Perhaps most surprising is the fact that not only was there never a shortage of volunteers for such a desperate enterprise, there was actually great competition to be selected. This may have been understandable in the case of lower-ranking officers, for promotion was often given to the survivors of a successful storm, so that the risk of life and limb might be seen as a worthwhile chance of gaining advancement, especially for those lacking influence or wherewithal to achieve promotion in the usual way. 'A gold chain or a wooden leg' was a common British expression which encapsulated the sentiments involved, or as Major Peter O'Hare remarked before the storm of Badajoz, 'lieutenant-colonel or cold meat in a few hours'.[3] Such was the competition for such suicidal duties that when William Napier discovered that another officer had been appointed to lead the forlorn hope at San Sebastian, he complained directly to Wellington, who said 'it was hard and that I was ill-used, but that it must stand; thus I was cut off from promotion and one of the most splendid opportunities of gaining reputation that could have offered itself. Under all these circumstances I wish to quit the army',[4] an odd reaction, it might be thought, for having escaped the most dangerous duty imaginable!

Volunteers from the rank and file were equally forthcoming, though they could expect neither promotion nor financial reward, nor even the opportunity of being first in among the treasures to be looted, for members of a forlorn hope could scarcely hope to survive so long. Instead, volunteering seems to have been nothing more than a combination of cold courage and bravado, and the idea that it was honourable for a soldier to participate in the forefront of a particularly ferocious battle, although it is difficult now to think of 'honour' in circumstances of such downright butchery. Nor was ignorance an excuse, for those who volunteered for one storming-party and survived usually volunteered on the next occasion, in the full knowledge of what the business entailed. So prized was the privilege of being first in the attack that strange practices had to be used to select the necessary numbers from all those who volunteered, to avoid charges of favouritism; for example, to select a storming-party of the 51st at Badajoz in 1811, the regimental adjutant chose the 'stormers' by a charade of blind man's buff, passing down the ranks of volunteers blindfolded, selecting those whom he touched at random.[5] Perhaps such volunteers had in mind what John Kincaid of the 95th believed, that it made little difference if one went first or last, as even those in the rear of the attack were just as likely to be shot!

The importance of the border fortress of Badajoz has been mentioned in the previous chapter, and accordingly, the Allies having failed to capture it in 1811, it was the second target for the opening of the 1812 campaign, following the capture of Ciudad Rodrigo in January. Accordingly, on 16 March 1812 Wellington's army opened the second Allied siege of Badajoz, which progressed along the usual lines. Two factors made their task especially difficult. The first was the lack of trained engineers, a serious failing in the British Army at this time: for a huge engineering task such as the construction of the trenches and batteries at Badajoz in 1812, for example, there were only nineteen engineer officers (of whom four were killed and nine wounded) and 115 artificers, supplemented by 120 men seconded from the 74th Foot. All the remaining manual work was carried out by untrained infantrymen, working in shifts; at Badajoz on 26/27 March, for example, 1,200 men began work at dusk, relieved by 1,200 more at midnight, supplemented by 600 more at day-break and another 600 at noon, with more than the number of diggers standing to arms to protect them from any sally by the garrison.

The scale of such an enterprise is demonstrated by the amount of ammunition expended in the bombardment of Badajoz: prior to the assault the Allies fired no less than 31,861 roundshot with a total weight of more than 306 tons of metal, 1,826 shells and 1,659 rounds of heavy (grapeshot) or ordinary canister.

The second hindrance to the progress of the siege was the strength of the fortress and the ability of its governor and garrison. General

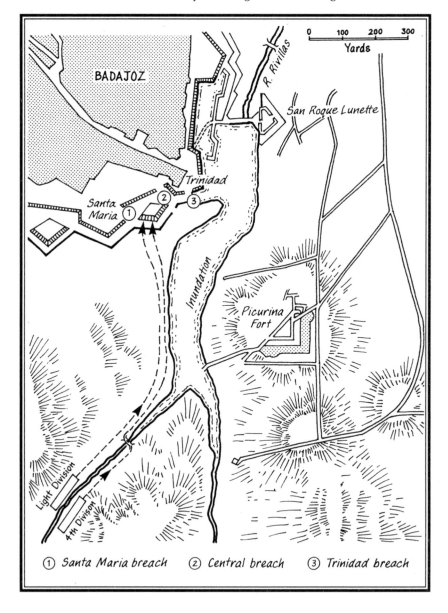

① Santa Maria breach   ② Central breach   ③ Trinidad breach

Armand Philippon was an experienced soldier who had successfully defied the Allies in 1811, and though an unimpressive commander in the field was an inspirational and ingenious leader behind the walls of a fortress. The strength of his garrison is uncertain: Belmas lists some 5,003 men, but this includes some 'round numbers' which seem to be estimates, and 256 non-combatants,[6] while a return of the garrison fit for duty on the day before the assault lists 157 officers and 3,921 other ranks, including 40 invalids. Although comparatively few in numbers, the troops were of excellent quality, including one battalion from each of the 9th *Léger*, 38th, 58th, 88th and 103rd Line, two companies of the 64th Line and two battalions of the Hesse-Darmstadt Regiment.[7] The city of Badajoz was one of the best fortified places in the entire Iberian peninsula, its location on the Spanish-Portuguese border accounting for its history of sieges and its strength; even the cathedral, dating from 1258, resembled a fortress. The castle of Badajoz was situated on an eminence at the north-east corner, and the entire northern wall of the city was made safe from assault by backing on to the River Guadiana. The remainder of the city's perimeter was studded by eight arrow-shaped bastions rising thirty feet from the base of the ditch which ran around the base of the wall, and the curtain-wall which linked the bastions was about 22 feet high. The broad ditch had a masonry counterscarp (the face of the ditch farthest from the wall) about seven feet high, and detached works covered the important sections of the walls.

Wellington's siege-works were constructed to the east of the city, the main target being the south-east corner of the city wall, between the Trinidad and Santa Maria bastions, the former being the south-east corner and the latter the next one along the south wall, running west. This position was covered by a prominent outwork, the Picurina Fort, which had to be reduced before the main section of the wall could be targeted. Despite the best efforts of Philippon and his garrison, the siege progressed until the breaching-batteries were able to open fire on 25 March upon the Picurina Fort and the wall behind it. The fort was captured that night in a violent assault which cost the storming-party more than half its strength; batteries were then established behind the fort, although counter-bombardment from the city caused such delays that not until 30 March could the new batteries begin to fire upon that section of wall between the Trinidad and Santa Maria bastions which had been selected as the site of the breaches.

Gradually the wall began to crumble and fall into the ditch, the resulting piles of rubble making the ascent from the ditch easier; so the defenders sent out parties at night to clear the rubble and deepen the ditch, a most hazardous task as the bombardment continued throughout the hours of darkness, with canister being fired into the ditch to kill those working there. The besiegers were unable to overcome one hazard in the approach to the breaches, however: between the siege-trenches around Picurina and the wall was a water-filled gully, the result of the defenders' blocking of the course of the small River Rivillas as it joined the Guadiana. This inundation was sealed by a dam at the San Roque *lunette* (outwork) which protected the section of Badajoz's eastern wall between the castle and the Trinidad bastion, and despite attempts to bombard it or blow it up during a nocturnal raid from the trenches, the besiegers were unable to cut the dam. This meant that an assault on the

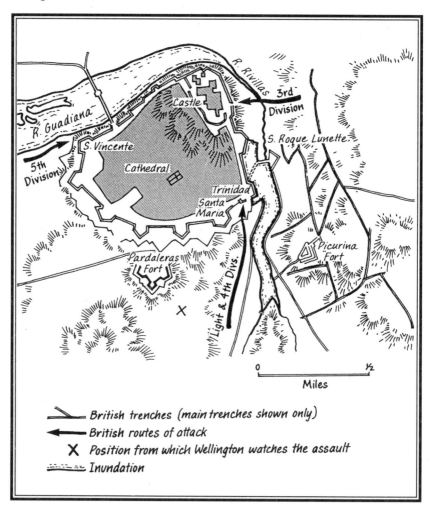

breaches would have to be made from the south, not from the protection of the trenches which were still separated from the city by the flooded terrain.

Two breaches were opened in the selected section of wall, one in the Trinidad bastion and one in the Santa Maria; despite the efforts of the garrison to repair the damage, by the morning of 5 April both breaches were reported to be practicable. There was some urgency on the part of the Allies, as Marshal Soult was reported to be en route with a relief-force, though not yet near enough to cause any disruption in the siege. As it was known that the French were constructing a second line of defence behind the breaches, in order to make the most determined resistance possible, Wellington decided to delay the assault for a day to enable his artillery to open a third breach in the wall between the bastions. By the afternoon of 6 April this was as practicable as the other two, and the assault was ordered for 7.30 that evening. In the event, it was postponed until 10 p.m., giving the defenders a few more hours to make the breaches as defensible as possible. To reconnoitre these defences as fully as possible, an intrepid officer of the Royal Engineers, Major William Nicholas, swam across the Rivillas inundation on the night before the attack, to make a personal inspection of the route which would be taken by the storming-parties.

The attack on the breaches was allocated to the Light and 4th Divisions of Wellington's army, the former arguably the élite of the entire Allied force in the Peninsula. In order to occupy the defenders' attention, diversionary attacks were also authorised, the most significant of which were an attempt to take the castle by escalade, suggested by General Sir Thomas Picton and using his 3rd Division, and a similar attack mounted by Sir James Leith's 5th Division on the San Vincente bastion at the extreme north-west corner of the city. Among attacks on outworks, the trench-guards furnished by the 4th Division were to attempt the semi-ruined San Roque *lunette* with the intention of breaching the dam. All these attacks involved heavy fighting, especially the two principal escalades; but it is upon the terrible events at the breaches that this account will concentrate.

The three breaches might have appeared practicable, but in and behind them Philippon and his garrison had constructed such an array of deadly obstacles as had scarcely ever been seen in siege-warfare. Behind the breaches were 'retrenchments' (earthen parapets strengthened with sandbags), and in the breaches and ditch had been piled all manner of lethal obstructions. Mines and barrels of explosives were laid in the ditch, with fuses running to the interior of the defences, and although much of the rubble had been cleared, piles of less climbable material had been thrown in to impede the progress of the attackers – damaged boats, overturned carts, broken gabions, rope entanglements, and beams and doors studded with nails to impale the feet. Among these were scattered caltrops (four-pointed iron stars calculated to cripple anyone who stepped upon them), and at the very summit of the breaches a series of *chevaux de frise*, beams into which sword-blades had been set, chained down at each end, made an almost impassable barricade. Deadly as these devices were, their main purpose was to slow down the attackers and expose them to the defenders' fire, from artillery sited to play upon the breaches and from the infantry allocated to the defence of the sector: the élite companies of all Philippon's French battalions and the four fusilier companies of the 103rd Line, about 1,200 men in all. Even their musket ammunition was particularly frightful, each round containing not only the ordinary lead ball but also a wooden cylinder packed with lead slugs, which scattered like grapeshot when the musket was fired. Such was the strength of the position that the disparity in numbers, between the defenders and the vastly more numerous attacking force, counted for nothing.

Orders for the attack were issued during the day. The 4th Division (less the trench-guards who were to attack the San Roque outworks) were to storm the breach of the Trinidad bastion, and the Light Division, which was to precede the 4th, the Santa Maria breach; the latter was also to furnish a party of marksmen to keep down the heads of the defenders as soon as the attack was discovered. Both divisions were to be preceded by a forlorn hope of 500 men, carrying twelve ladders and bags of grass to throw into the ditch (to soften the landing of troops who jumped into the ditch, should the ladders be broken). A late addition to the orders, inserted by Wellington, was an instruction to the 4th Division's commander, Sir Charles Colville, to ensure that his command also assailed the new breach in the curtain-wall.[8] The units involved included, in the 4th Division, the 7th and 23rd Fuzileers, 27th, 40th and 48th Foot, and Collins' Portuguese brigade; and in the Light Division, the 43rd and 52nd Light Infantry, 95th Rifles and 1st and 3rd Portuguese *Caçadores*.

The forlorn hopes were organised during the day, with the usual problem of an excess of volunteers. John Kincaid, as adjutant, had to select the men from his battalion of the 95th, a task which presented the usual difficulties: 'There were as many applicants for a place in the ranks as if it led to the highest honours and rewards ... there was as much anxiety expressed, and as much interest made by all ranks to be appointed to the post of honour, as if it had been sinecure situations, in place of death-warrants, which I had at my disposal.'[9] Two buglers were required for the forlorn hope; one of those selected was William Green, a Corunna veteran, but his companion Bugler West was so anxious to go that he gave the bugle-major two dollars to allow him to go in Green's place. Incensed, Green reported the bugle-major to Kincaid for taking the bribe; Kincaid threatened the bugle-major with demotion and restored Green to his rightful place. So great was the demand for places in the assault that even the officers' servants resumed their places in the ranks, Kincaid having to entrust his baggage to a convalescent to permit his own servant to join the attack.

Officers equally vied for places; Lieutenant George Simmons of the 95th recalled his disappointment when his superiors took the vacancies in the forlorn hope as privilege of rank. Lieutenant William Johnstone of the 95th was luckier; similarly excluded, he was authorised by the commander of the Light Division, Sir Andrew Barnard, to *precede* the forlorn hope with a small party equipped with ropes, to lasso and drag down the *chevaux de frise*, a hopelessly desperate enterprise. Captain James Fergusson of the 43rd had been severely wounded leading the stormers at Ciudad Rodrigo; with a ball still lodged under his spine he insisted on serving at Badajoz, was wounded again on 26 March, yet with his wounds still open he declared himself fit again to lead the stormers from his regiment. (He was wounded again, but survived). Lieutenant H. Harvest of the 43rd had just been informed of his promotion to captain, but insisted on accompanying the stormers so as not to impugn his honour; Quartermaster William Surtees of the 95th regarded his death at the breaches as 'an almost censurable excess' caused by 'his too refined sense of honour'.[10]

Forlorn hope men were given the remainder of the day off duty; Bugler Green took the opportunity to bathe, so as to be clean when he was wounded, as he expected to be. As the time for the attack approached, there was a perceptible tension in the Allied camp, but not one suggestive of trepidation. William Grattan, whose 88th Foot was part of the 3rd Division destined to attack the castle, described a 'desperate calm' which settled on the camp in place of the usual gaiety, as if the men were impatient to begin. The ladders and storming-equipment were distributed at 5 p.m.; the assembly was to be sounded at eight. The hours dragged by, each seemingly longer than the last;

173

and as the batteries fell silent, the town clock of Badajoz could be heard quite clearly, striking the hour.

Like most officers, Surtees of the 95th joined his friends for dinner. With Lieutenants Arthur Carey and Christopher Croudace he took a final glass – two in Croudace's case because he enjoyed his wine – and as they left, Croudace made him custodian of his entire wealth, half a doubloon in a purse. Surtees was so disconsolate on seeing them leave that although he was a non-combatant, he decided to join the stormers, so slung his haversack containing his pistol and set off; but on the way met his opposite number in the 43rd, who convinced him that they would only be in the way, so they retired to a small hill to watch the attack. General Leith entertained his friends to dinner in the usual way, until at 8 p.m. the orderly sergeant reported the division under arms. Leith and his companions rose from the table and went to their appointed positions in complete silence, which especially impressed one of the general's guests. Another staff officer, knowing that he would not be involved in the assault, sat for several hours upon a hillock with his friends Major James Singer and Captain William Cholwich of the 7th. On parting, Singer shook his hand and remarked, 'Tomorrow I shall be a lieutenant-colonel or in the kingdom of heaven.'[11] Lieutenant-Colonel George Elder, late 95th and now commanding the *Caçadores*, entertained five friends to dinner, during which not a word was spoken about the impending attack. At eight Elder's sergeant reported that the troops were assembled; the officers rose and Elder proposed a toast to their success, whereupon Major Peter O'Hare of the 95th, who had had a premonition of death, shook his hand and declared, 'By Jove, Elder, we have seen a great deal of service together, and we have had our share of hard knocks, and I sincerely hope that we shall meet tomorrow.'[12]

As the assembly-time approached, the bands of some regiments played to occupy the last hour; that of the 88th Connaught Rangers played Irish airs, which had an unforgettable effect upon the listeners. Tunes like *Savourneen Deelish* ('Dearest Darling') were melancholy at best ('Oh the moment was sad, when my love and I parted,/As I kissed off her tears I was near broken-hearted'), but under these circumstances they were especially poignant, causing the men to think of their homes and to reflect that the day was Easter Sunday, and doubtless how inappropriate it was to fight on such a holy day. Such thoughts were dispelled by the word to form their columns; knapsacks were piled (they were an unnecessary encumbrance in the storm of a fortress), stocks removed, jacket- and shirt-collars unfastened, ammunition checked and cartridge-boxes re-positioned (lowered or worn at the front for easier access), and trousers rolled up to the knee. 'Little, if any, directions were given; indeed, they were unnecessary, because the men, from long service, were so conversant with the duty they had to perform, that it would have been but a waste of words and time to say what was required of them ... their self-confidence, devoid of boast or bravado, gave them the appearance of what they in reality were – an invincible host.'[13]

As the Light Division's stormers assembled, Edward Costello of the 95th, having drunk a double ration of grog, took his place in the front rank. In front of him were two of the officers commanding the stormers, Major Peter O'Hare and Captain William (alias Jack) Jones of the 52nd, a fire-eating Welshman. O'Hare seemed in low spirits and confessed, 'Tonight, I think, will be my last.' 'Tut, tut, man!' replied Jones, 'I have the same sort of feeling, but I keep it down with a crop of the *cratur*', handing O'Hare his calabash. At this juncture Sergeant Flemming, a devoted companion of O'Hare's, announced that ladder-parties had yet to be selected, and detailed Costello for the task with a tap on the shoulder; when, recalled Costello, 'I now gave up all hope of ever returning.'[14]

Before the Light and 4th Divisions moved off, the four companies of sharpshooters moved forward silently and positioned themselves behind palisading on the glacis in front of the breaches. Their commander, Major Alexander Cameron, reported back to Sir Andrew Barnard, commander of the 95th and in temporary command of the division; Cameron, a most dauntless individual, appears to have been hardly able to contain himself. 'Now my men are ready, shall I begin?'; 'No, certainly not,' replied Barnard, anxious not to alert the French too early.[15] The riflemen had reached their position unobserved – Cameron and Kincaid had reconnoitred it earlier in the day – and each man lay with the muzzle of his rifle over the ditch, and though only a short distance from the French, a low-lying mist and the dark green of their uniforms prevented them from being seen. French sentries were visible, silhouetted against the sky; one challenged twice, '*Qui vive?*', and fired his musket, drums were heard to beat, but the riflemen remained still and silence descended again, the French evidently thinking it a false alarm.

The head of the Light Division silently approached the breaches, the forward elements under the command of Lieutenant-Colonel Charles Macleod of the 43rd, a young officer universally liked and admired throughout the army ('an ornament to his profession' was Wellington's opinion').[16] They aimed for the left-hand breach; the 4th Division, some way behind, went towards the Trinidad breach at the right, orders being given in whispers. Each ladder-party comprised six men, plus two men carrying hatchets to cut through obstacles in their path; some of those carrying bags of grass tied them in front of their bodies, hoping they might act as protection against bullets. Bugler Green, a veteran of 26 actions, recalled that he had never really known fear until those moments of marching in silence towards the breaches, when the thought came to him that he would be in hell before morning.

As the stormers reached the glacis, they were challenged by a French sentry; then all hell broke loose as every French gun within range opened to vomit death in the vicinity of the breaches. The mines and powder-barrels were set off, the rubbish in the ditch began to burn, and in the red light of the fires the forlorn hopes were clearly visible: '... the tumult at the breaches was such as if the very earth had been rent asunder and its central fires were bursting upwards uncontrolled ... a bright flame shooting upwards displayed all the terrors of the scene. The ramparts crowded with dark figures and glittering arms, were seen on the one side, and on the other, the red columns of the British, deep and broad, were coming on like streams of burning lava; it was the touch of the magician's wand, for a crash of thunder followed, and with incredible violence the storming-parties were dashed to pieces by the explosion of hundreds of shells and powder-barrels. For an instant the light division stood on the brink of the ditch, amazed at the terrific sight, then, with a shout that matched even the sound of the explosion, flew down the ladders, or disdaining their aid, leaped, reckless of the depth, into the gulf below; and nearly at the same moment, amidst a blaze of musketry that dazzled the eyes, the fourth division came running in and descended with a like fury ...'[17]

As soon as the French began to fire, Barnard called out to the sharpshooters, '*Now*, Cameron!'[18] and the riflemen began to pick off Frenchmen whose heads were visible above the ramparts; but it was the last advantage that the attackers were to enjoy that night. The first dreadful salvo of grapeshot and musketry was delivered while the attackers were still some thirty yards from the ditch. Only twenty minutes had elapsed since O'Hare and Jones had shared a drink; both were killed by the first blast, leaving Macleod the only senior officer at the head of the Light Division. Johnstone and his lasso-men never got near enough to use their ropes; all went down, Johnstone with a shattered arm (though he survived). Three of the men carrying Costello's ladder were struck down, and he fell under it as the men following dashed over him; but for the bag of grass tied to his chest he thought he would have suffocated. Drenched in the blood of his comrades, with difficulty he wriggled from under a pile of bodies and, having lost his rifle, drew his sword-bayonet and ran towards the ditch. He slid down a ladder into the base of the ditch but was knocked flat as men fell on top of him, and again had to extricate himself from under a pile of bodies. Having lost his bayonet and obviously disorientated, he moved along the ditch to the right, evidently into that part attacked by the 4th Division, for he fell into an inundation. He swam to the foot of the breach, and unarmed as he was began to climb, but received a violent blow on the chest from some missile (or even a musket-butt) and fell senseless back into the ditch.

Not many of the stormers got so far. Bugler Green was about to throw his bag of grass into the ditch when a ball went through his thigh and smashed his left wrist; he fell on the lip of the ditch and watched as burning shells were rolled from the breaches into the struggling mass of men in the ditch, each blowing up ten or twelve soldiers when it exploded. Sergeant Robert Fairfoot of the 95th passed and asked, 'Bill, are you wounded?'; 'Yes, and cannot get up.' Fairfoot passed him a flask of rum and went on, but fell as a musket-ball passed through the peak of his cap and lodged in his forehead (the wound was not fatal). Green lay under fire some time, until he heard the 95th's bugle-major sounding the call for advance in double-quick time; and wounded though he was, Green took up the call on his own bugle. An officer immediately commanded him to be silent, as he was drawing fire upon the troops nearby; somewhat aggrieved, Green replied 'I was only doing my duty.' It was the last time he ever blew a bugle; as he was of no use to the attackers any more, he crawled away with the rest of the wounded. Four bandsmen lifted him on to a stretcher made from two poles and a sack, and bore him away from the scene of carnage. His hand and wrist were permanently crippled – 29 pieces of bone came out of the wound – and he was discharged from the army.

The storming-parties were guided by engineer officers, but every one of them became a casualty, so the attack became terribly mixed-up. Arriving slightly later than those of the Light Division, the 4th Division's stormers jumped into a ditch, not realising that it was flooded to a depth of at least six feet; twenty of the 23rd, and about thirty of the Portuguese, were drowned in it. The remainder swerved to the left, some becoming entangled with the Light Division, and in the confusion only part of the Light Division assailed the Santa Maria breach, all the remainder making for the Trinidad. In front of the central breach was a partially completed and undefended ravelin, a detached fortification, which some mistook for the main defence; those who reached the top were confronted by a further ditch and, unable to proceed, began to exchange fire with the French, which served only to hold up the progress of the attack, and exposed them to the full fury of the defenders' fire. (It was for this reason that it was not uncommon for storming-parties to be sent in with unloaded muskets, to prevent 'the absurdity of firing at stone walls, or the impossibility of stopping fire if soldiers are suffered to load'.)[19] Because of this confusion at the ravelin it appears that no attempt whatever was made upon the central breach.

Harry Smith of the 95th, serving as brigade-major in the Light Division, was in the first wave that followed the initial storming-party. At the ravelin the fire was so hot that his pockets were filled with chips of stone thrown up by the impact of musket-balls; then he set off towards the ditch, linking arms with Lieutenant Charles Taggart of the 43rd, as they tried to keep their balance over ground strewn with bodies. Taggart was killed, but Smith got into the ditch, where he found the commander of the stormers, Charles Macleod, leaning upon a ladder with his hands on his breast. The young man, 'whose feeble body would have been quite unfit for war, if it had not been sustained by an unconquerable spirit',[20] had already been injured when a man behind him had been hit and in falling had run his bayonet into Macleod's back, but he had carried on until he was shot. He gasped, 'Oh, Smith, I am mortally wounded. Help me up the ladder.' Smith replied, 'Oh no, dear fellow.' 'I am,' said Macleod, 'be quick.'[21] Smith helped him out of the ditch, but to no avail; the wound was mortal.

Two of the 43rd's lieutenants were William Freer and his younger brother, 19-year-old Edward, a slight man 'of such surpassing and delicate beauty that the Spaniards often thought him a girl disguised in man's clothing [but] so vigorous, so active, so brave, that the most daring and experienced veterans watched his looks on the field of battle, and implicitly following where he led, would like children obey his slightest sign in the most difficult situations'.[22] In the assault William lost his right arm, shattered by a musket-ball (he also suffered a bruised knee from a stone thrown from the breaches, and a slug in the backside which worked out several days later), and young Edward was in the ditch when Smith returned from aiding Macleod. In the indescribable confusion, Smith found some troops intent on climbing back out of the ditch (hardly any other mention is made of troops attempting to escape from the fiery pit); little Freer and Smith were determined to stop them retreating: 'Let us thrown down the ladders; the fellows shan't go out.' The men in the trench had other ideas, saying 'Damn your eyes, if you do we will bayonet you,'[23] and such was the crush that the officers were forced back up the ladder. Smith's sash became entangled in the rungs and he almost suffered violence from those behind him, but by tugging the end came loose and he regained the glacis safely. Young Freer seems then to have ascended the ravelin – or at least some high point before the defences – and by the flash of gunfire and the light of burning debris was observed by both sides, unwilling to withdraw but unable to reach the French, picking up and hurling stones at the defenders of the breach. He was hit at least once – one account says three times – it was said in the abdomen, and he was carried off and laid in the same tent as his injured brother. By Edward Freer's own account, the shot he received was in the testicles, but when writing home he reported that it had not done any material damage;[24] thus he survived, only to fall, lamented by all, in the following year at Nivelle.

Confusion increased as the action progressed, with the Light Division mostly veering towards the Trinidad breach and becoming entangled with the 4th Division, which advanced making 'a most uncommon noise'.[25] Among them was the main body of the 7th Fuzileers, headed (probably) by Lieutenant-Colonel Edward Blakeney, to whom it is likely Kincaid referred: 'though a very little man, [he] shouted with the lungs of a giant, for the way to be cleared, to "let the Royal Fusiliers advance!" Several of our officers assisted him in such a laudable undertaking; but, in the meantime, a musket-ball found its way into some sensitive part, and sent the gallant major trundling head over heels among the loose stones, shouting to a less heroic tune – while his distinguished corps went determinedly on, but with no better success than those who had just preceded them.'[26]

The commanders of both the Light and 4th Divisions – Lieutenant-Colonel Andrew Barnard and General Charles Colville – did their best to prevent confusion. Colville went to the edge of the ditch before the Trinidad bastion with his personal staff: his ADC, Captain George Spottiswoode of the 71st, Assistant Quartermaster-General Major William Brooke of the 48th, Assistant Adjutant-General Captain D. James of the 81st, Captain William Latham of the Royal Artillery, and Major William Nicholas of the Royal Engineers. Harry Smith saw Colville on the glacis 'making a devil of a noise',[27] but he was quiet enough for Nicholas to ask whether the chaos in the ditch was not the grandest thing which could be imagined(!); Colville agreed that it was impressive if one could overlook the horrors taking place, which evidently Colville couldn't. Before he was able to get down into the ditch, Colville was hit twice: a shot through the thigh and another which removed the upper joint of the third finger of his right hand. For some time he appears to have lain where he fell, endeavouring to command his division through his staff, among whom James was especially commended for his efforts to maintain order and bring on successive waves of attackers. Colville's staff fared no better than he: James, Spottiswoode and Brooke were wounded and Latham killed. The three brigade-commanders of the 4th Division were similarly put out of action: Major-General Barnard Bowes, Brigadier-General William Harvey of the Portuguese, and Lieutenant-Colonel Charles Harcourt of the 40th. The loss of commanding officers must have greatly impaired the attackers' ability to reorganise or direct their efforts properly.

Some of the confusion was caused by successive waves of troops following the stormers into the ditch, irrespective of events. Harry Smith, for example, recorded that as soon as he had been forced out of the ditch, up came a Portuguese unit of the 4th Division in such style that Smith 'never saw any soldiers behave with more pluck',[28] and those who had recently left the ditch joined the Portuguese and went down into it again. The Light Division's commander, Andrew Barnard, accompanied the first wave himself, and left specific instructions that Lieutenant-Colonel George Elder, commanding the 1st and 3rd *Caçadores* and some companies of 95th, was to remain in reserve, fearing that Elder's impetuous character would lead him to rush straight on. Elder claimed that he was told not to advance until he saw the 43rd enter the ditch, and that when an officer of the 95th came to tell him that the 43rd *were* in the ditch, he led his men into the most 'frightful confusion',[29] which the presence of his own men only compounded. John Colborne (not present himself, having been wounded at Ciudad Rodrigo) said that when Elder arrived on the glacis, Barnard shouted to him: 'Ah, Colonel Elder, Colonel Elder, for your own glory you would throw away the whole British army.'[30] Elder recalled that he entered the ditch by a ladder, to see for himself what was happening, and met a wounded staff officer, Major Charles Broke, who told him that the attack on the Trinidad breach had failed, all the field officers were down, and that he was taking this news to Wellington. Elder thereupon pushed on further along the ditch and began to rally a party to attack the Santa Maria breach, when he himself was severely wounded. Some soldiers helped him out of the ditch, but on the glacis he was wounded again, and was borne away on the shoulders of some of his men.

The engineer William Nicholas, after leaving Colville's side, had led two rushes but was incapacitated by a shot through the left arm, breaking it below the elbow, other balls injuring his left wrist and grazing a kneecap, and a bayonet spiking his right calf. Despite these injuries, when he heard soldiers asking who would lead them in the next assault, he had himself lifted up by two men and, in the company of Lieutenant James Shaw of the 43rd, led about seventy men up the rubble at the foot of the Santa Maria breach. Few got even part way; one of the men supporting Nicholas was killed and Nicholas was hit again, a musket-ball entering his left side, breaking two ribs and exiting near the spine. He tumbled to the base of the ditch from where he observed Shaw, standing alone on the ascent of the breach, calmly pull out his watch and repeating the hour declare aloud that the breach could not be taken that night. Shaw and the few survivors drew off as further efforts were clearly hopeless; Nicholas was dragged clear and taken for medical attention. He appeared to be recovering but died eight days later.[31]

Successive waves of troops met the same fate. As Lieutenant George Simmons' party of the 95th approached the glacis they were mown down like grass, he recalled; he saw his captain, Charles Gray, fall wounded in the mouth, then went down a ladder into the ditch. There he found 'a most frightful scene of carnage ... the volleys of musketry and grapeshot that were incessantly poured amongst us made our situation too horrid for description. I had seen some fighting, but nothing like this. We remained passively here to be slaughtered, as we could do the besieged little injury from the ditch.'[32] Combustible illuminants or 'light balls' were thrown into the ditch to make the attackers easier to target; in a frenzy of impotent rage, Simmons began to stamp on one of these when another officer grabbed his arm and declared, 'Leave it, or when the light goes out your feet will be blown to pieces, as there is a live shell connected with it.'[33] There were even more remarkable escapes than this: Lieutenant Thomas Taylor Worsley of the 95th was hit under the ear by a musket-ball which made a circuit of his neck and turned his head permanently to the right. At Waterloo he was hit in a similar place under the other ear, which injury straightened his head again!

When Edward Costello recovered his senses he was lying amid the dead in the bottom of the ditch, from where he 'perceived our gallant fellows still rushing forward, each seeming to share a fate more deadly than my own. The fire continued in one horrible and incessant peal, as if the mouth of the infernal regions had opened to vomit forth destruction upon mankind. This was rendered still more appalling by the fearful shouts of the combatants and the cries of the wounded that mingled in the uproar. I now, strange to say, began to feel if my arms and legs were entire: for at such moments a man, I believe, is not always aware of his wounds. I now, indeed, lost all the frenzy of courage that had first possessed me, and actually seemed all weakness and prostration of spirit, while I endeavoured to screen myself from the enemy's shot among the dead bodies around me. As I lay in this position, the fire still continued blazing over me in all its horrors, accompanied by screams, groans, and shouts, and the crashing of stones and falling of timbers. I now, for the first time for many years, uttered something like a prayer.'[34]

The attacks continued; every time an officer gathered 50 or 100 men they would attempt to ascend the rubble to the top of the breach. Estimates mention forty or fifty separate assaults against breaches 'which yawning and glittering with steel, seemed like the mouth of some huge dragon belching forth smoke and flame'.[35] Not one man made it through the breach while it was defended, although one rifleman did reach the upper *chevaux de frise* and dived head-first beneath it, only for the French to batter his head with musket-butts. Captain Barney of the *Chasseurs Britanniques*, serving as an acting-engineer, saw a single man climb to the top of one of the breaches before he fell; in daylight he found a Portuguese grenadier dead on the ramparts, whom he presumed to be this intrepid man. Surtees also saw the body, but surmised that he had been blown up there from the ditch by the force of an explosion. Among those who fell was Captain Paul Saint-Pol of the 7th Fuzileers, 'a very fine young man',[36] who died after the amputation of a leg; he was the son of Louis Philippe, Duke of Orleans, to whom he bore a striking resemblance.

Much of the slaughter was clearly visible to those watching from afar. Quartermaster Surtees, from his vantage-point near the Duke of Wellington, recalled that the breaches seemed to blaze upwards, the flashes and fireballs so intense that the faces of Frenchmen on the ramparts could be seen clearly, though nearly a mile away. Even more unusual was the noise, unlike anything that even an experienced campaigner had ever heard, of the French fire being directed down into the ditch, the sound reverberating back from the enclosed space. So terrible was the situation at the breaches that a number of survivors could only find comparison with the infernal regions themselves: 'the scene that ensued furnished as respectable representation of hell itself as fire, sword and human sacrifices could make it; for, in one instant, every engine of destruction was in full operation'.[37] The engineer John Jones recorded that after a time it was only with difficulty that individual assaults could be made, as those who had watched the carnage 'could not be prevailed upon to make any effort; they stood patiently in the ditch to be slaughtered, rather than endeavour to extricate themselves by forcing the breaches'.[38]

In fairness, forcing the breaches was a task beyond human accomplishment, given the ferocity with which they were defended, even had not the confusion following the fall of so many officers resulted in the central breach remaining unattacked while the others were literally choked with dead. Jones presented a realistic assessment: 'Probably never since the discovery of gunpowder were men more seriously exposed to the effects of it than those assembled in this ditch this night; many thousand shells and hand-grenades, numerous bags filled with powder, every kind of burning composition, and destructive missile had been prepared, and placed behind the parapets of the whole front; these, under an incessant roll of musketry, were hurled into the ditch without intermission, for upwards of two hours, giving to its whole surface the appearance of vomiting fire, and creating occasional flashes of light more vivid than the day, followed by a momentary utter darkness – in fact it is beyond the powers of description to convey an adequate idea of the awful grandeur of the scene, and it is no small credit to the men that they quietly remained under it ... far from thinking ill of the troops for not forcing through [the breaches], it is rather a subject for pride and glory that they were such as dared to make the attempt.'[39] William Grattan, himself wounded in the attack on the dam near the San Roque *lunette*, expressed similar sentiments: 'To stand before such a storm of fire, much less endeavour to overcome a barrier so impregnable, required men whose minds, as well as frames, were cast in a mould not human: but, nevertheless, so it was ... [they] prolonged a struggle the very failure of which, taking into account the nature of the obstacles opposed to them, and their immense losses, was sufficient to immortalise them.'[40]

All this time Wellington had been waiting for news; Surtees overheard him repeating, as if to himself, 'What can be the matter?', symptom of the anxiety which he often felt but rarely showed.[41] James McGrigor, head of the army's medical staff, was standing nearby when a courier arrived from the breaches with news that the attack had failed. Wellington read the report by the light of a torch held by his ADC,

Charles, Earl of March; 'the countenance of Lord Wellington lit up by the glare of the torch; I shall never forget it to the last moment of my existence, and I could even now sketch it. The jaw had fallen, and the face was of unusual length, while the torchlight gave his countenance a lurid aspect; but still the expression of the face was firm.'[42] He read the message 'with a steady hand. His countenance was pale and expressed great anxiety. In his manner and language he preserved perfect coolness and self-possession.'[43]

Wellington thereupon ordered the Light and 4th Divisions to withdraw. Barnard received the order some time after midnight, but even after two hours of sustained butchery he was unwilling to retire as rushes were still being made from the ditch; but after leading some in person, with reluctance he gave orders for those still alive to pull back and re-form some 300 yards from the defences. Even the withdrawal was conducted with heroism and in good order. Ensign George Gawler of the 52nd was wounded and in the ditch when the Light Division bugles sounded the retreat. One of the soldiers with him grabbed Gawler by the belt and dragged him up a ladder, 'or', said he, 'the enemy will come out and bayonet you';[44] as Gawler reached safety he felt the soldier jerk backwards and fall into the ditch, shot dead. Gawler never knew his saviour's name.

Shortly after giving the order for withdrawal, Wellington received decisive news: Picton's 3rd Division had taken the castle by escalade; 'It is impossible to imagine the change this produced in the feelings of all around.'[45] Of even more significance to the troops just withdrawn from the breaches was the fact that Walker's brigade had penetrated the San Vincente bastion and was drawing defenders from the breaches. Immediately Wellington sent word to Picton that he must maintain his position, and ordered the Light and 4th Divisions to made a renewed attempt on the breaches. Hearing of Picton's success, Surtees ran off to the Light Division which was re-forming its shattered ranks, but those he told refused at first to credit the news. Surtees received only melancholy tidings in return: that his friends were both hit, Croudace shot dead and carried to the rear and Cary fallen but missing.

Wellington's order to return to the breaches was carried to the Light Division by Lord Fitzroy Somerset (the future Lord Raglan), who tried to find Barnard. Harry Smith met him with the news that Barnard was safe but that his whereabouts were unknown. Somerset thus gave the order to Smith: that Wellington desired them to storm again. "'The devil!" says I. "Why, we have had enough; we are all knocked to pieces." Lord Fitzroy says, "I dare say, but you must try again." I smiled and said, "If we could not succeed with two whole fresh and unscathed Divisions, we are likely to make a poor show of it now. But we will try again with all our might."'[46] At that moment a British bugle was heard, blowing from *inside* the breaches, signifying that the place had been taken. George Simmons was lying on the grass with what remained of his men, almost overcome by disconsolate thoughts, when he heard the order to advance; 'We moved back to this bloody work as if nothing had happened. Never were braver men congregated together for such a purpose.'[47]

This time the attackers encountered no opposition as they scrambled up and through the breaches; musketry sounded afar off, but otherwise the night was broken only by the shrieks and groans of the wounded, as they were trodden upon by those struggling through the breaches. As Kincaid described it, the ditch was a veritable charnel-pit, and heart-rending in that those advancing had to ignore the cries and pleas for help of the wounded. Even without opposition, the *chevaux de frise* could only be surmounted with the greatest difficulty. Lying half-stunned, Edward Costello heard the firing subside and then a shout from *within* the defences, 'Blood and 'ounds! Where's the Light Division? – the town's our own – hurrah!' On trying to stand, Costello found that he had been shot through the lower right leg, and not until blood began to run down his face did he realise that one of the balls that had pierced his shako had cut his scalp. As the Light Division came back into the ditch, Costello recognised one of the first as a rifleman named O'Brien, from Costello's own company. O'Brien exclaimed, 'What! is that you, Ned? We thought you ladder-men all done for.'[48] Using O'Brien's rifle as a crutch, Costello hobbled after the riflemen up the rubble of the breach, entering the city once the *chevaux de frise* had been unfastened and pulled aside.

If the events of the previous few hours had been singularly dreadful, what followed the capture of the city and the surrender of garrison was even worse. As if temporarily unhinged by the carnage, and taking advantage of the 'rule of war' which gave over a captured fortress to its conquerors if the assault had been resisted to the end, the victors ran wild. For two days officers were powerless to prevent every outrage of pillage, drunkenness, violence, brutality and rapine which could be imagined, all perpetrated upon the unfortunate inhabitants of Badajoz. Most of the survivors of the garrison were saved from the worst ill treatment, but the civilians were abused, looted and even murdered, until the erection of gallows provided a sufficient threat for the outrages to cease; or perhaps the perpetrators were simply sated. It was the most disgraceful episode in the annals of the Peninsular army. One of the few gleams of humanity which arose from it was the well-known romance of Harry Smith and the Spanish girl he saved from the lust of the troops, who became his wife and faithful companion in many campaigns and gave her name to the town of Ladysmith, where there occurred a siege even more famous than the one which brought Harry and Juana Smith together.

While much of the rank and file of the victorious army were ravaging the city, a few turned their attention to the breaches. All who saw them were consumed with the same horror as Quartermaster Surtees, who estimated that as many as 1,500 men lay within the space of an acre. Harry Smith, with his experience of campaigns in five continents, recalled: 'There is no battle, day or night, I would not willingly re-act except this. The murder of our gallant officers and soldiers is not to be believed. Next day I and Charlie Beckwith, a brother Brigade-Major, went over the scene. It was *appalling*. Heaps on heaps of slain ...'[49] Many survivors went in search of friends or kin. George Simmons found Major O'Hare lying dead with two or three balls in his breast; his faithful Sergeant Flemming, who had been at O'Hare's side in every action, lay beside him in death. Next morning the staff officer quoted above found a party of 7th Fuzileers at work, so inquired of his friends; when he mentioned Major Singer they said, 'We are throwing the last shovels of earth upon his grave,' the edge of which, the spot where he fell, was still marked with his blood. He asked about his other companion, Captain Cholwich, and was told that he had been wounded climbing over a palisade, had fallen into the inundation and been seen no more.

As soon as he could escape from these ghastly scenes, George Simmons retired to his tent. A moment later it was entered by his brother Maud, an officer of the 34th (and thus not involved in the assault), who had been told that George was dead; on finding him unhurt, Maud burst into tears and collapsed on the ground. 'Why, this is woman's work,' said George. 'You ought to laugh, I am sound and untouched,' but Maud had to lie down for some time to compose himself.[50]

John Kincaid was another who returned to the breaches at first light, where he received a scare greater even than the terrors of the night. In the grey half-light of morning, he observed, quite distinctly, a red-clad headless figure clambering over the piles of slain, sword drawn. Kincaid was convinced that it must be the ghost of one of the slain, searching for its corporeal body; but steeling himself, he approached closer and was greatly relieved to find that instead of a headless wraith it was only Lieutenant James McNair of the 52nd, with a red handkerchief wrapped around his head, which in the dim light blended with the colour of his jacket to give the impression of his being decapitated. McNair was sorting through the heaps of dead in search of his shako and scabbard, both of which he had lost in the assault; he found neither, but was presumably cheered by Kincaid's congratulations that his head had not gone the same way as his cap.

Most encounters at this location were far more melancholy. In the morning, Captain Charles Allix of the 1st Foot Guards went in search of his brother William, a lieutenant in the 95th. The officer in charge of burying the slain officers tried to spare Allix the ghastly sight of his dead brother, and sent him to the 95th's camp. There he learned the truth, and returned to the site of the slaughter where he encountered Harry Smith, who commented on Allix's downcast expression. Allix replied, 'Do you not know my brother in the Rifles was killed last night?' 'God help him and you!' said Smith. 'No, for I and we all loved him.' Allix burst into tears, pointed to a body, presented a pair of scissors to Smith and asked, 'Go and cut off a lock of his hair for my mother. I came for the purpose, but I am not equal to doing it'.[51]

One of the worst aspects of the immediate aftermath of the storming of the breaches was the neglect of the wounded, while so many of the troops were engaged in pillaging. Surtees and his sole surviving messmate, Captain William Percival of the 95th, who was lamed, spent the entire morning compelling – with the aid of Percival's stick – gangs of half-drunk and unwilling soldiers to help them move the wounded, the drunks frequently dropping the casualties or treading on them in their alcoholic haze. They worked through the morning, removing some wounded but leaving the most seriously hurt to die where they lay, rather than cause them more pain for no purpose; this in itself was heartrending. Before their task was completed, shortly before noon Surtees and Percival had to desist from sheer exhaustion and from the appalling smell which the hot sun had caused to rise from the dead and wounded. Surtees' last task was to recover his friend Cary, whom he found stripped naked by scavengers, lying under a ladder at the foot of the ditch, shot through the head but still alive. Surtees rounded up a sergeant and some men to carry him to camp, but they were so drunk that they dropped him; Cary never recovered consciousness and was buried next day behind the 95th's camp, Percival reading the burial service.

Lieutenant-Colonel Macleod of the 43rd was buried in a cornfield on the slope of a hill overlooking the regimental camp. Only six officers of the 43rd were fit to attend the interment, but his brother James, of the Royal Artillery, was also present; all were overcome with grief, and even the privates who carried the body were sobbing aloud. One of Macleod's men, Sergeant Thomas Blood, gave the most remarkable testimony: 'There was not a man in that corps [the 43rd] but would have stood between him and the fatal ball that struck him dead, so esteemed was he by all, and only twenty-seven years of age.'[52] He was commemorated by a marble monument in Westminster Abbey, erected by his brother officers and executed by the great sculptor Joseph Nollekins.

The statistics of casualties sustained in the assault of the breaches vary slightly in a number of sources, and it is possible that the losses sustained by the 2nd Battalion 95th may have been omitted from the published statistics in the *London Gazette* of 24 April 1812.[53] Excluding the losses of the Portuguese (a total of 53 officers and 677 other ranks, killed, wounded and missing on 6/7 April), in the attack on the breaches the 4th Division appears to have sustained about 925 casualties, the Light Division 977 (the *London Gazette* roll suggests 929 casualties for the Light Division, to which the losses of the 2/95th may have to be added). In regimental terms, the three regiments of the Light Division lost most heavily: the 43rd suffered 341 casualties, the 52nd 320 and the 95th 258 (plus the losses of the 2/95th, if they should be added).

It is perhaps difficult to account for the sustained and almost suicidal bravery of the troops involved, who actually vied with one another for the privilege of experiencing the greatest risk of death. High morale and regimental *esprit de corps* certainly played a part, and perhaps with a few foolish individuals the fear of missing the best plunder, or (as some writers averred) antipathy towards the inhabitants of Badajoz arising from their previous treatment of the British and the belief that they were French sympathisers. Nevertheless it caused great wonder among the witnesses that such appalling slaughter could occur without, apparently, much diminution of the determination of those involved. William Napier reflected some of this wonder when he noted that the 43rd and 52nd alone lost more men than the seven regiments which assaulted the castle, and observed of the assault on the breaches:

'Let any man picture to himself this frightful carnage taking place in a space of less than a hundred yards square. Let him consider that the slain died not all suddenly, nor by one manner of death; that some perished by steel, some by shot, some by water, that some were crushed and mangled by heavy weights, some trampled upon, some dashed to atoms by fiery explosions; that for hours this destruction was endured without shrinking, and that the town was won at last, let any man consider this and he must admit that a British army bears with it an awful power. And false would it be to say that the French were feeble men, for the garrison stood and fought manfully and with good discipline behaving worthily. Shame there was none on any side. Yet who shall do justice to the bravery of the soldiers? the noble emulation of the officers? Who shall measure out the glory of Ridge [Major Henry, 5th Foot, killed in circumstances of the greatest gallantry in the assault of the castle], of Macleod, of Nicholas, or of O'Hare, of the ninety-fifth, who perished on the breach, at the head of the stormers, and with him nearly all the volunteers for that desperate service? Who shall describe the springing valour of that Portuguese grenadier who was killed the foremost man at the Santa Maria? or the martial fury of that desperate soldier of the ninety-fifth, who, in his resolution to win, thrust himself between the chained sword-blades, and there suffered the enemy to dash his head to pieces with the ends of their muskets? ... Nor would I be understood to select these as pre-eminent, many and signal were the other examples of unbounded devotion, some known, some that will never be known; for in such a tumult much passed unobserved, and often the observers fell themselves ere they could bear testimony to what they saw; but no age, no nation ever sent forth braver troops to battle than those who stormed Badajos.'54

Written by a comrade of those troops, the last phrase might not be regarded as totally objective; indeed, even though it helped detract some of the defenders' resources away from the diversionary attacks which succeeded, the assault of the breaches was a failure. From the efforts made by the troops at those breaches, however, it is difficult to argue against Napier's contention.

NOTES

1. *Journaux des Sièges faits ou Soutenus par les Français dans la Péninsule de 1807 à 1814*, J. Belmas, Paris, 1838, III, p. 287.
2. *Journals of the Sieges undertaken by the Allies in the Years 1811 and 1812, with Notes*, J. T. Jones, London, 1814, pp. 333–4.
3. *A British Rifle Man; The Journals and Correspondence of Major George Simmons*, ed. Lieutenant-Colonel W. Verner, London, 1899, p. 232.
4. *Life of General Sir William Napier*, ed. H. A. Bruce, London, 1864, I, p. 145.
5. This strange practice is described in *Bonaparte vs. Blainey*, W. Blainey, Union Springs, N. Y., 1988, p. 14.
6. Belmas, *op. cit.*, IV, pp. 364–6.

7. Ibid., IV, p. 364; the statistics given by Belmas are slightly at variance with Jones's calculation based on 'the Governor's papers, found after the assault' which give a strength of 4,499 men plus 243 sick at the commencement of the siege (Jones, p. 144).

8. The full instructions can be found in *Dispatches of Field Marshal the Duke of Wellington*, ed. J. Gurwood, London, 1834–8, IX, pp. 36–40.

9. *Random Shots from a Rifleman,* Captain Sir John Kincaid, London, 1835; Maclaren's combined edn. (with *Adventures in the Rifle Brigade*, London, 1830), London, 1908, p. 273.

10. *Twenty-Five Years in the Rifle Brigade*, W. Surtees, London, 1833, p. 152.

11. 'Table-Talk of an Old Campaigner', by 'A Constant Reader', in *United Service Journal*, 1834, III, p. 51.

12. Ibid., p. 56.

13. *Adventures with the Connaught Rangers, 1809–1814*, W. Grattan, ed. Sir Charles Oman, London, 1902, p. 197; the text was originally published in *United Service Journal*, and in book form in 1847.

14. 'Memoirs of Edward Costello', in *United Service Journal*, 1839, III, p. 41; published in book form in London, 1857.

15. *The Autobiography of Sir Harry Smith*, ed. G. C. Moore Smith, London, 1910, p. 64; this names him as 'Old Alister Cameron'.

16. Wellington's *Dispatches*, IX, p. 44.

17. *History of the War in the Peninsula*, W. F. P. Napier, London, 1832–40, IV, p. 422.

18. Smith, *op. cit.*, p. 64

19. 'Mr. Alison's History and the Attack on Buenos Ayres' by 'Bayonet', in *United Service Journal*, 1838, I, p. 108.

20. Napier, *op. cit.*, IV, p. 425. Napier's description of Macleod, who was a dear friend, is perhaps deceptive: Macleod's youngest brother described him as 'a lithe supple figure, but very active and muscular' ('Lieutenant-Colonel Charles Macleod', in *The Oxfordshire Light Infantry Chronicle*, ed. A. F. Mockler-Ferryman, 1895, IV, p. 109).

21. Smith, *op. cit.*, p. 65.

22. Napier, *op. cit.*, VI, p. 360.

23. Smith, *op. cit.*, p. 65.

24. See *Letters from the Peninsula: The Freer Family Correspondence*, N. Scarfe, Leicester, 1953, p. 24 (from *Transactions of the Leicestershire Archaeological Society*, 1953, XXIX).

25. Smith, *op. cit.*, pp. 65–6.

26. Kincaid, *op. cit.*, pp. 281–2. The officer is not identified by Kincaid, but is likely to have been Blakeney, who recovered from his wound and rose to achieve the rank of Field Marshal in 1862. Kincaid presumably mistook his rank – Blakeney was a lieutenant-colonel from 20 June 1811 – though it could perhaps refer instead to Major James Singer, although Kincaid would surely not have written with such levity about his wound, for Singer was killed.

27. Smith, *op. cit.*, p. 66.

28. Ibid. p. 65.

29. 'Table-Talk', p. 55.

30. *The Life of John Colborne, Field Marshal Lord Seaton*, G. C. Moore Smith, London, 1903, p. 176.

31. *Royal Military Chronicle*, February, 1813, pp. 271–2, gives a detailed account of Nicholas and his injuries. James Shaw is better known as Sir James Shaw-Kennedy, taking the latter name upon his marriage to Mary Kennedy in 1820.

32. Simmons, *op. cit.*, p. 229.

33. Ibid.

34. Costello, *op. cit.*, pp. 42–3.
35. Napier, *op. cit.*, IV, p. 425.
36. 'Table-Talk', p. 56.
37. Kincaid, *Adventures*, p. 66.
38. Ibid., p. 141.
39. Jones, *op. cit.*, pp. 150–1.
40. Grattan, *op. cit*, pp. 202–3.
41. Surtees, *op. cit.*, p. 139.
42. *The Autobiography and Services of Sir James McGrigor, Bart.*, London, 1861, p. 273.
43. 'Table-Talk', p. 50.
44. *Historical Record of the Fifty-Second Regiment,* W. S. Moorsom, London, 1860, p. 167.
45. 'Table-Talk', p. 51.
46. Smith, *op. cit.*, p. 66. Apparently the Prince of Orange also carried the same message from Wellington to Barnard; it was not unusual for more than one courier to be sent to ensure that at least one got through (see account of Captain Barney, Chasseurs Britanniques, Napier, *op. cit.*, IV, p. 575).
47. Simmons, *op. cit.*, p. 230.
48. Costello, *op. cit.*, p. 43.
49. Smith, *op. cit.*, pp. 66–7.
50. Simmons, *op. cit.*, pp. 232–3.
51. Smith, *op. cit.*, p. 67. Kincaid's account of Allix's arrival does not name him, and Smith calls him 'Allen', but it is obvious that it was the Allix brothers who were involved.
52. 'Lieutenant-Colonel Charles Macleod', in *The Oxfordshire Light Infantry Chronicle*, p. 114.
53. See *History of the Peninsular War*, Sir Charles Oman, Oxford, 1914, V, pp. 594–5; and *History and Campaigns of the Rifle Brigade*, Colonel W. Verner, London, 1919, II, pp. 381–2; the latter may be mistaken in the case of the officers referred to: Captain Thomas Diggle (killed) and Lieutenant Henry Manners (wounded) *were* listed in the dispatch, and the third, Lieutenant Walter Bedell, had been severely wounded at Ciudad Rodrigo and appears not to have been at Badajoz (he did not receive that clasp for the Military General Service Medal).
54. Napier, *op. cit.*, IV, pp. 432–3. 'Badajos' is the alternative spelling.

— 9 —

On the Banks of the Styx
THE BEREZINA
27–28 November 1812

Probably the least regarded, and certainly the least celebrated, parts of an army were the 'supporting services', which although fulfilling a vital operational role are often overlooked when the events of great campaigns are recounted. Troops such as engineers, transport and commissariat personnel were sometimes even disregarded by their fellows; yet there were occasions when they assumed the guise of heroes, and surely one of these was at the Berezina.

Napoleon's invasion of Russia in 1812, the most ambitious undertaking of his career, involved an army of unprecedented size, which in every sense justified its name of *la Grande Armée*. The invasion force numbered about 450,000 men, Napoleon's own command almost a quarter of a million strong; the second-line reserves numbered about 165,000, intended as reinforcements, and including as its largest formation Marshal Victor's IX Corps, 33,000 strong; with a third-line reserve of about 60,000 men. Roughly half the infantry and one-third of the cavalry were contingents drawn from allied or French-satellite states, including Germans from the *Rheinbund* (the 'Confederation of the Rhine', states allied to Napoleon), Italians from the Kingdoms of Italy and Naples (whose sovereigns were Napoleon himself and his brother-in-law Joachim Murat respectively), Poles from the Duchy of Warsaw (a state created by Napoleon), Netherlanders from the ex-Kingdom of Holland (incorporated into France in 1810), and smaller contingents of Portuguese, Spanish and Greeks. There were even (somewhat unenthusiastic) contingents from two of Napoleon's erstwhile most bitter enemies, Prussia and Austria, the latter providing an entire corps for the enterprise.

Even this mighty force proved unable to accomplish the task it was set, though this was less a reflection upon the troops than upon the miscalculation of their commander and the magnitude of the project. The principal intention of Napoleon's strategy was always to destroy the enemy's field army, and thereby his ability to resist, rather than the

192

occupation of territory; but in 1812 the Russian commanders avoided giving battle, and thus denied Napoleon the opportunity for achieving the decisive victory he desired. After considerable division and friction within the Russian command, the Tsar felt compelled to appoint old General Mikhail Kutuzov to overall command of the Russian forces on 20 August 1812. He halted the retreat of the Russian forces into the interior to make a stand at Borodino, where on 7 September he engaged Napoleon in a ghastly, bloody but indecisive battle, which cost perhaps 44,000 Russian casualties and 30,000 of the *Grande Armée*, and then recommenced his retreat. Napoleon determined to press on to capture Moscow, believing that this, if nothing else, would compel the Tsar to negotiate a peace on Napoleon's terms; but Kutuzov declared that the loss of Moscow would not mean the loss of Russia, and was content to permit Napoleon to advance ever farther into Russia, stretching his already tenuous lines of communication. Napoleon duly entered Moscow as the bulk of the civilian population was leaving; and almost immediately much of the city was consumed by fires, probably mostly the work of incendiaries ordered to deny Napoleon the advantages of his capture. Enough of the city remained unburned to provide quarters for Napoleon's army, however, as he waited there for an answer to his demand that the Tsar surrender. No reply was forthcoming.

Napoleon later admitted to making two mistakes: in going to Moscow, and in staying there too long; if the first were an understandable error, arising from a miscalculation of Russian determination, the second was probably avoidable. Realising the impossibility of spending the winter in Moscow, Napoleon finally determined to retire by a more southerly route than that used in his journey to Moscow; but when this new route was blocked by Russian forces, he decided to withdraw the way he had come, over territory which had already been stripped bare of resources by his advance.

During the progress of this retreat from Moscow, the Russians held off from a full-scale engagement, pursuing instead a policy of harassment of the flanks and rear of the *Grande Armée*, for which the Russian army's hordes of Cossacks and similar light horse were uniquely suited. A major battle was not necessary: climatic conditions, the breakdown of the supply system and the exhaustion caused by traversing vast distances at speed were alone sufficient to cause the disintegration of Napoleon's army. Burdened by large numbers of camp-followers and by baggage – the loot of the unburned part of Moscow, most of which was gradually abandoned by the wayside – weakened by malnutrition and

exhaustion, frozen as the first snows of winter forced down the temperature and turned already poor roads into morasses, the troops of the
Grande Armée starved to death, were killed by the cold, by the Cossacks
or by vengeful Russian peasants who massacred any defenceless stragglers who fell into their hands. Discipline survived in some regiments,
survivors staunchly marching with their Colours; elsewhere morale collapsed and the fight for survival revealed the most base of human
instincts, which spared neither woman, child, comrade or helpless
invalid in the desperate attempt to find sufficient food to prolong the
agony of life for another day, or secure enough warm clothing to survive
the plummeting temperatures of the night. The weak were killed for
morsels of food, the dying stripped for scraps of clothing, the plight of
comrades ignored in the ghastly struggle for survival; which, in so many
cases, was in vain. Excluding the declining number of stalwarts who
clung to their officers and their Colours, in little over a month that part
of the force which had begun the withdrawal from Moscow was transformed from an army into a crowd of fugitives who experienced almost
all the excesses that human imagination can conjure.

Effective though their tactics were, the Russians were not content
to rely entirely on the Cossacks, the cold and starvation to harry
Napoleon's army out of existence. About midway between Smolensk
and the comparative safety of the River Niemen (the border of Russian
territory), the River Berezina cut across Napoleon's path of retreat, providing the Russians with the opportunity to capture or destroy the remnant of his army. While Kutuzov's main force followed the staggering
column, two other Russian contingents prepared to trap the *Grande
Armée* in a triple pincer around the Berezina: from the north, an army
under Ludwig Wittgenstein, the son of a Prussian general in Russian service; and from the south, another army under Admiral Pavel
Tchitchakov, the anglophile ex-minister of the navy who had been
raised in England and became a naturalised Briton in later life; acknowledged to be an honest and well-meaning man, he lacked military talent
and (at least in the eyes of some of his subordinates) common sense and
good manners. These three forces intended to converge, Wittgenstein
and Tchitchakov to hold the line of the Berezina to bar Napoleon's route
of escape from Kutuzov's pursuit. Of approximately 95,000 members of
the *Grande Armée* who had left Moscow under arms, Napoleon had perhaps 25,000 men still capable of fighting in a cohesive body, and a
horde of fugitives and stragglers at least as great, if not more. Kutuzov
stated that he had 80,000 men, but probably had rather fewer; in the

north Wittgenstein had some 30,000 men and in the south Tchitchakov led about 34,000 more.

Had these been the only forces involved, surely nothing could have prevented the complete annihilation of Napoleon's army; but as it was only a part of the army had got as far as Moscow, other forces had remained in the rear. Napoleon's own force comprised I, III, IV, V and VIII Corps, Murat's reserve cavalry and the Imperial Guard, and it was the remnants of these which were now staggering back towards the Berezina. Farther west, however, were three corps that had not reached Moscow and which, although they had been engaged by outlying Russian detachments, were still strong, properly nourished, fully equipped and with morale unshaken by the catastrophe which had befallen the 'Moscow army', about which they knew nothing: II, VI and IX Corps. IX Corps was commanded by Marshal Claude Victor, an old companion of Napoleon's in the Italian campaigns, who, though having recently suffered defeats in the Peninsula, proved to be a competent commander. II Corps was led by Marshal Nicolas Charles Oudinot, one of the 'characters' of the army, if for no other reason than that he was probably its most wounded soldier. Hardly an action occurred in which Oudinot was unscathed, so that his survival was truly miraculous. True to form, he had been hit in the shoulder by grapeshot on 17 August which had compelled him to relinquish his command, but he returned to it in October. Gouvion Saint-Cyr's VI Corps was composed of Bavarians, and after he had been wounded command had passed to the Bavarian General Carl Philipp Wrede; but in the operations which permitted the escape of the *Grande Armée* this formation, stationed well to the north of the Berezina crossing, was largely uninvolved. As Tchitchakov moved up from the south, on 16 November he captured Minsk, a vital supply depot which Napoleon had been relying on to replenish his exhausted troops; and this devastating blow put Tchitchakov to the *west* of the line of the Berezina, so that Napoleon's army would find itself with the almost impossible task of fighting its way over a defended crossing, while encumbered by an immense concourse of non-combatants and stragglers, and under threat of attack from flanks and rear. The situation was critical, and Napoleon responded with the necessary speed. He ordered the destruction of all unnecessary wagons and baggage, which were duly burnt or abandoned around the town of Orsha on 20 November, but permitted the vast number of private carriages, many transporting the booty of Moscow, to remain with the army, thus choking the route westward which was already littered by the human wreckage of the army. The pontoon-train was also destroyed at Orsha, in the belief that there could be no further use for it at this stage of the campaign. It could have proved the most costly mistake of all.

While thus endeavouring to quicken the pace of his staggering army, Napoleon sent messages to his forces farther west. He ordered General Dombrowski, commanding the 17th Division of V Corps, which had been stationed south and east of Minsk, to hold a bridge over the Berezina at Borisov, at all costs; Oudinot's II Corps was ordered to counter-attack Tchitchakov's forces which were threatening the Berezina crossing; and Victor's IX Corps was ordered to form a defensive position to the north of the projected river-crossing, to hold back Russian forces under Wittgenstein which were approaching from the north. With that, Napoleon hoped to protect the crossing over the Berezina

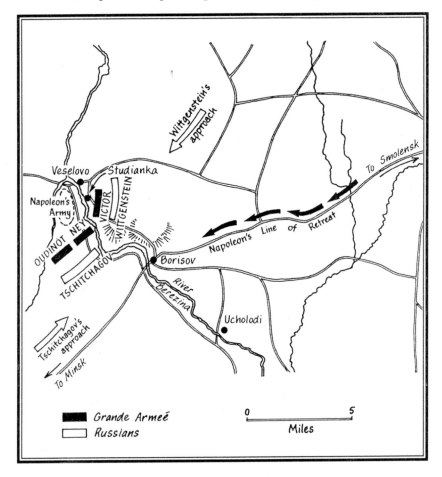

long enough for his army to escape before the Russians could sever his route. It was a vain hope.

As the remnant of Napoleon's 'Moscow army' retired westwards, the appalling privations they had endured became evident to the soldiers of II and IX corps who were profoundly shocked to encounter 'a train of spectres covered with rags, with female pelisses, pieces of carpet, or dirty cloaks, half-burnt and holed by the fires, and with nothing on their feet but rags of all sorts ... faces black with dirt and hideous bristly beards, unarmed, shameless, marching confusedly, with their heads bent, their eyes fixed on the ground, and silent, like a troop of captives. But what astonished them more than all was the number of colonels and generals scattered about and isolated, who seemed only occupied about themselves, and to think of nothing but saving the wrecks of their property, or their persons; they were marching pell-mell with the soldiers, who did not notice them, to whom they no longer had any commands to give, and of whom they had nothing to expect, all ties between them being broken, and all ranks effaced by the common misery. The soldiers of Victor and Oudinot could not believe their eyes.'[1] In fairness, however, despite their appearance, parts of Napoleon's force were still operational, even if very considerably reduced in numbers.

The River Berezina ran approximately south-east to north-west, and was crossed at the town of Borisov by the main road from Smolensk to Minsk, that which formed the route of Napoleon's retreat. North-west of Borisov the river's winding course increased in width, with marshy ground on both banks until past the village of Studianka (or 'Studenka') where there was no official road-bridge; higher ground was some way east of the river, with marsh between it and the river. Possession of the Borisov bridge was therefore of paramount importance; and when news was received on 22 November that the bridgehead had been lost on the previous day, the effect on the morale of the retreating army must have been profound.

The defence of the vital bridge had been entrusted to a Polish officer, Bronikowski, who had previously failed to defend the storage depot of Minsk. He was reinforced by the 17th Division's commander, General Jean Henri Dombrowski (or 'Dabrowski'), who arrived on the night of 20/21 November to find that some attempt had been made to create a fortified bridgehead on the west bank of the Berezina, but the works were incomplete. No further improvements had been made when Dombrowski was attacked on the following dawn by General Lambert, commanding Tchitchakov's advance-guard. Dombrowski held his position for some time, but not long enough for support to arrive from Oudinot's corps; and with considerable losses Dombrowski withdrew eastwards over the Berezina by the Borisov bridge, and was pursued for some way towards the head of the retreating *Grande Armée*. Tchitchakov himself arrived that night and established his headquarters in the town, choking its narrow streets with wagons and baggage, but not (at least in the opinion of his most critical subordinates) taking adequate measures to protect the bridge. He had, however, blocked Napoleon's route home.

Learning of the fall of Borisov even as he advanced to its relief, Oudinot realised that he must recapture the route over the Berezina, so pushed on with all haste. On the morning of 23 November Tchitchakov deployed his advance elements between Borisov and the likely approach of the French, but his reconnaissance was so imperfect that he had no knowledge of the proximity of Oudinot's men; he was sitting down to dine in Borisov at 1 p.m. when he was interrupted by the sound of gunfire. Within a short time Oudinot's leading units drove the Russian picquets back into Borisov, where total chaos ensued; instead of defending the town or withdrawing in an orderly manner, Tchitchakov was involved in an undignified scramble to regain the western bank of the river, leaving behind not only his dinner but his plate, clothes and documents as well. So complete was the Russian disorganisation that all their wounded were abandoned in Borisov, and Lambert, who had been wounded on the previous day, was only saved by his wife who rounded up a few Russian hussars and shamed them into carrying the injured man over the bridge. Yet although the French had so rapidly re-possessed the town, the bridge was a very different matter, covered as it was by Russian positions on the west bank.

The troops who had hustled the Russians back across the river were Castex's brigade of light cavalry, the 23rd and 24th *Chasseurs à Cheval*, serving as corps cavalry with Oudinot. Perhaps they delayed vital moments in looting the abandoned baggage – Marbot, commanding the 23rd, described how Castex apportioned the 1,500 wagons into two lots, one for each regiment, but implies this happened later in the day, though some looting at the first opportunity would have been almost inevitable. Whatever the cause of the delay in pursuing the Russians over the bridge – Marbot said that the streets of Borisov were so choked with baggage that only with difficulty could they *find* the bridge – light cavalry were not the ideal troops to consolidate their hold on the town, but the infantry required were still several miles away. There was also no possibility of crossing the river by any other means than by the bridge;

there was no known ford, and the weather was not sufficiently cold for ice to form strong enough to support the weight of a man. (It is often stated that it was the cold, Russia's 'General Winter', which destroyed the *Grande Armée*, and there is much truth in this statement; but at this juncture it was the unexpectedly mild weather that did not freeze the river, which caused disaster.)

At this point Oudinot arrived and attempted to remedy his dearth of infantry by ordering Castex to dismount three-quarters of his men (the remainder acting as horse-holders) and to attempt to secure the bridge on foot, even though their short carbines without bayonets were suited only to skirmishing. Marbot thought the desperate enterprise was feasible as great confusion could still be seen among the Russians on the western bank of the Berezina. He ordered that the first men across should fortify houses near the end of the bridge, so that both ends would be held until Oudinot's infantry came up. However, perhaps because of the delay caused by the abandoned baggage, when the attempt was made the Russians were sufficiently composed to open a furious cannonade upon the *chasseurs*, and forced them back. As the French recoiled, a party of Russian engineers took advantage of the moment to set the wooden bridge on fire, but as their operations had compelled the Russian artillery to fall silent, the *chasseurs* were able to renew their attack, hurling many of the Russians into the water and extinguishing the fires. Then they, in turn, were again driven back by a battalion of Russian grenadiers, and under their cover the bridge was again set alight. So many torches were employed that the whole structure was soon engulfed in flame, the heat compelling both sides to withdraw from their respective ends of the bridge.

Defeated in his attempt to secure the army's route home, Oudinot drew off most of his troops from Borisov, leaving only Castex's *chasseurs* to watch the Russians on the opposite bank; but to offset his defeat, Oudinot received the information which was to save what remained of the *Grande Armée*. The second brigade of his corps cavalry, commanded by General Jean-Baptiste Corbineau, comprising the 7th and 20th *Chasseurs à Cheval* and 8th *Chevau-Léger-Lanciers*, had been 'borrowed' by Wrede and removed to VI Corps far to the north, according to Marbot without authorisation and much to Corbineau's dissatisfaction. Eventually he challenged the Bavarian to produce the written orders authorising the transfer, and when these were not forthcoming Corbineau took his brigade back in the direction of II Corps, which he hoped to join by following the Berezina to Borisov, crossing by the bridge there and then riding east until he rejoined Oudinot. This march was somewhat hazardous, being entirely without support, but greatly assisted by the fact that the 8th *Chevau-Léger-Lanciers*, originally the lancers of the Vistula Legion, was Polish in composition and thus could elicit information from local civilians, a facility not available to most French regiments whose personnel had no knowledge of the local language. When he approached to within about half a day's march of Borisov, Corbineau was told by the peasants that the town was occupied by Tchitchakov, and realised that he had no chance of crossing the river. These same peasants advised him go to a point on the Berezina opposite the village of Studianka, about eight miles north of Borisov, where the river was sufficiently shallow to be forded. Corbineau found the ford, crossed safely to the east bank and rejoined Oudinot east of Borisov late on 23 November. The whereabouts of the ford were passed immediately to Oudinot, and thence to Napoleon, and proved the salvation of the army.

With the crossing at Borisov impossible, and with no known fords farther south, Napoleon had considered marching north towards Wrede, hoping to hold off Wittgenstein's army closing in from the north, but this would have been hazardous in the extreme because of the bad roads and a temporary thaw which had turned the terrain into mud. Now, escape by the Studianka ford was possible, though it required much planning. Kutuzov's army, though still following the *Grande Armée*, was not pushing on. It appears that either Kutuzov was content to let exhaustion and the climate finish the job, or was unwilling to have the French emperor annihilated for fear that it might create a power vacuum in Europe, allowing Britain to dominate (Sir Robert Wilson, the British attaché to Kutuzov's headquarters, reported Kutuzov expressing just such a fear). For whatever reason, however, Kutuzov's slow progress meant that Napoleon would be opposed by many fewer Russians than might have been the case, once he began to force the line of the Berezina.

Before this could be attempted, however, there remained the problem of Tchitchakov, whose forces were strung along the west bank of the Berezina from a position opposite Veselovo (a village north of Studianka) to beyond Borisov. Napoleon ordered Oudinot to make a demonstration miles to the south of Borisov, around the village of Ucholodi, to fool the Russians into believing that a ford had been found there. The ruse worked: Tchitchakov concentrated his forces to cover the imaginary river-crossing south of Borisov, and left the actual ford opposite Studianka virtually unguarded. This removed one obstacle, albeit temporarily, but another remained: the river itself. Not too difficult an obstacle when Corbineau had crossed, flood waters had increased its width considerably. Witnesses reported the river as being anything from about 25 to almost 200 yards in width, explained by the fact that though the east bank was firm, the west bank was marshy, so that although the temperature was again dropping, the ground was sufficient only to bog down anything which attempted to cross it, rather than presenting the firm footing as it would have in the coldest weather. In places the river flowed quickly, and its depth also increased in mid-stream so as to present difficulties even for a mounted man; and the majority of the army was afoot. A bridge was required; but at Orsha Napoleon had burned his pontoon-train in the belief that it was no longer needed, and so that the teams could be transferred to the artillery, in an attempt to preserve some of the army's guns.

In the event, the army's saviour was General Jean-Baptiste Eblé, a 54-year-old artillery officer who had been commissioned in the days of the *ancien régime* and had enjoyed a career both in the field and in administrative duties (Minister of War in Westphalia 1808–10). Although recently commandant of the artillery in Masséna's Army of Portugal (when he had supervised the sieges of Ciudad Rodrigo and Almeida), for the 1812 campaign Eblé had been given command of the pontoon-train (pontoneers in the French army being a branch of the artillery). Perhaps suspecting that the destruction of the pontoons was premature, on his own initiative Eblé had managed to preserve two field forges, two wagonloads of charcoal and six of tools and nails, and had instructed each of his men to carry an implement of some kind and some metal fastenings, which comprised a sufficient quantity of materials to make the construction of bridges across the ever-swelling Berezina a possibility. (Eblé had protested against the burning of the pontoon-train, pleading to be allowed to preserve just fifteen pontoons, but had been over-ruled.)

The task of throwing bridges over the Berezina by Studianka was entrusted to Eblé and his pontoneers (about 400 strong), and to the army's chief engineer, General François Chasseloup-Laubat, four years older than Eblé, and who had served as Napoleon's chief engineer as early as the Italian campaigns of 1796. Although his engineers were skilled, they had none of the equipment which Eblé had preserved. Marbot believed that progress on the bridges was hampered initially by jealousies between the two officers, but whether this was true or not, it was soon discovered that there were insufficient materials to construct the three bridges planned, so it was decided to build just two, Chasseloup-Laubat putting his men under Eblé's supervision.

In the evening of 25 November Eblé arrived at Studianka to find Corbineau's men already pulling down the wooden houses of the village and constructing trestles from the wood. Eblé thought them insufficiently strong, and put his mobile forges into operation to make additional metal fittings, while the demolition of the village continued. Napoleon met Oudinot at Veselovo early in the morning of 26 November, and remarked to the Marshal, 'you shall be my locksmith and open the passage for me';[2] in reality, the key was provided by Eblé and his pontoneers, whose efforts were nothing less than heroic.

To secure the crossing Corbineau forded the Berezina with a few of his troopers, each carrying an infantryman behind his saddle; more infantry were ferried across on small rafts constructed by Eblé's men, and they were sufficient, with covering fire from artillery on the east bank, to drive off the few Cossacks and two Russian guns covering the ford. With both banks secure, Eblé began to construct his bridges, one for infantry and a more robust one for wheeled traffic, about 130 yards downstream. For each bridge 23 trestles were constructed, held by supports planted in the muddy bottom of the river. To fix these in place the pontoneers had to stand breast- or shoulder-high in the icy river for hours at a stretch. François Pils, Oudinot's batman, stood on the bank and watched these men – whom he rightly described as heroes – as they laboured unceasingly in the freezing water, with ice forming around them, and described how the cold and exertion proved too much for some who sank beneath the water and disappeared in the downstream current. Despite the death of their comrades, the rest worked on undaunted.

During the work of construction, Napoleon stood on the east bank, watching the progress of the bridges, and seemed less than impressed with the difficulties being encountered by the pontoneers. Louis Bégos, a captain of the 2nd Swiss Regiment in Oudinot's corps was stationed near the bridges and overheard Napoleon's conversation with Eblé as the emperor became progressively more impatient: 'It's taking a very long time, General, a very long time.' Eblé was unsympathetic to his master's demands, forcibly pointing out that his men were being hampered by ice-floes and were working up to their necks in freezing water, with neither food nor brandy to sustain them. 'That will do,' scolded Napoleon; and after a few moments staring at the ground with a worried expression, he began complaining again.[3] All the while, the pontoneers were toiling, and in some cases dying, in the icy water; while infantrymen were employed in the less arduous task of fashioning fascines from brushwood and straw, to provide a firmer footing to the muddy approaches to the bridges. Eventually, at about 1 p.m. on 26 November, the last planks were put into position on the first bridge, and the second was completed at about 4 p.m.[4]

The completion of the bridges did not signal an end to the pontoneers' work, however, because the need to improvise meant that both were fairly ramshackle affairs. The 'right bridge' – intended for infantry and cavalry – was made principally of boards taken from the roofs of Studianka, laid upon trestles, which the passage of horses' hooves would continually kick out of place so had to be repaired almost constantly. The 'left bridge' for vehicles and artillery had an uneven surface made of logs, and the weight and movement of heavy traffic caused the supports, fixed in the loose and muddy river-bed, to collapse. These supports gave way at 8 p.m. on 26 November, requiring three hours' work to repair; at 2 a.m. the following morning two supports collapsed, needing four hours' work; and two more supports collapsed at 4 p.m. on 27 November, requiring a further three hours' labour. So the pontoneers were continually being dragged away from their meagre bivouac fires to repair the bridges, plunging time and again into the bitter water and working without sustenance or complaint, until the bridges were again operational. No praise could be too high for Eblé and his devoted band of craftsmen.

As soon as the first bridge was completed, Napoleon ordered Oudinot's corps to begin to cross, to establish a strong force on the west bank to oppose Tchitchakov who might be expected to return as soon as Napoleon's ruse was discovered; and to secure the wooden causeway through the marshes on the route west from the Berezina crossing. The Russian failure to destroy this causeway, which would have been the doom of the *Grande Armée* irrespective of what happened at the Berezina, was perhaps the most serious error perpetrated by the Russians during the whole of Napoleon's retreat. When the second bridge was completed, the artillery and transport began to cross, and throughout 27 November that part of Napoleon's force which was still in a cohesive body passed over the river. Victor's corps, still comparatively fresh, did not cross with the remainder but formed the rearguard on the east bank, holding back Wittgenstein's pressure from the north. By that evening only Victor's men remained on the east bank, together with an immense horde of tens of thousands of stragglers, some of whom had begun to press in on the bridges in the afternoon, forming a human obstacle for those units attempting to cross in an orderly manner. Witnesses who crossed with their regiments wrote of the need to force a passage through the throng, even beating the stragglers with the flat of their sabres to push them back. Eblé's pontoneers were formed into squads to do duty at the bridges in relays, to enable them to get some rest from the constant process of renovation and major repair of the bridges; and some now stood at the approaches to the bridges, attempting to control the crowds and open the way for those men still under arms. So unsteady had the bridges become that cavalry had to dismount and lead their horses, and some vehicles had to be manhandled across, to prevent shaking the woodwork to pieces; while teams of pontoneers still stood shoulder-deep in the water, repairing the bridges as they deteriorated and casting into the river any debris which collected on the 100-yard length of the bridges, vehicles that broke down or horses that dropped dead during the crossing. (The bridges had no guard-rails, which facilitated the task of pitching such impediments into the water.) In places the bridges were scarcely a foot above the river, and on the marshy western bank the water even came to ankle-depth over the surface, caused by the piles of the bridge sinking and the water level rising.

Napoleon had intended the bridges to be used by day and night, but perhaps because of the dangers of crossing a rail-less bridge in the dark, few of the huge body of stragglers attempted a nocturnal crossing, but, leaderless and unwilling to obey orders, huddled on the east bank around whatever paltry fires they could light, awaiting the dawn. Writing of that night, Eugène Labaume reflected on what he considered the very worst aspect of the campaign, 'to what a degree of brutality excess of misery would debase human nature. In one place we saw several soldiers fighting for a morsel of bread. If a stranger, pierced with the cold, endeavoured to approach a fire, those to whom it belonged inhumanly drove him away; or, if tormented with raging thirst, one asked for a single drop of water from another who carried a full supply, the refusal was accompanied by the vilest abuse. Often we heard those who had once been friends, and whose education had been liberal, bitterly disputing with each other for a little straw, or a piece of horse-flesh, which they were attempting to divide. This campaign was, therefore, the more terrible, as it brutalised the character, and stained us with vices to which we had before been strangers. Even those who were honest, humane, and generous, became selfish, avaricious, dishonest, and cruel.'[5]

Realising his error, Tchitchakov marched northwards parallel to the west bank of the Berezina, and from early on 27 November began to attack Oudinot, whose troops held a position south of Studianka, preventing Russian pressure upon the bridgeheads. Oudinot's troops held the right and centre of the line, Ney's III Corps – such of it as existed – held the left, as the rest of the army crossed the bridges. On the east bank, Wittgenstein thrust against Victor's rearguard, which gave ground gradually until it was holding a position south-west of Studianka, extending to Borisov, preventing the Russians from attacking *that* end of the bridges. So well did Victor's IX Corps appear to be holding, that on the afternoon of 27 November Napoleon thought it safe to order part of Victor's command, the Baden brigade of General Daendels' 26th Division, to cross the bridges. Victor's rearguard action, however, was put into severe jeopardy when one of his divisions disappeared.

General Louis Partouneaux (or 'Partonneaux') with his 12th Division of Victor's corps had been holding around Borisov, until ordered to abandon the town and retire on Studianka, to rejoin the rest of IX Corps. Ten days earlier Partouneaux had asked to be relieved of his command on the excuse of physical weakness (though he was probably considerably despondent), but had been told to remain in command. At about 3 a.m. on 28 November he began to withdraw, but took the wrong path and marched straight into Wittgenstein's army. Partouneaux himself went off to reconnoitre, was captured, and after holding its position for the remainder of the night, not knowing what was happening, his division found itself completely surrounded, and surrendered. The loss of these 4,000 excellent infantry, 500 cavalry (Saxon and Berg) and four guns put Victor in a most hazardous position. Only about 160 of Partouneaux's men were able to break free and rejoin Victor, bringing with them news of the débâcle. (It was said that these only escaped because their commanding officer ordered them to follow him and threatened to shoot the first man who spoke of surrender.)

Napoleon was furious at the news of Partouneaux's capture, but more than anger was required to enable Victor to hold the eastern end of the bridges; so the Emperor ordered the Baden contingent to re-cross the Berezina, back into the scenes of horror and devastation. There was no hesitation; though comparatively small, the Baden contingent was among the very best elements of the *Grande Armée*, and obediently trudged back, somehow managing to force a way through the crush which was again building around the bridges; but they were unable to clear the way sufficiently to take their artillery with them.

On the morning of 28 November the Russian commanders made a concerted effort against their respective opponents (having repaired the Borisov bridge, Tchitchakov was able to communicate more easily with Wittgenstein and they were able to co-ordinate their operations).

On the west bank, Tchitchakov attacked with something less than total commitment, but the Russian pressure threatened to break Oudinot's line. Amid falling snow which at times reduced visibility to 30 yards, the French hung on, their commander, as usual, quite careless of his personal safety. Oudinot sat his horse amid the flying shot, humming to himself 'You shan't catch me just yet,'[6] when suddenly he pitched from his saddle and, with foot caught in his stirrup, was dragged for some way along the ground. He had been shot low in the body by a ball which proved impossible to extract even though the surgeons probed for six or seven inches into the wound, the Marshal refusing restraint and merely biting a napkin during the operation. Probably thanks to his constitution he survived, and carried the bullet for the rest of his life. Marshal Ney took command of the fight against Tchitchakov, and no more determined replacement could have been found.

Although the situation had been so severe that Napoleon had ordered forward elements of the Imperial Guard (his last reserve, usually held back), Oudinot had steadied the line before his injury; and under Ney's command the battered French turned back the Russian advance. A decisive blow was struck on the left of the Russian position by General Doumerc's 3rd Heavy Cavalry Division, officially part of III Cavalry Corps but attached to Oudinot's II Corps, which made a devastating charge against the Russian 18th Division. Formed in column and unsuspecting a cavalry attack because of the woodland which surrounded them, the Russians were ridden down by Doumerc's 4th, 7th and 14th Cuirassiers which had passed through the woods and re-formed before making their charge which inflicted some 2,000 casualties on the Russians. On their right, another decisive advance was made by Berthezène's brigade of the 1st Imperial Guard Division (4th *Tirailleurs*, 4th and 5th *Voltigeurs*), and together these halted the Russian advance. Napoleon's position on the west bank of the Berezina was secured.

On the east bank, the situation was even more critical. Having lost most of its French element with the capture of Partouneaux's brigade, Victor's IX Corps now comprised the recalled Badeners, and brigades of Poles, Saxons and Bergers; the only remaining cavalry were some 350 troopers of the Baden Hussars and Hessian *Chevauxlegers*, commanded by General François Fournier.[7] Victor's own artillery was supported by a battery posted by Napoleon on the west bank, to provide covering fire across the river. The Russians engaged Victor along virtually the whole of his front and, overlapping his flank, began an artillery bombardment upon the bridges and the hordes of fugitives who had not yet crossed the

Berezina. This initiated a panic and the same mad scramble as had occurred on the previous afternoon, with thousands of desperate men and women attempting quite literally to fight their way across the river. For some 200 yards around the approaches to the bridges there was a ghastly half-circle of dead horses and trampled people, crushed beneath the stampeding multitude in a press so tight that once on the bridges, countless unfortunates were pushed off to freeze and drown in the water below. When the 'artillery' bridge again broke down, those attempting to cross tried to turn back, only to be precipitated into the river by those following, unaware that the bridge had been severed.

General Philippe de Ségur, who wrote a noted (if not entirely unbiased) history of the campaign, described the horror and confusion which ensued as the Russian fire began to fall among the fugitives:

'... the first Russian bullets ... were the sign of universal despair. Then it was, as in all cases of extremity, that dispositions exhibited themselves without disguise, and then were seen actions the most base, and actions the most sublime. According to their different characters, some furious and determined, with sword in hand, cleared for themselves a horrible passage. Others, still more cruel, opened a way for their carriages by driving them without mercy over the crowd of unfortunate persons who stood in their way, and were crushed to death. Their detestable avarice made them sacrifice their companions in misfortune to the preservation of their baggage. Others, seized with a disgusting terror, wept, supplicated, and sunk under the influence of that passion, which completed the exhaustion of their strength ... nothing was heard but cries of rage and suffering. In this frightful medley, those who were trod under and stifled, struggled under the feet of their companions, to whom they fastened with their nails and teeth, and by whom they were repelled without mercy, as if they had been enemies. Among them were wives and mothers, calling in vain for their husbands and their children, from whom they had been separated but a moment previously, never more to be united: they stretched out their arms and entreated to be allowed to pass in order to rejoin them; but being carried backwards and forwards by the crowd, and overcome by the pressure, they fell under without even being remarked. Amidst the tremendous noise of a furious hurricane, the firing of cannon, the whistling of the storm and of the bullets, the explosion of shells, vociferations, groans, and the most frightful oaths, this infuriated and disorderly crowd heard not the complaints of the victims whom it was swallowing up.'[8]

Even in this hellish scene there occurred what Ségur termed 'actions the most sublime': men attempting to save their comrades, choosing not to desert their wounded officers, and risking their own lives, such as the gunner who deliberately jumped off the bridge successfully to rescue a child who had slipped under an ice-floe.

Oblivious to these terrible events, Victor's men were still fighting to hold a precarious defensive perimeter. Both the Berg and Baden brigades made heroic bayonet-charges, the former unsuccessful, to stave off Russian attacks. Then, when Victor's centre was in danger of collapse, his small force of cavalry stepped into the breach. The Baden Hussars were acknowledged as a superb regiment, but had already lost their colonel, von Cancrin, killed a fortnight earlier; they were accompanied by the Hessian *Chevauxlegers*, and together, led by Fournier, they charged upon the flank of an advancing Russian column which threatened to split Victor's centre. Fournier was wounded at the outset, so command of the 350-odd cavalrymen passed to the Baden colonel von Laroche. Taking the advancing column in flank, they rode down the Russian 34th *Jägers*, taking 500 prisoners, and threw back the other two regiments; then charged on against a body of Russian grenadiers and two squadrons of cuirassiers. Von Laroche, bayoneted in the first charge, was wounded again and taken prisoner, but was rescued by *Wachtmeister* Martin Springer of the Baden Hussars. The two regiments then retired and rallied amid Victor's troops; but only about 50 men from each regiment had returned. Their so-called 'Charge of Death', however, had stabilised Victor's centre, and the fighting died down, the Russians content to use only skirmishing and artillery fire as Victor slowly pulled back to the bridgeheads.

At 9 p.m. Victor received orders to evacuate the east bank, and what remained of his exhausted command began to file over the bridges, the operation taking less time than expected because of their losses suffered in the day's fighting: for example, Damas' Berg brigade had only about 60 men left under arms. Once again, Eblé and his pontoneers had to open a path through the crowds of fugitives still on the east bank, to allow Victor's men to pass, and by about 6 a.m. on 29 November the last combatant elements of the *Grande Armée* were safely across the Berezina.

As on the previous night, the dangers of a nocturnal crossing of the river, and the cessation of the Russian offensive, had engendered a feeling of apathy among the fugitives. Entreaties that they should attempt to save themselves by crossing during the night went largely unheeded, and on the morning of 29 November Eblé was ordered to destroy the bridges which he and his men had laboured so long to keep open. In vain he tried to galvanise the pathetic horde on the east bank, by declaring that the bridges would have to be burned. At about 5 a.m., in the hopes of moving them, he had some abandoned carriages set alight; he called out that at 7 a.m. the bridges would be destroyed, but as there was still no general movement, he waited until 8.30 a.m. before, with reluctance but in the absolute necessity of closing the passage over the Berezina, he ordered the bridges to be broken down and burned. This, at last, forced the mob into movement, initiating another ghastly scene: 'several thousand men and women, and some children, were abandoned on the hostile bank. They were seen wandering in desolate troops on the borders of the river. Some threw themselves into it in order to swim across; others ventured themselves on the pieces of ice which were floating along: some there were also who threw themselves headlong into the flames of the burning bridge, which sunk under them; burnt and frozen at one and the same time, they perished under two opposite punishments. Shortly after, the bodies of all sorts were perceived collecting together and driving with the ice against the trestles of the bridge. The rest awaited the Russians. Wittgenstein did not shew himself upon the heights until an hour after Eblé's departure, and, without having gained a victory, he reaped all the fruits of one.'[9]

After these appalling scenes, Napoleon's retreat continued, but without another major action; the Russians were content to allow the pathetic remnant of the *Grande Armée* to stumble home with only the harassment of the Cossacks, allowing the weather, starvation and exhaustion to complete the work of destruction. For all that, the battle of the Berezina could be seen as a victory for Napoleon, for against all the odds he had found a way out of what appeared to be a hopeless trap, had established a bridgehead and defended it long enough for that part of his force still under arms to extricate itself. The cost, however, was horrific: probably between 20,000 and 30,000 of the *Grande Armée's* combatants fell in the battle to keep open the bridges, and an untold number of stragglers either drowned or were trampled in the crush, or died of cold and starvation after falling into Russian hands. Oudinot and Victor's corps, those parts of the *Grande Armée* least affected by the retreat, probably lost more than half their number in the fighting around the Berezina. Russian losses may have been as high as 10,000 killed and many thousands wounded.

The worst and most obvious characteristic of this terrible battle was the fate which befell the army's stragglers. So many tragedies and heart-rending scenes were recorded by the survivors – even of mothers strangling their own infants to end their misery – that the impression of such ghastly tales is such that it is possible to overlook the heroism of those troops who fought so hard to preserve what remained of the army. Admittedly most of these were the troops of Oudinot and Victor, who had thus far been spared the horrors which had overtaken the remainder, but their devotion to duty was remarkable, especially when opportunities existed of desertion to join the huge mass of stragglers who were not faced with the immediacy of combat. Oudinot and Victor – and by extension their men – might be hailed as the heroes of the battle of the Berezina, but at least equal praise must be reserved for Jean-Baptiste Eblé and his force of pontoneers, engineers and pioneers.

Even after almost superhuman efforts to build and keep open the bridges, Eblé and his men could not rest, for as the retreat continued their immediate task was to destroy the causeway away from the Berezina once the army had passed, to slow Russian pursuit. Only about forty of Eblé's men survived the campaign. Eblé himself had worked as hard as any, sharing the tasks of his men and marching on foot with them, a severe trial for a middle-aged man. He remarked, surely with every justification, that the construction and maintenance of the Berezina bridges was the most valuable service he had ever rendered his country, but it took its toll, as he demonstrated by exhibiting the waistband of his breeches, now hopelessly large, as evidence of how his body had wasted. When the army's artillery chief, Lariboisière, fell ill (fatally) on 9 December, Eblé took over, and on 2 January 1813 Napoleon appointed him Chief Inspector of Artillery. Eblé never learned of this promotion; totally worn out, he had died at Königsberg on 30 December 1812. Having overlooked the honour during Eblé's lifetime, it was to his widow that Napoleon granted a patent of nobility as *comtesse* in April 1813; and, according to French military tradition, the right to wear golden spurs claimed by *pontonnier* officers originated with a grant made to the heroic and devoted Eblé.[10] If this were so, it was little enough reward for the man who saved the *Grande Armée*.

Courage in the face of battle is one thing; but a different type of determination is required to risk death by the exhaustion of manual labour, especially when opportunities existed for desertion and a more certain preservation of life. If the 'Charge of Death' at Studianka represents one end of the range of military valour, then surely those who built and maintained the Berezina bridges are equally deserving of laurels, for devotion to duty of the highest order was required to continue working when exhausted, repeatedly soaked through and frozen in such a climate, with little chance of finding dry clothing. Oudinot's ADC Le Tellier, while exaggerating slightly a story which needed no embellishment, provided a final comment: 'When the foundations of that historic bridge, the sole hope of safety offered us, had to be laid in at the Berezina, at the voice of their chief those men of duty and resolution marched silently into the water, never interrupting their work save to turn aside the huge pieces of ice which threatened to cut them in two like a sword. They drove in the piles, the ground-work of the construction, and went on striking their blows until the moment came when they felt death seize them. Not one came out alive, but others stepped in to complete the work – the work of a day which should leave an immortal memory!'[11]

Memories were not quite the only thing left after the battle of the Berezina. Ten years later, but for a few months, a Prussian engineer officer, Major Blesson, made a tour of the battlefields of the war and discovered that the locations of the two bridges were still visible from the heaps of debris, leatherwork, metal fittings and bones which marked the path of the *Grande Armée*. Tranquil now, an artificial island and three boggy mounds had been formed in the river, originally composed of vehicles and bodies which had fallen off the bridges or slipped from the banks into the river, and which, covered with mud and silt swept down river, had become permanent reminders of the tragedy of the Berezina. The mounds, observed Blesson, were covered with forget-me-nots.

NOTES

1. *History of the Expedition to Russia*, General Count P. de Ségur, London, 1825, II, p. 284.
2. *Memoirs of Marshal Oudinot*, Duchesse de Reggio and G. Stiegler, trans. A. Teixeira de Mattos, New York, 1897, p. 171.
3. Bégos' account is in *Soldats Suisses au Service étranger*, Geneva, 1909; this translation is in *1812*, A. Brett-James, London, 1966, p. 257.
4. These are the times which seem most accurate, although alternative schedules exist; Pils, for example, thought that the first bridge was completed shortly before 11 a.m.
5. *Circumstantial Narrative of the Campaign in Russia*, E. Labaume, London, 1814, pp. 350–1.
6. Oudinot, *op. cit.*, p. 176.
7. At this date his name was 'Fournier'; only after the Second Restoration was he elevated to the status of *comte* and permitted to use the name Fournier-Sarloveze, the latter name from his birthplace, Sarlat.
8. Ségur, *op. cit.*, II, pp. 312–14.
9. Ibid., p. 317.
10. This tradition is recorded in *Swords Around a Throne*, Colonel. J.R. Elting, London, 1989, p. 253.
11. Oudinot, *op. cit.*, pp. 177–8.

'With the Utmost Gallantry'[1]
HOUGOUMONT

18 June 1815

Fortifications did not play as crucial a role in Napoleonic warfare as in some other conflicts; but if protracted sieges were the exception, the defence for a shorter duration of fortified posts was of some significance. Even in actions or campaigns based on manoeuvre, the advantages of a defensible position were obvious, and although the construction of fieldworks was rare, more common was the rapid fortification of a building for use as a strong-point. Probably no case was more important than the defence of the château of Hougoumont at the battle of Waterloo, one of the turning-points of that climactic end to the Napoleonic Wars.

It is unnecessary to describe in much detail the events of the battle of Waterloo, for the action at Hougoumont was a battle within a battle, fought almost in a vacuum and for much of the day oblivious to events unfolding elsewhere on the field. What was important, however, was the tactical significance of the post, which demonstrates how vital it was that the position be held.

Having returned from exile and re-possessed his throne, Napoleon's only real chance of keeping it was to defeat the forces which were massing against him in the Netherlands, and on the strength of that defeat then negotiate with the Allied powers bent on his overthrow, but who might well be willing to compromise in the wake of the destruction of these two armies. They comprised a Prussian army under Marshal Gebhard von Blücher, and a mixture of contingents commanded by the Duke of Wellington, an assemblage of Netherlandish, Hanoverian and Brunswick troops, all believed to be of dubious value, with a reliable British nucleus (in the event, the other contingents performed better than Wellington's original description of 'an infamous army' might have implied).

Napoleon's plan to defeat them employed the standard tactic he used when facing an enemy of superior strength; to interpose himself between the two enemy armies and defeat them in detail. It came near to success: on 16 June 1815 he mauled the Prussians at Ligny while containing Wellington at Quatre Bras, but both Allied forces were able to withdraw. On 17 June Wellington retired to a position along the ridge of Mont St-Jean, to hold off Napoleon's assault until Blücher could come up upon his left, allowing the Allies to tackle Napoleon together. In the battle of 18 June, known as Waterloo from the village to the rear of the Mont St-Jean position, Napoleon had conversely to destroy Wellington before the Prussian arrival tipped the balance against the French.

Wellington's position was moderately strong, especially if one considers his immense skill in fighting defensive actions (although to describe him as a 'defensive general' does little justice to his all-round ability). On his right flank, just in front of the ridge, was a perfect defensive position, the château of Hougoumont, which the Duke realised at once would be a crucial post. From Napoleon's viewpoint, it could be the focus of an important if essentially diversionary attack: he hoped that by making a heavy attack on Hougoumont, the Duke would be compelled to divert his reserves to keep his right flank secure, when Napoleon would strike Wellington's centre, consequently weakened by having troops diverted to Hougoumont, and thus deliver the decisive blow in breaking the Allies' centre. Thus could Wellington be overthrown before the Prussians could save him.

One thing could frustrate this plan: if Hougoumont could be held without pulling in so many reinforcements as to denude Wellington's centre. Even worse for Napoleon would be the situation in which Hougoumont was defended so vigorously that it actually consumed some of Napoleon's reserves, which would have been employed more valuably elsewhere. Yet that is what happened: so important did the capture of Hougoumont become to the French commanders in the vicinity that they used increasing numbers of troops in their attacks, making the defence of the post doubly destructive to Napoleon's plans. Such heroism was displayed at Waterloo that it is difficult to single out any one feature as being more important than the rest; but as it transpired it might not be too fanciful to suggest that the fate of Europe might have hinged upon the small château at the right front of Wellington's line.

Hougoumont was not a castle or great house as might be understood by the term 'château'; a better English approximation might be a combined manor-house and farm, the gaps between buildings closed by walls, forming a roughly oblong structure. Nor was the name originally 'Hougoumont'; though this name was in use by 1815, Maxwell, who described it as 'a quiet country house, with its rustic environment',

213

termed it a 'ghost name',[2] perpetuated by its use in the dispatches of the battle. At least 17th century in origin, its proper name was the Château de Goumont, and in 1815 its absentee owner was the octogenarian Chevalier de Louville; the château itself was thus unfurnished and unoccupied, the farmhouse and its buildings being used by a tenant farmer named Dumonceau.

Lying in a roughly north-south position, the rectangular compound had the château approximately across the middle, dividing the enclosure into two courtyards. The château was a two-storeyed building with a small tower at one side and a small chapel built on to the south-

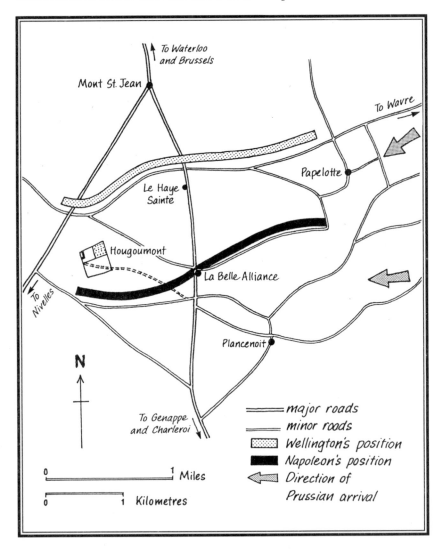

facing wall. On the east wall of the château was the farmer's house, two-storeyed and overlooking the northern courtyard, which on the north and east was bounded by an L-shaped cowshed, and on the west by a barn and cart-shed. Between the cart- and cowsheds was a wall with a double gate (the North or Great Gate), the principal entrance. The southern courtyard was bounded by the château and farmer's house on the north side, by stables adjoining the barn on the west, by a gardener's two-storeyed house on the south, and by more stables on the east. On the east side of the compound, these stables and the farmer's house were joined by a wall pierced by the 'garden gate', giving access on to a narrow terrace and thence to a formal garden. Next to the gardener's house, and with rooms above it, was the South Gate; the only other entrance was the small West Door giving access from the barn into the lane which ran along the western perimeter. The walled formal garden at the east was considerably larger in size than the entire built-up compound, and to the north of the garden was a small orchard, and beyond that a hedge-lined 'hollow way' running roughly west to east, to the north of which rose the slopes of the ridge upon which Wellington's right wing was posted. A small kitchen garden adjoined the south wall of the gardener's house, and to the east of the formal garden was a large orchard, surrounded by hedges and ditches. Within the compound the two court-yards were joined by an arched doorway between the barn and the château. To the south was a thickly wooded area, and between it and the gardener's house the farm's haystack was situated.

By the evening of 17 June Wellington's army had taken up its position along the Mont St-Jean ridge; most spent a miserable night as the weather was extremely wet and the shelter very sparse. On the slopes to the rear of Hougoumont was Major-General George Cooke's 1st Division, arguably the élite of the army, being the only division composed entirely of British troops, and the élite of the British army at that. Major-General Peregrine Maitland's 1st Brigade was composed of the 1st and 3rd Battalions of the 1st Foot Guards, and Sir John Byng's 2nd Brigade of the 2nd Battalions of the 2nd (Coldstream) and 3rd (Scots) Foot Guards. The rank and file of these units were acknowledged as among the best in the army, and the officers included a greater proportion of aristocracy and landed gentry than any other formation save the Household Cavalry.

On the evening of the 17th, the division's four light companies were sent down to occupy Hougoumont, the two 1st Guards companies taking over the orchard and those of the 2nd Brigade the château and

215

farm. Alexander Woodford, senior officer of the 2/ Coldstreams, reported the place 'well calculated for defence ... with small doors and windows',[3] and even the hedges were thick and impenetrable: Ensign George Standen of the 3rd Guards remarked that in all his life he never saw such a 'bullfincher' (a hedge difficult to cross on horseback),[4] and another witness noted that the stems of the bushes were as thick as a man's arm and up to twelve feet high, 'so close that nothing larger than a cat could pass between them'.[5] This first detachment sent to

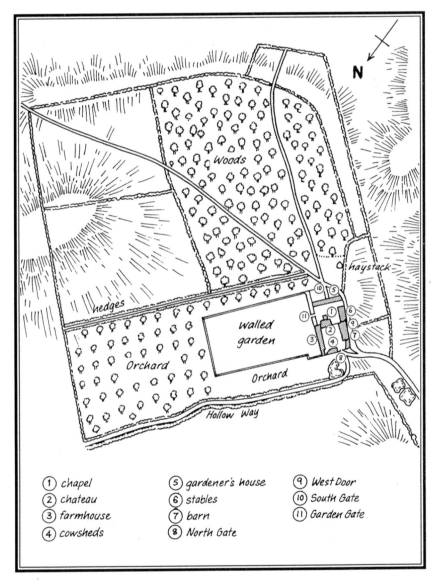

① chapel   ⑤ gardener's house   ⑨ West Door
② chateau   ⑥ stables   ⑩ South Gate
③ farmhouse   ⑦ barn   ⑪ Garden Gate
④ cowsheds   ⑧ North Gate

Hougoumont was commanded by Captain and Lieutenant-Colonel (a unique system of 'double rank' pertained in the Foot Guards) Alexander, Lord Saltoun of the 3/1st Guards, a most intrepid and capable officer, and he had to fight for possession of the position, a brief exchange of shots in the early evening of 17 June repelling a French detachment which had also been sent to investigate it. To assist this detachment, Wellington sent three companies of Hanoverian riflemen from Kielmansegge's *Jägers*, some 330 strong; they were deployed with the Guards' advance picquet under Lieutenant and Captain George Evelyn and Ensign George Standen of the 3rd Guards, which moved into the wood, where it was observed that the trees were not so thick as to inhibit the free movement of infantry, and was devoid of undergrowth. Lieutenant and Captain Robert Ellison of the 1st Guards was on picquet duty in the orchard.

To command the two light companies in the château (those of Captain and Lieutenant-Colonels Henry Wyndham, 2nd Guards, a natural son of the Earl of Egremont, and Charles Dashwood of the 3rd), Captain and Lieutenant-Colonel James Macdonell of Glengarry, 2nd Guards, was sent, arriving at about 7 p.m. This large, powerful Highlander must have been acknowledged as a particularly formidable individual, for Wellington seems personally to have arranged for him to take command. The Duke, who throughout took a particular interest in the events that unfolded at Hougoumont, was questioned early on the day of the battle by his Prussian liaison officer, General Müffling, about the weakness of the position and the smallness of the detachment sent to hold it. 'Ah!', replied the Duke. 'You do not know Macdonell'; which was apparently all he thought necessary to quell Müffling's fears. (At the same time, the Duke did heed Müffling's warning about the possibility of Hougoumont being outflanked on the right, to prevent which he had an abatis thrown across the Nivelles road and manned by the 51st Light Infantry.)

To improve his defences, Macdonell had loop-holes hacked in the outer walls, platforms erected to permit the defenders to fire over the walls, gates and doorways barricaded, (except the North Gate, left open for supplies and reinforcements); and early next morning the troops in the orchard cut holes in the hedges, the very concept of loop-holing a hedge being testimony to the strength of it. Lack of adequate tools, however, precluded any entrenching or the felling of trees to form defensive abatis. With these preparations in hand, one of the small band of guardsmen who settled down for a cold and wet night was Matthew Clay of the 3rd Guards, who wrote an account of the battle for

Hougoumont. He spent the night in a ditch at the rear of the orchard, without rations (which had never arrived) and attempts to sleep constantly interrupted by the vigorous Saltoun (still in command in the orchard despite Macdonell's arrival at the château), who spent the night riding up and down his positions, ensuring that his men remained alert.

On the early morning of Sunday, 18 June, when it was obvious that Napoleon was going to attack, Wellington rode over to Hougoumont to tell Macdonell that he must expect to be attacked immediately, and that he must 'defend the post to the last extremity'. Matthew Clay and his fellows were more concerned with finding firewood and something to eat; all Clay received was an ounce lump of bread and a piece of half-cooked pig's head which had been found in the farm, which was so nauseating that he could manage little more than a mouthful, even in his famished state. He was, however, able to change his underwear (having found some clean garments on the body of a dead German the day before), and collected some straw from the farmyard, which he carried back to his ditch, to sit upon instead of on the soaking grass. At about 10 a.m. Wellington ordered up a battalion of the 2nd Nassau Regiment, some 600–700 strong, who were posted in the orchard, wood and buildings, which allowed Saltoun and his two companies to rejoin his regiment on the ridge (encountering Wellington on the way, who was apparently unaware that Saltoun had been ordered to retire).

That part of the French army which assembled opposite Hougoumont was II Corps, commanded by General Honoré Reille, an experienced commander who had served some years against Wellington in the Peninsula. The commander of one of his four infantry divisions was Napoleon's youngest brother Jérôme, ex-king of Westphalia, who has taken much of the blame for becoming obsessive about Hougoumont, ordering up increasing numbers of troops when it was obvious that they were achieving little; nevertheless, despite his family connections, Jérôme commanded only his own division, and it was Reille who was ultimately responsible for the expenditure of the troops who exhausted themselves against the walls of Hougoumont when they could have been employed to greater effect elsewhere. Jérôme later claimed that Napoleon had personally urged him to take Hougoumont 'at all costs', which would seem to absolve him of some of the blame; and there is perhaps some truth in Maxwell's remark about Reille's 'gross mismanagement'.[6]

The battle opened at about 11.20 a.m. with Jérôme's first attack, mounted by Bauduin's brigade (1st *Léger* and 3rd Line Regiments) which, preceded by its skirmishers and an artillery bombardment, advanced through the woods towards the southern defences of Hougoumont. (Edward Cotton, later a resident guide at the battlefield, was told by two separate officers that the first French column advanced to support the skirmishers at 11.50 a.m.) Their approach was visible to those on the ridge; Rees Gronow of the 1st Foot Guards recalled that there was first a burst of music from French bands, then their artillery opened, and finally, before their approach was hidden by gunsmoke, the French came on to the rapid drum-beat of the *pas de charge*, so familiar to Peninsular veterans and which, he said, not even the bravest could hear without an unpleasant sensation.

The Hanoverian *Jägers* and apparently three companies of Nassauers (the remaining three companies remaining in the buildings) disputed the woods for some time, causing heavy casualties (Bauduin himself was killed by a shot through the body). Weight of numbers, however, forced them back; and while the Germans apparently put up a sterling resistance, at least some of the Nassauers appear to have given way temporarily (in fairness, they had been mauled at Quatre Bras where they had lost their commanding officer, Major Sattler, and were commanded at Hougoumont by Captain Buschen). Wellington observed their flight and remarked to General Vincent, the Austrian attaché, 'Do you see those fellows run? Well, it is with these that I must win the battle, and such as these.'[7] However, he succeeded in rallying them; but perhaps at this stage – the exact time is not certain – some of the Nassauers are said to have fired on Wellington, fortunately without effect, and whether by accident or design is unknown. To what extent they aided the defence is unclear; early British accounts, which in general were not very generously disposed towards their Netherlandish allies (the Nassauers were part of the Netherlands army), refer mostly to their initial retirement, for example Daniel Mackinnon, who joined the action shortly after and wrote 'all attempts to rally these men proving fruitless'.[8] Another account, written shortly after the battle, expresses dissatisfaction at the retirement of 'the Dutch', and another was even more dismissive, claiming that after the Nassauers had been forced back, 'not a man was to be found on the ground after one o'clock, with the exception of *one officer*, who made his appearance about eight at night, after the action was over, for the purpose of asking a certificate of the loss of the colours of that corps by fire. This certificate was granted upon *his representation of the fact*, and no doubt at this moment forms a conspicuous proof and document of the *hard services* and *gallantry* of that distinguished body of troops.'[9]

Initially, the British Guards advanced to meet the French and maintained a sharp action for some time, to the right of the buildings and in the woods; they only withdrew into the defences as more French troops came up. The fight ebbed and flowed: George Standen recalled that the haystack near the south-west corner of the buildings was used as a rallying-point, 'behind which we repeatedly formed and charged',[10] and that it was set on fire during this stage of the action. On reaching the northern edge of the wood, the French found it impossible to cross the thirty-yard strip of open ground to the south wall of Hougoumont by virtue of the weight of fire directed against them from the buildings (even the roofs were loop-holed) and through and over the walls.

At this juncture, having lost perhaps 1,500 men already, it would have been prudent for Jérôme to have consolidated his position, for the woods were sufficiently extensive to shield from Wellington's view any concentration of troops preparing to drive around the right flank of the château. Instead he determined to take the château, which might have had the same effect as an outflanking movement in its potential for drawing in Wellington's reserves, but which would be most costly to the attackers. The failure to breach the walls with artillery – guns were available had Jérôme requested them – was perhaps the greatest error on the part of the attackers. It was not that Jérôme lacked advisers; his own chief-of-staff, General Guilleminot, urged against renewing the assault, and as corps commander Reille could have over-ruled him, but did not. In fairness it should be mentioned that the wood considerably inhibited the field for artillery-fire; this point was noted as early as 1816 by Sir John Sinclair, Bt. in his editorial to the translation of Müffling's *History of the Campaign*, (London, 1816, pp. 145–6). Sinclair only visited the field as a tourist, but as ex-commander of the Rothsay and Caithness Fencibles, his military opinion is worth consideration, and is confirmed by one of the defenders, who stated that the post's real strength was the wood which prevented direct artillery-fire upon the buildings which, he thought, were so ill-made that they would have been as impervious to cannon-fire as brown paper, and could have been reduced to rubble in ten minutes. Nevertheless there were sufficient French resources available to protect a battery which could have been established on the far left of the French position, to breach Hougoumont's west wall, which would have rendered the post untenable.

Instead, Jérôme ordered the advance of his 2nd Brigade under General Soye, 8,000 men of the 1st and 2nd Line, which allowed the mauled battalions of the 1st Brigade to swing around Hougoumont's right flank. The approach of Soye's brigade through the wood was noticed by Wellington from his position on the ridge, which coupled with the retirement of the Nassauers gave cause for concern. The commander of Wellington's horse artillery, Sir Augustus Frazer also observed it, and after receiving permission from his immediate superior, the Earl of Uxbridge (Wellington's cavalry commander), sent for the one battery in the Allied army which was equipped entirely with howitzers, Major Robert Bull's troop of Royal Horse Artillery. Cooke's divisional artillery (Captain Sandham's battery of Royal Artillery and Major Kuhlmann's troop of King's German Legion Horse Artillery) had already been providing supporting fire to the château – an officer in the attacking columns told Edward Cotton that their very first shot had struck down seventeen men – but only the arching trajectory of howitzers was capable of 'indirect fire', i.e., over obstacles or friendly troops.

When Frazer notified Wellington of Bull's arrival, the Duke quickly explained the delicacy of the task, that the wood held Frenchmen but that part of it (presumably meaning the orchard) still had Allied troops in it. Frazer expressed complete confidence in Bull's ability, then watched as he laid down a bombardment of 'spherical case-shot' (shrapnel which burst over the heads of the enemy, showering them with musket-balls). Within ten minutes the attack had been halted as Soye's men were cut down in swathes, forcing them out of the wood; Bull ceased fire on Wellington's orders, but when French troops were again observed, Bull recommenced and remained in action until withdrawn for replenishment of ammunition in the early afternoon.

The withdrawal of the Nassauers opened the château's left flank to possible attack; so Saltoun's two light companies were again hustled down the slope, into the hollow way, and, once more encouraged by Wellington, passed through the northern hedge of the orchard and cleared it of Frenchmen. They found the southern hedge so broken down that they were unable to maintain a permanent defensive position, so that as Saltoun described: 'The whole was a succession of attacks against the front of that post attended with more or less partial success for the moment, but in the end always repulsed.'[11] During this back-and-forth fight in the orchard, one attack was so heavy that Saltoun's men were driven out of the orchard entirely and into the hollow way; the French thereupon lined what remained of the southern hedge and brought up a gun in support. Again Saltoun charged across the orchard with his own men and about 50 Hanoverian riflemen, attempted but failed to take the gun, but re-established his hold on the southern hedge, and was never again driven from it. During this fighting he had no fewer than four horses shot from under him, but his conspicuous leadership and carelessness of danger must have provided an inestimable boost to the morale of his men during this desperate contest. In these attacks, the French came under constant fire from the loopholed garden wall, against which so much musketry was directed from behind the southern hedge that it was thought the red brick glimpsed through the hedge caused the French to believe it was redcoats in line. On other occasions the French attackers were so bold that they ran right up to the wall and tried to pull the guardsmen's muskets out of the loopholes.

The French attacks seem to have come in rushes, between which a continuous fusillade was maintained by French sharpshooters. Probably in an attempt to drive these away, Captain Charles Dashwood led his 3rd Guards' light company out of the defences into the open ground at the south-west corner, engaging the sharpshooters in the fringes of the woods and from the hedges to the west of Hougoumont. Matthew Clay was one of the last to quit the shelter of the kitchen garden and move into the open, where he observed Ensign Standen waving his shako in one hand and his sword in the other, calling upon his men to follow him in a charge. Clay and an experienced old hand, Guardsman Gann, took cover behind the haystack and began to exchange shots with the sharpshooters, failing to notice the retreat of their comrades in the face of an attack launched by Bauduin's brigade, which passed the west wall and made for the great North Gate. Clay and his pal decided that it was time for them to retire also, but not before Clay took post on some higher ground by the west wall, hoping it would provide a better vantage-point from which to shoot; but as French bullets whistled around his ears and hit the wall behind him, he realised that his red coat had made *him* the more prominent target, so he sheltered instead behind a stack of clover. Clay and Gann remained outside the defences until a lull in the fighting enabled them to follow their comrades and re-enter Hougoumont by the North Gate, where they found a scene of considerable carnage.

What had occurred was probably the most famous episode in the story of the defence of the château. As Dashwood's company retired along the west side of the farm, the French pursued them and made to enter the open North Gate. Dashwood's men had something of a running fight until they were able to regain the defences, in the course of which Sergeant Ralph Fraser of the 3rd Guards was attacked by Colonel Cubières of the 1st *Léger*, leading the brigade after Bauduin's death.

Somehow Fraser managed to unhorse the colonel (the story that this was achieved by hooking Cubières from the saddle by his spontoon[12] must be questionable, as sergeants of light companies did not normally carry that unwieldy polearm, but a musket or carbine instead); and leaving Cubières wounded on the ground, mounted the horse himself and rode it through the gate and into the courtyard. Although Cubières lay wounded for some time at the foot of the wall, the British refused to shoot at him, and he was able to make his way to safety; in later years he recalled the incident whenever he spoke of Waterloo, Alexander Woodford remarking that when he conversed with Cubières, 'he says ... he owes us much for many good years since', and that of the circumstances of his escape 'he always makes a great deal'.[13]

Dashwood's company closed the North Gate with the French literally at their heels; as Lieutenant George Evelyn was helping to close the gates he dropped to his knees, not knowing where he had been hurt until he saw his arm hanging limp: he had been shot through a hole in the gate. Seven or eight men of his company gathered around, declaring that as the French were breaking in, they would defend him to the last man; but he was helped inside one of the buildings until he could be evacuated with the walking wounded.

The French did, indeed, break in. Lieutenant Legros of the 1st *Léger* (a powerful man known as *l'enfonceur* – 'the smasher') seized a pioneer's axe and swung it against the double doors; as the wood splintered he led a charge into the farmyard, followed by probably some 30 or 40 men (accounts which claim as many as 100 got inside are probably exaggerations). At once the yard was filled with furious hand-to-hand combat as the French rush drove back the defenders, who retired to the surrounding buildings and began to fire upon the intruders, as did others from the château windows. One of the garrison's officers (sometimes described as a Hanoverian but apparently the Nassauer Lieutenant Diederich von Wilder) attempted to seek refuge in the farm-house, but as he was opening the door a French pioneer swung his axe and cut off von Wilder's left hand. Other defenders took refuge 'within a low range of hog-styes that occupied one side of the farmyard, but concealed, as they might have remained [but] their bold spirit spurned such compromise with their duty; even from such a refuge ... and from the air-holes of the styes, on the very level of the ground, and surrounded with straw, which a spark might have ignited and suffocated every man, they opened a musketry fire of great accuracy and constancy, and maintained it until the farmyard was evacuated by the French'[14]

When the French broke in, James Macdonell was by the garden gate, but alerted by shouts of '*Vive l'Empereur!*', he hurried to the archway which connected the two courtyards. Here he found a party of the 1st *Léger* in a desperate tussle with some Hanoverian riflemen, and as the Frenchmen went down under the Hanoverians' musket-butts, Macdonell realised the necessity of securing the North Gate before any more Frenchmen got inside. Calling for assistance, he ran across the farmyard towards the open gate, followed by Captain Henry Wyndham and Ensigns James Hervey and Henry Gooch, all of the Coldstream. They were joined by some of the defenders from the adjoining buildings, Corporals James and Joseph Graham, Irish brothers in the Coldstream, and a handful of 3rd Guardsmen including Sergeants Ralph Fraser, Joseph Aston and Bruce McGregor, and Private Joseph Lester (there are various accounts of exactly who was involved; Joseph Graham may have been wounded by this time, for example).

Macdonell and James Graham, both powerful men, each put their shoulders to a gate, and closed the opening just as more French arrived outside; one of these, more audacious than the rest, climbed upon the shoulders of his comrades to look over the wall, and levelled his musket at Wyndham, who was just inside the gate, instructing James Graham where to deposit a baulk of timber to barricade the gates. Wyndham was holding a loaded musket, and seeing the Frenchman taking aim, calmly handed it to Graham (who had dropped his burden) and pointed out the Frenchman; they fired simultaneously, the Frenchman's shot going wide but Graham's taking his adversary in the head, and the Frenchman fell back among his comrades on the outside of the gate. As some of the defenders piled scrap wood against the gates, others hunted down those French who had broken in, all of whom were killed or wounded; it was said that only a drummer was spared. (Although it is generally assumed that there was only one French incursion, some sources refer to the gate being forced a second time, either at this point or later; conceivably the original attack was seconded by a second party before the gate was finally secured.)

The French still outside the north and west faces of Hougoumont presented a grave danger, but help for the garrison was at hand. Observing the fighting around the North Gate from his position on the ridge, Major-General Byng ordered the 2nd Battalion Coldstream Guards to advance; their commanding officer, Colonel Alexander Woodford, immediately sent two companies to attack the French on the west side of Hougoumont: the grenadier company of Captain and Lieutenant-

Colonel 'Dan' MacKinnon and No. 1 Company under Lieutenant and Captain Thomas Sowerby. MacKinnon, the commander of this detachment, was one of the army's great 'characters'; an inveterate practical joker (in the Peninsula he once impersonated the Duke of York at a grand Spanish function, dispelling the illusion by diving head-first into a bowl of punch), he was also acknowledged as the greatest athlete in the army, a man of immense strength and athleticism who could win bets by scrambling over roof-tops. Such daring doubtless stood him in good stead as he led his two companies into action, driving the French from the west wall. The regiment's No. 4 company then followed (that commanded by Captain and Lieutenant-Colonel the Hon. Edward Acheson), and together the three companies pushed the French back into the wood where they remained to dispute the ground for some time. Here Acheson had a narrow escape when his horse, Moses, was shot dead and pinned its rider underneath when it fell; stunned by the fall, Acheson appeared dead and thus was left alone by the French as the fight raged over him. After recovering his senses, it was only with difficulty that Acheson was able to drag himself from under the horse, leaving his boot behind. MacKinnon was also wounded in this fight, by a musket-ball in the knee-cap; but he remained on duty despite the agony, and in a letter written five days later expressed more concern over the loss of a fine grey horse which was killed at the same time.

It was evidently after the North Gate had been cleared of Frenchmen that Clay and his comrade regained the inside of the compound, passing Captain Dashwood and Lieutenant Evelyn who were making their way to the rear in search of medical treatment. Entering the yard, Clay noticed Macdonell carrying a tree-trunk to help barricade the gate; his cheek was bloodstained and his horse lay dead a short way off. Clay noticed that the gates were riddled with shot-holes, and remarked upon the heaps of bodies inside the gateway, so muddy and trampled that they were scarcely identifiable; but he noticed in particular the body of a French officer, though did not record why it so attracted his attention. Presumably it was from the size of the man, for it must have been the gallant Legros, *l'enfonceur*, who was killed in the farmyard shortly after he broke in.

Woodford followed MacKinnon's three companies down the outside of the west wall, and being assured that the French had gone, entered the compound by the door in that wall. MacKinnon's companies then retired into the defences, and as a further reinforcement Woodford brought down the remainder of the battalion, leaving companies Nos. 7 and 8 on the ridge to protect the unit's Colours. Although the senior officer, Woodford declined to take command from Macdonell, so they took on the defence of the post together. Additional supporting fire was now available from the Bremevörde battalion of Hanoverian *Landwehr* and from elements of the Brunswick Corps (*Leib-Bataillon* and riflemen from the *Avant-Garde)*, ordered by Wellington to the north-west of Hougoumont, though not within the compound. In a fight so confused and incessant, it is difficult to be precise about the time; Woodford thought that he was sent to reinforce Hougoumont at about noon or just after, but it was surely later, perhaps nearer 1.30 p.m. Even in question is the number of attacks made upon the château; accounts vary between three main assaults and seven, and under such conditions it is difficult to be precise about the sequence of various events.

What is not in doubt is that shortly after Woodford's arrival, or perhaps simultaneous with it, another major attack was mounted upon the east of the orchard, by fresh troops: Gauthier's Brigade of Foy's 9th Division, comprising the 92nd and 93rd Line. To help Saltoun's mauled and doubtless exhausted men, the grenadier and No. 1 companies of the 3rd Guards were sent down from the ridge; it was apparently about this time that Saltoun made his unsuccessful attempt to capture the French gun. Saltoun's men must have been almost fought to a standstill, so observing the continuing conflict around the orchard, Sir John Byng sent down the remainder of the 3rd Guards to relieve him; less a guard for their Colours, which like those of the Coldstream, remained on the ridge. The first reinforcement was led by Captain and Lieutenant-Colonel Douglas Mercer, but the battalion's commanding officer, Colonel Francis Hepburn, soon joined; apparently the various companies were sent down the slope separately, and guided in turn into Hougoumont by Sergeant-Major McGregor. Hepburn thought it was about 1 p.m. when Byng ordered him to Hougoumont, but this would appear to be another case of mistaken timing: by Saltoun's calculation, it was about 2 p.m. when Hepburn met him in the hollow way behind the orchard, and formally took over command of that sector. Saltoun retired to the ridge with the remnant of his own men for a welcome rest before they participated in their regiment's triumphs later in the day.

Saltoun must have pulled his men back upon Hepburn's arrival, for the latter recalled how he assembled his companies in the hollow way, and after a pause advanced through the orchard and drove the French from the hedge, 'which I considered my post'.[15] Hepburn remained in command of that sector for the remainder of the day, though of his regiment it was Captain and Lieutenant-Colonel Francis Home, Macdonell's deputy in the château, who received the praise in Wellington's dispatch, Hepburn being overlooked. The omission is the more marked if one takes into account the fact that Hepburn had assumed command of the entire brigade after Byng had to take over the division when Cooke was wounded. (Staff officers were just as much at risk as ordinary soldiers in such circumstances; indeed, Byng's ADC, Captain Henry Dumaresq of the 9th Foot was shot through the lungs at Hougoumont while carrying a message to Wellington, but succeeded in delivering it. He survived though the ball was never extracted.) The matter of Home's authority was the cause of some acrimonious correspondence in 1836, when an officer who had been present claimed that Hepburn had only arrived after 4 p.m. and made no contribution to the fight, an opinion strenuously refuted by others, including Byng, who stated that it was shortly before 2 p.m. that he sent Hepburn to Hougoumont, who 'received my orders with marked pleasure, and with alacrity obeyed them' (though Byng admitted that after looking at his watch when the action began – 11.35 a.m. he thought – he didn't consult it again until 4 p.m.).[16]

As virtually an entire brigade was now deployed to defend Hougoumont, with others in support, one may question whether Napoleon's plan to divert Wellington's resources had succeeded. In fact, it had not, for the only troops used were those positioned on the right wing anyway, and troops had not been pulled in from the centre as Napoleon had intended. Had Hougoumont been outflanked to the west, Wellington's planning would have been more seriously disrupted (though the force he maintained much farther west, around Hal, could have acted against any serious outflanking manoeuvre); but with the defenders of Hougoumont holding firm, and with Jérôme's intention to take the post, the château soaked up all the French efforts on that wing.

Between 2 and 3 p.m. the defenders of Hougoumont appear to have experienced a slight respite, except for continuous skirmish-fire. Another fresh formation, General Bachelu's 5th Division of Reille's corps, approached from the south, but devoid of the cover of woodland and in front of Wellington's line; it was so severely mauled by artillery that the attack was pulled back before ever reaching the Hougoumont defences. Concerned about the increasing number of casualties being sustained in what was intended only as a diversionary action (yet perhaps unwilling to admit weakness by abandoning the attempt), probably shortly before 3 p.m. Napoleon turned his personal attention to Hougoumont. He ordered a concentration of howitzers against the post, in the hope that if his troops were unable to evict the defenders, they might perhaps be burned out. Accordingly – and belatedly – the French fired carcasses (incendiary shells) into the compound; within moments the château and large barn were ablaze. The defenders were evidently still fully occupied in firing at the French outside, so with little that they could do to extinguish the flames, the fire took hold so quickly that they simply had to suffer the heat and smoke. Even Woodford, in his very matter-of-fact account, noted that 'the heat and smoke of the conflagration were very difficult to bear' – surely an extreme understatement – and that 'several men were burnt, as neither Colonel Macdonell nor myself could penetrate to the stables where the wounded had been carried'.[17] This must have been the worst part of the entire day: the wounded had been placed under cover to keep them safe, only for the helpless men to be killed by the flames. The interior of Hougoumont at this stage must have possessed more than a passing resemblance to the infernal region itself.

The smoke and flames immediately attracted Wellington's attention. Ever vigilant, he pencilled a rapid note to the commander of the defenders (it was not addressed because the Duke would have had no way of knowing who was alive in Hougoumont). It read:

'I see that the fire has communicated from the Hay Stack to the Roof of the Château. You must however still keep your Men in those parts that the fire does not reach. Take care that no Men are lost by falling in of the Roof or floors. After they will have fallen in occupy the Ruined walls inside the Garden; particularly if it should be possible for the Enemy to pass through the Embers in the inside of the House'.[18]

The message was carried by Major Andrew Hamilton of the 4th West India Regiment, ADC to Sir Edward Barnes, the adjutant-general; at Hougoumont he handed it to Francis Home, which led to the minor confusion about who was actually in command. At least according to the witness whose statements about Hepburn were subsequently contradicted, on his arrival at Hougoumont Home he sent a sergeant to find either Macdonell or Woodford to report his arrival, but the man returned saying that he could not find them (he cannot have looked far!), and so when Hamilton rode in with the Duke's message, Home believed himself the senior officer present, and told Hamilton so. The latter must have had doubts, for having repeated verbally the order that the post had to be held 'to the very last, and on no account give it up or abandon it', he rode away but returned shortly, asking if Home were sure he understood the full extent of the order, as the Duke 'holds the maintaining of this post to be essential to the success of the operations of the day. It must on no account be given up'.[19] Upon Home affirming that the Guards *would* hold, Hamilton transmitted the reply to the Duke, and hence it was Home's name which appeared in the dispatch. When the true facts became known, while the Guards were quartered in Paris, a meeting was convened in the presence of both Home and Hepburn to determine how the mistake had occurred.

And hold on the Guards did, despite the increasing ferocity of the blaze. Matthew Clay had been posted in an upper room in the château from where he and his comrades were able to fire down upon the French skirmishers. As the château began to burn, the officer in command, Ensign Henry Gooch of the Coldstream, placed himself at the door to prevent any man leaving, until the fire became so intense that they feared the floor was about to collapse. Only at the very last moment did they quit their post, several being injured as they made their escape. As the fire raged, Corporal James Graham (one of the heroes of the gate) left his post at the wall to ask Macdonell if he might be excused for a moment. Knowing the man's bravery, the colonel inquired the reason; Graham answered that his wounded brother lay helpless in one of the burning buildings; and not until he received permission did the heroic Graham drag his brother clear of the flames, and then return to his post. Something else impressed Ensign George Standen at this dreadful time: he recalled how three or four of the officers' horses rushed out of the burning stables, but with no one free to attend to them, they re-entered the burning building and were lost.

The château was entirely consumed, but for the wounded who had been placed in the small chapel it seemed as if a miracle occurred. The flames entered the doorway and began to burn the feet of the figure of Christ which hung above the door; but having singed the base of the figure, the flames suddenly retreated, leaving the chapel and its occupants safe. Standen confirmed that the story: 'the fire burning only to the foot of the Cross is perfectly true, which in so superstitious a country made a great sensation'.[20] The burning of the place seems also to have been the cause of the exit of the only civilians to remain there once the fighting had begun. According to the information gleaned by Sir John Sinclair on his trip to Waterloo shortly after the battle, those who lived at the farm had left on the evening of the 17th, including the gardener, his wife and child, but returned for a short time on the morning of the 18th to take away some goods. Evidently the gardener and his 5-year-old daughter remained behind too long and became caught up by accident in the battle; they had been treated with every kindness by the Guardsmen, who had broken up some of their biscuits to feed the child, but after the buildings began to burn it must have been decided that they should be taken to safety, and they were escorted out of the North Gate.

The conflicting evidence concerning the time at which various events occurred also involves another famous incident, the replenishment of the garrison's ammunition. MacKinnon's history states that 'About one o'clock a cart of ammunition, which had been sent for early in the day, was brought into the farmyard of Hugomont [sic], and proved most seasonable',[21] yet the officer apparently responsible for its arrival was certain that it happened late in the day. In any event, ammunition was running dangerously low when apparently Ensign Berkeley Drummond, acting adjutant of the 3rd Foot Guards, asked one of the Earl of Uxbridge's ADCs for help in procuring a fresh supply. This officer, Captain Horace Beauchamp Seymour of the 18th Hussars (reputedly the strongest man in the British Army), stated in his own account that he was 'called by some Officers of the 3rd Guards defending Hougoumont to use my best endeavours to send them musket ammunition'. He encountered a private of the Royal Waggon Train with a tumbrel of ammunition on the ridge; Seymour gave him no order (obviously because of the hazardous nature of the service) but 'merely pointed out to him where he was wanted'. The man immediately drove his horses straight down the ridge and into the North Gate; Seymour was surprised to see him arrive, because of the intense fire flying all around, and was surely correct in commenting that 'I feel convinced to that man's service the Guards owe their ammunition'.[22] The hero's name was not recorded at the time, but almost certainly he was Joseph Brewer, a member of the Waggon Train who later transferred to the 3rd Guards (presumably in recognition of the service he had performed for them), rose to the rank of corporal and received a medal from the regiment.[23]

Elsewhere on the field, the great French cavalry attacks were mounted, which the defenders of Hougoumont witnessed but in which they were not involved. Instead, they were occupied by another assault on the orchard, by two regiments of Foy's division and the survivors of Bachelu's. Hepburn's 3rd Guards in the orchard were forced back to the hollow way; but as the French followed them across the orchard they received such a fire from the Coldstreams, enfilading from behind the garden wall, that they were 'completely staggered',[24] which enabled Hepburn's men to counter-attack and repossess the orchard. (The trees were by now so shot to pieces that they provided little cover for the French, hence the destructiveness of the musketry over the garden wall.) Casualties among the 3rd Guards' officers were especially heavy; a sergeant had to take over No. 7 company after Lieutenant and Captain the Hon. Hastings Forbes (son of the Earl of Granard) was killed, and Ensigns Charles Lake and David Baird were wounded (the latter the nephew of the renowned general Sir David Baird, to whose baronetcy the ensign succeeded in 1829). The company's fourth officer, Lieutenant and Captain R. H. Wigston, was one of three officers of the battalion guarding the unit's baggage at Waterloo.

During this time Matthew Clay was still defending the buildings of Hougoumont, though his account is somewhat confused (not surprisingly, given the conditions); he wrote of French artillery twice bursting open the gates (presumably the South Gate), one roundshot penetrating and striking a pile of the farm's firewood, sending it flying in all directions, a trivial memory but one which lends credence to the story. Clay mentioned how a party of French gained entry but were driven out, all except a drummer boy who was captured and under Clay's supervision was lodged in an outhouse; but this must refer to the break-in at the North Gate. Finally, Clay helped defend a breach in the wall, evidently in an upstairs room, the masonry having fallen among the bodies of dead defenders. The other side of the breach was defended by Sergeant Joseph Aston, one of the few 'other ranks' of the regiment at Waterloo who subsequently gained a commission (as quartermaster in 1833).

Towards the end of the day, a final assault was made on the farm by Jérôme and on the orchard by Foy. Once again Hepburn's men were outflanked and withdrew to the hollow way, and again the enfilading fire over the garden wall repelled the French. As they fell back, Hepburn advanced through the orchard and his men lined what remained of the southern hedge. At last he received reinforcements; he described them as *Landwehr* but apparently they included Brunswick light infantry and riflemen. With this augmentation, Hepburn was able to take the offensive, sending the newly arrived troops and two of his own companies into the wood, where they engaged the French in a heavy fire-fight. It is sometimes stated that elements of du Plat's King's German Legion brigade were engaged at Hougoumont comparatively early in the action; some may have been, but Beamish's history of the K.G.L., evidently drawing upon an account by Adolphus Hesse, adjutant of the 2nd K.G.L. Line Battalion, states that du Plat's and part of the 3rd Hanoverian Brigade 'had stood in column without being employed, during the early part of the day, but when, about four o'clock, the enemy's cavalry, passing through the intervals of the squares, penetrated to the second line, their front was changed, and they were moved in the direction of Hougoumont',[25] and it was evidently subsequent to this that the K.G.L. came into action at Hougoumont itself.

Demonstrating how Hougoumont was a battle within a battle, even though he commanded the brigade (Byng having stepped up to lead the division), Hepburn commented that throughout the fighting, 'I knew nothing of what was passing elsewhere',[26] which must have been even more true for his bloodied and exhausted men. For an hour after the final attack Hepburn held his position, occupied only by the fighting in the wood, and perhaps by desultory skirmish-fire still incoming; then a staff officer came up at a gallop, bearing orders for an immediate advance, as the entire army was moving forward in pursuit of the French, who were at last withdrawing and disintegrating under the combined pressure of Wellington's dogged defence and the arrival of the Prussians on the French right. It was probably at this time that the K.G.L. took their part in the fighting at Hougoumont, as the 2nd Line Battalion and the skirmishers of the rest of the brigade 'threw themselves into the ditch by which the place was surrounded'[27] and helped drive off the French (though from a reference in Beamish's account to this fight taking place in 'the garden' – perhaps actually the orchard – it may refer to an earlier stage in the fighting). In the final advance, what had been du Plat's brigade (he was killed in the fighting) moved forward to the left of Hougoumont, presumably with the 2nd K.G.L. Line Battalion nearest the château; but the Salzgitter Battalion of Hanoverian *Landwehr* was positioned even farther right, and charged into the Hougoumont woods; this was presumably the *Landwehr* reinforcement to which Hepburn referred.

As Hepburn ordered his men forward, over the hedge and into the fields beyond, the French retired 'in no order',[28] scarcely firing a shot. It was presumably during this brief advance that Henry Wyndham was reported to have almost captured Jérôme Bonaparte, who leaped out of one door of his carriage as Wyndham entered by another. If the French had finally cracked after such battering upon the walls of Hougoumont, neither were the Guards in any state to pursue, being utterly exhausted; so having ascertained that the French retreat was irreversible, Hepburn ordered his men into a field at the rear of Hougoumont, to bivouac for the night. The regimental picquets posted in the woods for the night were drawn from the companies which throughout the day had remained on the ridge with the Colours.

As evening drew on, the fires in Hougoumont subsided, but the remains of the buildings continued to glow, casting an eerie light upon the scenes of slaughter. Stood-down from his post after the fighting ended with the retreat of the French, Matthew Clay began to cast around for something to eat, having hardly tasted a morsel for two days. Entering the kitchen of one of the surviving buildings, he found it full of wounded, of all nationalities; and some foreign troops, who he thought were Belgians, began to menace the French wounded with their bayonets. The British intervened and prevented the Belgians doing them any further harm. Finding a glowing fire in the ruins, Clay took from his haversack the piece of half-cooked pig's head and laid it in the embers to finish cooking; but on closer examination saw that the glow was emanating from a burning corpse, and hungry though he was, Clay found the prospect of eating his pork cooked in such a way so revolting that he could not stomach it. Instead, he found a small cooking-pot, its contents covered with dust, ash and debris, but just edible, so ate that instead. Even now his duties were not ended; together with Robert Brooker, a private in his company who had been almost blinded by an explosion of gunpowder, he was ordered to carry firewood from the château to the field at the rear, to supply the camp-fires of the Guards' bivouac. The exertions of the day caught up with him and he almost collapsed under the weight of wood, only just managing to negotiate a bank between the château and the field, but arrived in time to answer his name in the evening calling of the roll.

The morning of 19 June revealed a quite ghastly sight around Hougoumont. Cavalié Mercer, who had commanded a troop of horse artillery during the battle, set off for a sight-seeing trip around Hougoumont, the ferocity of the fighting having 'rendered it an object of interest'. He found awful scenes: 'The immediate neighbourhood of Hougoumont was more thickly strewn with corpses than most other parts of the field – the very ditches were full of them. The trees all about were most woefully cut and splintered, both by cannon-shot and musketry. The courts of the Château presented a spectacle more terrible even than any I had yet seen. A large barn had been set on fire, and the conflagration had spread to the offices, and even to the main building. Here numbers, both of French and English, had perished in the flames, and their blackened swollen remains lay scattered about in all directions. Amongst this heap of ruins and misery many poor devils yet remained alive, and were sitting up endeavouring to bandage their wounds. Such a scene of horror, and one so sickening, was surely never witnessed. Two or three German dragoons were wandering among the ruins, and many peasants. One of the former was speaking to me when two of the latter, after rifling the pockets, &c., of a dead Frenchman, seized the body by the shoulders, and raising it from the ground, dashed it down again with all their force, uttering the grossest abuse, and kicking it about the head and face – revolting spectacle! – doing this, no doubt, to court favour with us. It had a contrary effect, which they soon learned. I had scarcely uttered an exclamation of disgust, when the dragoon's sabre was flashing over the miscreants' heads, and in a moment descended on their backs and shoulders with such vigour that they roared again, and were but too happy to make their escape.'[29]

Leaving this infernal scene, Mercer entered the garden, where he found a transformation, 'long straight walks of turf overshadowed by fruit-trees, and between these beds of vegetables, the whole enclosed by a tolerably high brick wall'. After three days of death and exertion, it seemed a glimpse of Heaven, with birdsong and the hum of insects replacing the recent cacophony of battle. 'Nature in repose is always lovely: here, and under such circumstances she was delicious. Long I rambled in this garden, up one walk, down another, and thought I could dwell here contented for ever. Nothing recalled the presence of war except the loopholed wall and two or three dead Guardsmen; but the first caused no interruption, and these last lay so concealed amongst the exuberant vegetation of turnips and cabbages, &c., that, after coming from the field of death without, their pale and silent forms but little deteriorated my enjoyment. The leaves were green, roses and other flowers bloomed forth in all their sweetness, and the very turf when crushed by the feet smelt fresh and pleasant.'[30]

Such idyllic scenes were not repeated on the other side of the garden wall. Rees Gronow of the 1st Guards, who also made a sightseeing trip that morning, found the orchard strewn with heaps of bodies. The scavengers had not yet been at work, for the corpses were still clad in their uniforms, red (Guardsmen), blue (French) and green (Germans); so ghastly was the sight that it seemed to Gronow that not less than 2,000 men must be lying dead or stricken in the orchard. He noticed especially the apple trees, their trunks riddled and with shattered branches hanging down, so that it appeared they had been transformed into weeping willows. The analogy was appropriate, for instead of Mercer's pleasant reverie, Gronow could think only that upon that spot he had lost some of his dearest friends. The surrounds of the orchard were similarly piled with dead; a senior officer later told Edward Cotton that although he had fought in most of the Peninsular War battles, only at a breach had he seen the dead lie thicker than along the hedge.

Others visited Hougoumont that morning for more practical reasons than sightseeing, for the well was one of the few sources of water on the battlefield. Mercer's battery drew water from it, but when Matthew Clay and a corporal were sent back to Hougoumont they found the well almost empty and surrounded by soldiers clamouring for a drink. Clay wandered off, found some biscuit on the body of a dead Guardsman, some butter by the body of a Frenchman, picked some unripe fruit from the garden and made a passable breakfast. He then entered the wood, which he found carpeted with French bodies, testimony to their own persistence and to the effectiveness of the British musketry. By the burned haystack he found the remains of many of his comrades, the bodies dried and shrivelled from the heat of the burning hay. As he made his way back to his unit he passed parties of soldiers collecting the wounded, and compelling local inhabitants (out seeking plunder) to carry off the injured in blankets; Clay noticed particularly a wounded Frenchman sitting by the side of the garden, unable to rise but imperiously declining the assistance he offered. Clay rejoined his battalion in time to accompany them in pursuit of the defeated French, and not until the end of that day's march did they have the opportunity to wash off the grime of battle, and finally receive some rations.

It is difficult to ascertain casualty-figures for the defence of Hougoumont, at least for units that did not spend the entire battle there, but may have suffered losses elsewhere; this is especially true for the light companies of the 1st Foot Guards and the Nassau and Hanoverian troops. It is easier to evaluate the losses of the 2nd and 3rd Foot Guards.

On the morning of 18 June the official roll showed that the 2nd Foot Guards mustered 31 regimental and five staff officers, 58 sergeants (including three 'present sick', i.e., ill or injured but still with their unit), sixteen drummers and 988 rank and file (one and 49 'present sick' respectively); and the 3rd Foot Guards 32 regimental and three staff officers, 55 sergeants (two 'present sick'), 10 drummers and 998 rank and file (one and 41 'present sick' respectively).[31] (These statistics may not be absolutely precise: for example, Dalton's *Waterloo Roll Call* lists 27 regimental and four staff officers, and 34 and four respectively for the 2nd and 3rd Guards, and the situation is further complicated by the fact that both regiments also had officers serving in detached staff duties, and other circumstances; for example, Lieutenant and Captain John Stepney Cowell of the Coldstream was taken ill on the evening of the 17th and was sent to Brussels.)

From these figures, the first published casualty returns showed that the Coldstream lost one officer, one sergeant and 53 rank and file killed; seven officers, thirteen sergeants and 229 rank and file wounded; and one drummer and three rank and file missing, representing a loss of 28 per cent; and the 3rd Foot Guards three officers, two sergeants and 37 rank and file killed; nine officers, ten sergeants and 178 rank and file wounded, representing a loss of almost 22 per cent.[32] The Coldstream had one officer, a sergeant and 27 other ranks subsequently die of their injuries, and the 3rd Foot Guards three sergeants and 44 other ranks. MacKinnon's list does not specify which officers were actually engaged at Hougoumont, and is not entirely clear about the companies to which the various officers belonged (for example, he states that Charles W. Short of the Coldstream was an officer of the 5th Company, whereas by his own testimony[33] he was with the 7th and 8th Companies on the ridge). Siborne's list of officers 'present at the defence of Hougoumont'[34] includes officers who were in fact in staff appointments, Cowell who had gone to Brussels ill, those who were with the baggage-guard and some who were apparently not even at the battle, at least according to MacKinnon and Dalton, as well as those who were with the companies on the ridge. Siborne's list also includes Short, despite the fact that the officer in question had personally informed Siborne that he was on the ridge; and Siborne notes that 'I know not the names of the remaining officers of the light companies of the 1st Brigade of Guards detached to Hougoumont',[35] although these had been published by MacKinnon as early as 1833.

Severe though the officer casualties were, it is interesting to note that the 'other rank' losses among one of the most heavily engaged companies were not as severe as might have been expected, given the nature of the fighting. The roll of the Coldstream light company, completed shortly after the battle by Sergeant John Biddle[36] shows the loss of two NCOs and eleven privates dead or died of wounds, five NCOs and 20 privates wounded, and one drummer and one private captured but returned after the battle.

Among the wounded of the 3rd Foot Guards (but of course not mentioned in the official returns) was the newly married wife of Private

George Osborne (or Osbourn) of No. 1 Company. She had accompanied her husband throughout the battle, tending the wounded and using her spare clothing as bandages, until she was herself shot in the arm and left breast. She survived and was duly rewarded for her courage at the instigation of her husband's company commander, Captain and Lieutenant-Colonel Edward Bowater, himself one of the wounded attended by Mrs. Osborne.

French losses in the assaults on Hougoumont are impossible to quantify with exactitude; estimates range from about 5,000 to a more improbable 'above 10,000'. Probably the former figure is the most likely, though detailed calculations are complicated by the unresolvable problem of deciding whether casualties sustained by units manoeuvring in the vicinity of Hougoumont should be included, even were it possible to determine at what stage of the battle certain casualties were incurred. Of more significance than even such dreadful loss of life is the tactical effect of the attacks on Hougoumont, in occupying so much of Napoleon's army to virtually no advantage, and in frustrating his plan to compel a fatal weakening of Wellington's centre.

Indeed, the significance of Hougoumont was never in doubt from the very beginning, though at times the site has been neglected: Sir William Fraser, Bt. complained that when he visited Hougoumont for the third time he found the kitchen garden newly covered with vegetables, and the memorial plaque at the grave of Captain Thomas Craufurd of Kilbirnie, 3rd Guards 'removed, I am quite certain without the knowledge of the proprietor, in order to make room for a few more beans'.[37] (Craufurd's remains, like those of Lieutenant and Captain John Lucie Blackman of the Coldstream, who was buried where he fell in the orchard, were removed to Evre Cemetery in 1890; commemorative plaques are now in place.)

Wellington himself had no doubts about the significance of the defence of Hougoumont. On the evening of the battle, mindful of Müffling's earlier doubts about its defensibility, the Duke raised his telescope and remarked to his Prussian colleague, 'You see, Macdonell has held Hougoumont,' one of his few exclamations of satisfaction at the close of that dreadful day. He was more fulsome in his dispatch, remarking that Napoleon 'commenced a furious attack upon our post at Hougoumont. I had occupied that post with a detachment from General Byng's Brigade of Guards, which was in position in its rear; and it was for some time under the command of Lieutenant-Colonel Macdonell, and afterwards of Colonel Home; and I am happy to add that it was maintained throughout the day with the utmost gallantry by these brave troops, notwithstanding the repeated efforts of large bodies of the enemy to obtain possession of it.'[38] Thomas Creevey recorded that the Duke remarked at this time that no other troops could have held Hougoumont other than British, and only the best of them. This opinion was apparently shared widely; Rees Gronow remembered the reaction of General Maitland to Lord Saltoun and Lieutenant and Captain Charles Parker 'Charley' Ellis when they rejoined their regiment with the wreckage of their 1st Foot Guards' light companies: that their defence of Hougoumont had saved the army, that nothing could have been more gallant, and that every man deserved promotion. Saltoun replied that it had been touch and go, a matter of life and death, and that every one of the defenders had sworn never to surrender. Lieutenant and Captain James Gunthorpe of the 1st Guards, Maitland's brigade-major, who must at some time have been involved in the fighting at Hougoumont (though not listed as such) added that the officers had been determined not to yield, and that the men resolved to stand by their officers to the last.

Wellington's opinion of the importance of Hougoumont was confirmed by his answer to a singular request. In August 1815 he was contacted by the Revd. John Norcross, rector of Framlingham, Suffolk, who wished to bestow a pension of £10 p.a. for life upon a Waterloo soldier. The Duke requested Byng to choose a member of the 2nd Brigade as a tribute to the defence of Hougoumont, and it was to James Graham (by then promoted to sergeant) that the annuity was awarded. It ceased after two years upon the bankruptcy of the donor, but by the Reverend's will, £500 was left to 'the bravest man in England'. Asked to choose the beneficiary, Wellington wrote to Norcross' executors that 'The success of the battle ... turned upon the closing of the gates of Hougoumont',[39] and nominated Sir James Macdonell (he had been knighted subsequently). Generously, Macdonell recognised that he alone was not responsible, and shared the bequest equally, remarking that 'I cannot claim all the merit due to the closing of the gates of Hougoumont; for Sergeant John Graham, who saw with me the importance of the step, rushed forward, and *together* we shut the gates.'[40] Perhaps due to Macdonell's mistake, even the name of the hero has been confused, and is recorded elsewhere as John, whereas it was actually James Graham. The official rolls note that the other Graham in the company (obviously James's brother) was Corporal Joseph Graham; despite James's dragging him from the burning building, Joseph died of his wounds on 23 June. The Norcross money was not the only reward received by James Graham for his bravery: the sergeants of the regiment presented him with a medal 'in commemoration of his gallant conduct and devotion to duty'.[41] James Graham died at the Royal Hospital at Kilmainham in April 1843; the memorial plaque erected there was later transferred at the behest of his regiment to the church in his birthplace in Co. Monaghan. Other noted defenders lived long into the century; Alexander Woodford died in August 1870, having attained the rank of field marshal in 1868, and Ensign the Hon. Henry Montagu of the 3rd Foot Guards, who was just 17 years old at Waterloo, was one of the longest-lived Waterloo veterans. Succeeding his brother as 6th and last Baron Rokeby in 1847, he rose to the rank of general, served in the Crimea, became colonel-in-chief of his old regiment in 1875 (as had Woodford before him), and died in May 1883.

Hougoumont became a place of pilgrimage for British tourists from the earliest; among the first accounts was that of three English gentlemen who visited in July 1815, at a time so near to the battle that the imprint of horses' hooves were still visible in the hardened mud, the field was scattered with clothing and accoutrements, and huge piles of human ashes surrounded Hougoumont, marking the cremation-pyres of many of the fallen. In the garden they found a glorious scene of roses and geraniums, tended by the gardener who told them that he had been present during the battle, having not dared to leave once the fighting started. The tourists found the brick outer walls still pierced with two tiers of loop-holes, and contrasting with the garden, the château was just a mouldering ruin and 'scene of desolation'.[42] By the time William Siborne wrote his history of the campaign, the garden had vanished under weeds and wild flowers, the wood was entirely gone, and although the barn had been re-roofed and the gardener's house occupied by the farmer, the remainder 'present to the eye nothing more than crumbling walls, scattered stones, bricks and rubbish'; yet, as is to this day the case with the more carefully preserved ruins, 'there is not, perhaps ... any single feature of the field of Waterloo so well calculated to excite the interest of visitors as Hougoumont'.[43]

It remains to explain how it was that two battalions, with the assistance of some other units at various times and some artillery support, were able to withstand the combined attacks of approximately 15,000 members of an army which, by the general consensus of the victors, performed throughout the day with conspicuous heroism. Some British veterans of the Peninsular War even claimed that the French had never fought better, which is high praise indeed.

Part of the reason for the successful defence of Hougoumont must lie with the mistakes of the French command, in not deploying artillery, particularly in an attempt to breach the west wall. Perhaps the attacks could have been better co-ordinated, and it may be because separate assaults were made on individual sectors of the defences that Alexander Woodford remarked that after the first, most furious attempt, 'it always struck me that the subsequent attacks were feeble',[44] hardly an adjective that would generally be used to characterise the desperate fighting in the orchard in particular. Another participant even thought the merits of the defence 'somewhat overrated', in that the troops were in a defensive position, unlike those on the ridge, and that it was the tactical importance of the post which contributed to its fame.[45] It is also noteworthy that only the light companies of the 2nd and 3rd Guards were in action throughout: fresh troops were introduced at times, and those that had fought to a standstill (notably the remnants of Saltoun's 1st Foot Guards light companies) were withdrawn.

Such tactical points notwithstanding, the defence of Hougoumont must have depended heavily upon the nature of the troops involved. The Foot Guards were regarded as among the élite of the army, a fact proven in the most obvious way at Hougoumont; though they might be killed or the place burned around them, retreat or surrender was never even considered. The quality of leadership must have reinforced their inherent discipline and morale; that the troops had confidence in their leaders is unquestioned. As Sir William Fraser remarked, it was as if Wellington had been 'above humanity', and with him in command 'they no more believed that the French could beat them than that they could fly over their heads';[46] and the commanders involved personally at Hougoumont seem to have been not only militarily capable, but able to inspire by personal example. The comparatively fluid nature of the defence is evidence of tactical ability: by using the buildings of Hougoumont as a redoubt, but wherever possible endeavouring to engage the enemy outside these defences, the garrison was able to retire to comparative safety when the pressure grew too great, and to sally once again when the French had drawn off, hence the protracted fighting to the south and west of the compound, and the almost constant change of possession of the orchard. The leaders were also able to motivate by personal example, none more so than Macdonell, whose bravery under fire was tantamount to recklessness. That his conduct at Waterloo was no fluke seems proven by Sir William Fraser's encounter with him, in Macdonell's old age, at a shooting-party in dense woodland, when Macdonell calmly marched a fair distance in front of the other guns quite unconcerned that he was in danger of being shot in the back! The demeanour of other officers, such as Wyndham's calm reaction when he realised that he was the target of a sharpshooter, can only have reinforced the morale of their troops; and surely no compliment could have been greater than Wellington's description of Saltoun: 'a *thorough* soldier'.

Such factors led to what MacKinnon described as the 'calm and stubborn gallantry, that alone could have enabled so small a force to resist the repeated and fierce assaults'.[47] Wellington remarked that 'the Division of Guards ... set an example which was followed by all',[48] and as Sinclair wrote, they 'so gallantly maintained the high character they have so long established for firmness, intrepidity, and valour'.[49] This combination of regimental *esprit de corps*, training, discipline, leadership and the morale they combined to engender, and perhaps that most intangible of qualities, the character of the individual soldiers, produced a lasting fame. Scott wrote that the name of Hougoumont would be remembered when Agincourt, Crécy and Blenheim were forgotten, and it is characteristic of the public perception of the action that Tennyson went even further, implying that Hougoumont was the watershed which laid the path for wider successes later in the century, by those for

> 'whom the roar of Hougoumont
> Left mightiest of all peoples under Heaven'.[50]

NOTES

1. Wellington to Earl Bathurst, 19 June 1815; *Dispatches of Field Marshal the Duke of Wellington*, ed. J. Gurwood, London, 1834–8, XII, p. 481.
2. *The Life of Wellington*, Sir Herbert Maxwell, London, 1900, II, p. 56.
3. *The Waterloo Letters*, ed. Major-General H. T. Siborne, London 1891, pp. 263–4.
4. Ibid., p. 269.
5. 'More Reminiscences of Waterloo: The Defence of Hougomont', by 'W', in *United Service Journal*, 1836, II, p. 352.
6. Maxwell, *op. cit.*, II, p. 72.
7. *Personal Reminiscences of the Duke of Wellington*, Francis, Earl of Ellesmere, ed. Alice, Countess of Strafford, London, 1903, p. 157.
8. *Origin and Services of the Coldstream Guards*, Colonel D. MacKinnon, London, 1833, p. 217.
9. 'More Reminiscences ...' by 'W', p. 354.
10. *Waterloo Letters*, p. 268.
11. Ibid., p. 246.
12. See *With Napoleon at Waterloo*, E. B. Low, ed. MacK. MacBride, London, 1911, p. 127.
13. *Waterloo Letters*, p. 262.
14. 'Waterloo and the Waterloo Model', anon., in *United Service Journal*, 1839, II, p. 202.

15. *Waterloo Letters*, p. 266.
16. The argument regarding the status of Hepburn and Home was covered in *United Service Journal*, 1836, II, pp. 351–7, III, pp. 78–80, 255–8; the quotation from Byng is in ibid., III, p. 257.
17. *Waterloo Letters*, p. 262.
18. Illustrated in, for example, Maxwell, *op. cit.*, II, p. 74; this is the exact wording, which appears in a slightly different form in some sources.
19. 'More Reminiscences ...', p. 355.
20. *Waterloo Letters*, p. 269.
21. MacKinnon, *op. cit.*, II, p. 216.
22. *Waterloo Letters*, pp. 19–20.
23. Elsewhere his name appears as 'Gregory Brewster' (as given by Sir Arthur Conan Doyle and Sir Henry Irving, the latter on the stage), but 'Brewer' appears to be correct.
24. *Waterloo Letters*, p. 267.
25. *History of the King's German Legion*, N. L. Beamish, London, 1837, II, p. 379.
26. *Waterloo Letters*, p. 267.
27. Beamish, *op. cit.*, II, p. 379.
28. *Waterloo Letters*, p. 267.
29. *Journal of the Waterloo Campaign*, General A. C. Mercer, Edinburgh and London, 1870, I, pp. 347–8.
30. Ibid., pp. 349–50.
31. Statistics prepared by Lieutenant-Colonel J. Waters, Assistant-Adjutant-General, in *Dispatches of Field Marshal the Duke of Wellington*, XII, p. 486.
32. Statistics prepared by Waters, in *London Gazette*, 8 July 1815.
33. *Waterloo Letters*, p. 265.
34. *The Waterloo Campaign*, W. Siborne, London, 1844, II, p. 501.
35. Ibid.
36. The author is grateful to Alan Harrison for the opportunity to consult this document.
37. *Words on Wellington*, Sir William Fraser, Bt., London, 1889, pp. 258–9.
38. *Dispatches*, to Earl Bathurst, 19 June 1815, XII, p. 481.
39. Quoted in *A Voice from Waterloo*, E. Cotton, Brussels, 1900, p. 278 (9th edn.: orig. pubd. 1849).
40. Quoted in Low, *op. cit.*, p. 132.
41. *British and Irish Regimental and Volunteer Medals*, J. L. Balmer, Loughborough, 1988, I, p. 81.
42. 'A View of the Field of Waterloo a Few Weeks after the Engagement', anon., in *The Memorable Battle of Waterloo*, C. Kelly, London, 1817, pp. 108–11.
43. Siborne, *op. cit.*, I, pp. 343–4.
44. *Waterloo Letters*, p. 262.
45. 'More Reminiscences ... ', p. 356.
46. Fraser, *op. cit.*, p. 219.
47. MacKinnon, *op. cit.*, II, p. 218.
48. *Dispatches ...*, XII, p. 483.
49. *History of the Campaign ... in the Year 1815*, by 'C. de M.' (F. C. F. von Müffling), ed. Sir John Sinclair, London, 1816, p. 146.
50. 'To the Queen', Alfred, Lord Tennyson.

POSTSCRIPT

T
he foregoing chapters recount extraordinary feats of heroism, determination and endurance, performed for the most part by soldiers who probably would have regarded themselves as entirely unexceptional, and who after their momentous deeds mostly slipped back into obscurity, perhaps to reflect upon their past career, when each

'Sat by his fire, and talked the night away,

Wept o'er his wounds, or, tales of sorrow done,

Shouldered his crutch, and showed how fields were won.'[1]

For most of these individuals, their appearance belied their conduct in the great events in which they participated, and which they helped to form. As a boy, the war correspondent Archibald Forbes (1838–1900) once accompanied his minister father on a visit to a house at Auchin-roath, at the mouth of Glen Rothes. Forbes senior went inside, leaving the lad to look after their dogcart, and as he waited for his father's return, he was greeted by 'a very queer-looking old person, short of figure, round as a ball, his head shrunk between very high and rounded shoulders, and with short stumpy legs. He was curiously attired in a whole-coloured suit of gray; a droll-shaped jacket the great collar of which reached far up the back of his head, surmounted a pair of voluminous breeches which suddenly tightened at the knee'.[2] Young Forbes imagined him to be the butler, so hinted to the old person that a meat sandwich would be very acceptable, as the drive had made him ravenously hungry. The 'butler' asked him into the house for breakfast, but Forbes demurred, thinking that a servant would not have the authority to invite him indoors. Amid strong language, the old person declared imperiously, 'I am master here!', whereupon Forbes asked if he were the lord whom Forbes senior had come to visit. 'Of course I am!' said the old person; 'Who the devil else should I be?'

After breakfast, and with the permission of Forbes senior, the old man marched off with young Archibald to the Spey, into which he plunged up to the armpits, and showed the lad how to cast a rod; and with the aid of his drunken old gillie, landed a 15-pound salmon which he presented to young Forbes as a gift for his mother, and accompanied it with a half-sovereign so that the lad could buy himself a decent trout rod. All this time the old man had been answering the boy's questions about the great exploit of his life, describing with great 'spirit and vehemence' the braving of musketry and cannon fire, and of hand-to-hand bayonet-fighting, to which the young man listened with rapt attention, his disappointment at the unimpressive appearance of his host long forgotten.

The little old man may have looked nothing like a hero, but his animation and spirit were undimmed from his one great day of four decades earlier: he was Lord Saltoun, the defender of Hougoumont.

NOTES

1. *The Deserted Village*, Oliver Goldsmith.
2. *Camps, Quarters and Casual Places*, A. Forbes, London, 1896, pp. 155–6.

BIBLIOGRAPHY

Works of especial relevance to each chapter are listed below; further sources are listed in the footnotes.

General works

Chandler, D. G. *The Campaigns of Napoleon*, London, 1967.

– *Dictionary of the Napoleonic Wars*, London, 1979.

Esposito, V. J., and Elting, J. R. *Military History and Atlas of the Napoleonic Wars*, London, 1964; superb maps, covering all the campaigns in which Napoleon commanded.

Haythornthwaite, P. J. *The Napoleonic Source Book*, London, 1990.

Rothenberg, G. E. *The Art of War in the Age of Napoleon*, London, 1977.

Villers-en-Cauchies

Anon. 'Copies of the Official Testimonies proving the gallant Conduct of the 15th Light Dragoons on the 24th of April, 1794, in the Affair of Landrecies', in *British Military Library or Journal*, London, 1799–1801, I, pp. 105–8.

Anon. 'Sketch of the Action fought on the 24th of April, 1794, at Villers en Couché ...', in *British Military Library or Journal*, London, 1799–1801, II, pp. 176–8.

Cannon, R. *Historical Record of the Fifteenth, or, The King's Regiment of Light Dragoons, Hussars*, London, 1841.

Fortescue, the Hon. Sir John. *History of the British Army*, London, 1906, vol. IV.

Martin, E. J. 'A Note on the 15th Light Dragoons & Villers-en-Cauchie Medal', *Bulletin of the Military Historical Society*, 1955, VI, p. 43.

Matthews, A. S. 'The 15th Light Dragoons and the Battle of Villers en Cauchies', in *Journal of the Society for Army Historical Research*, 1964, XLII, p. 53.

Oman, Sir Charles, 'The 15th Light Dragoons at Villers-en-Cauchies, 24th March [*sic*] 1794', in *Journal of the Society for Army Historical Research*, 1937, XVII, pp. 12–14.

Randolph, E. H. (ed.). *Life of Sir Robert Wilson from autobiographical memoirs, journals, narratives, correspondence, &c.*, London, 1862; Wilson was present at the action. A modern biography is *A Very Slippery Fellow: The Life of Sir Robert Wilson 1777–1849*, M. Glover, Oxford, 1978.

Wood, General Sir Evelyn. *Achievements of Cavalry*, London, 1897.

Wylly, Colonel H. C. 'Avesnes-le-Sec and Le Cateau Ambresis, trans.

and abridged from the *Kavalleritis-che Monatshefte'*, in *Cavalry Journal*, London, 1913, VIII, pp. 249–54 (Austrian account).
– *XVth (The King's) Hussars 1759 to 1913*, London, 1914.

Marengo

Anon. 'Other Interesting Particulars respecting the Battle of Marengo', by 'C. J.', in *British Military Library or Journal*, London, 1799–1801, II, pp. 422-3.

Chandler, D. G. *On the Napoleonic Wars: Collected Essays*, London, 1994.

Coignet, J.-R. *The Note-Books of Captain Coignet*, intr. the Hon. Sir John Fortescue, London, 1929.

Foudras, 'Citizen'. 'French Account of the Battle of Marengo', in *British Military Library or Journal*, London, 1799–1801, II, pp. 417-21.

Furse, G. A. *Marengo and Hohenlinden*, London, 1903.

Haythornthwaite, P. J. *Napoleon's Campaigns in Italy*, London, 1993.

Lunt, J. *Charge to Glory!: A Garland of Cavalry Exploits*, London, 1961.

Martha-Beker, F. *Le Général L. C. A. Desaix*, Paris, 1852.

Sargent, H. H. *The Campaign of Marengo*, Chicago, 1901.

Wood, General Sir Evelyn. *Achievements of Cavalry*, London, 1897.

Eylau

Barrès, J.-B. *Memoirs of a Napoleonic Officer*, ed. and intr. M. Barrès, trans. B. Miall, London, 1925.

Fraser, E. *The War Drama of the Eagles*, London, 1912.

Marbot, A. M. *Memoirs of Baron de Marbot*, trans. A. J. Butler, London, 1913.

Petre, F. L. *Napoleon's Campaign in Poland 1806–07*, London, 1901; r/p. with intr. by D. G. Chandler, London 1976. Contains a good short bibliography of relevant early works, pp. xii–xiv.

Saragossa

Belmas, J. *Journaux des Sièges faits ou soutenus par les français dans la Péninsule, de 1807 à 1814*, Paris, 1836, vol. II. The most invaluable of the contemporary works, a day-by-day account of the siege which includes orders-of-battle and transcripts of documents and proclamations issued during the siege.

Cavallero, M. *Défense de Saragosse ou Relation des deux sièges soutenus par cette ville en 1808 et 1809*, Paris, 1815.

Lejeune, Baron L.-F. *Memoirs of Baron Lejeune*, trans. and ed. by Mrs. A. Bell, London, 1897, vol. I.

Napier, W. F. P. *History of the War in the Peninsula*, London, 1832–40. Classic early history, but not the most unbiased!

Oman, Sir Charles. *History of the Peninsular War*, vols. I (Oxford 1901) and II (Oxford 1903).

Rudorff, R. *War to the Death: The Sieges of Saragossa 1808–09*, London, 1974. Best modern study, containing a comprehensive bibliography.

Vaughan, C. R. *Narrative of the Siege of Saragossa*, London, 1809.

Aspern-Essling

Castle, I. *Aspern and Wagram 1809: Mighty Clash of Empires*, London, 1994.

Coignet, J.-R. *The Note-Books of Captain Coignet*, intr. by the Hon. Sir John Fortescue, London, 1929.

Lejeune, Baron L.-F. *Memoirs of Baron Lejeune*, trans. and ed. by Mrs. A. Bell, London 1897, vol. I.

Marbot, A. M. *Memoirs of Baron de Marbot*, trans. A. J. Butler, London, 1913, vol. I.

Müller, W. *Relation of the Operations and Battles of the Austrian and French Armies in the Year 1809*, London, 1810.

Petre, F. L. *Napoleon and the Archduke Charles: A History of the Franco-Austrian Campaign in the Valley of the Danube in 1809*, London, 1909; r/p. with intr. by D. G. Chandler, London, 1976.

Quennevat, J.-C. *Atlas de la Grande Armée: Napoléon et ses campagnes 1803–1815*, Paris 1966; includes photographs of existing locations, including the Essling granary and the house in which Lannes died.

Rothenberg, G. E. *Napoleon's Great Adversaries: The Archduke Charles and the Austrian Army 1792–1814*, London, 1982; excellent account of the Austrian army and its operations.

Tranié, J., and Carmigniani, J. C. *Napoléon et l'Autriche: la Campagne de 1809*, Paris 1979; contains many contemporary illustrations and modern photographs of the locations, including the Essling granary.

Barrosa

Aspinall-Oglander, C. *Freshly-Remembered: The Story of Thomas Graham, Lord Lynedoch*, London, 1956; includes only a limited description of Barrosa.

Beamish, N. L. *History of the King's German Legion*, London, 1837, vol. II.

Blakeney, R. *A Boy in the Peninsular War*, ed. J. Sturgis, London, 1899.

Daniell, D. S. *Cap of Honour: The Story of the Gloucestershire Regiment (The 28th/61st Foot) 1694–1950*, London, 1951.

Napier, W. F. P. *History of the War in the Peninsula*, London, 1832–40.

Oman, Sir Charles. *History of the Peninsular War*, vol. IV, Oxford, 1911.

Verner, Colonel W. *History and Campaigns of the Rifle Brigade*, vol. II, London, 1919.

Albuera

Beresford, Viscount. *Strictures on Certain Passages of Lieut. Col. Napier's History of the Peninsular War which relate to the Military Operations and Conduct of General Lord Viscount Beresford*, London, 1831; and *Further Strictures on those parts of Col. Napier's History ...*, London, 1832 (in answer to Napier's criticisms).

Cooper, J. S. *Rough Notes of Seven Campaigns*, Carlisle, 1914.

Knight, C. R. B. *Historical Record of the Buffs*, London, 1935.

Napier, W. F. P. *History of the War in the Peninsula*, London, 1832–40; classic account though clouded by personal animosities.

Oman, Sir Charles. *History of the Peninsular War*, vol. IV, Oxford, 1911.

– *Studies in the Napoleonic Wars*, London, 1929; includes Major William Brooke's 'A Prisoner of Albuera', originally published in *Blackwood's Magazine*, 1908.

Sherer, M. *Recollections of the Peninsula*, London, 1823.

Woollright, H. H. *History of the Fifty-Seventh (West Middlesex) Regiment of Foot 1755–1881*, London, 1893.

Personal accounts concerning the problem of Hardinge, Lowry Cole and the advance of the 4th Division appeared in the *United Service Journal*, including: Sir Henry Hardinge, 1840, III, pp. 246–9; Sir Galbraith Lowry Cole, 1841, I, pp. 539–41; William Napier, 1840, II, pp. 537–8; Thomas Wade, 1840, II, pp. 395–6, 1841, I, pp. 536–9; 'An Old Soldier', 1840, III, pp. 106–9.

Badajoz

Belmas, J. *Journaux des Sièges faits ou soutenus par les Français dans la Péninsule de 1807 à 1814*, Paris, 1837, vol. IV.

Costello, E. *Memoirs of Edward Costello*, London 1857; originally pubd. in *United Service Journal*, 1839; re-pubd. as *The Peninsular and Waterloo Campaigns: Edward Costello*, ed. A. Brett-James, London, 1967.

Fletcher, I. *In Hell Before Daylight*, Tunbridge Wells, 1984; excellent modern account of the storming of Badajoz.

Green, W. *A Brief Outline of the Travels and Adventures of Wm. Green*, Coventry, 1857; re-pubd. as *Where Duty Calls Me*, ed. J. and D. Teague, West Wickham, 1975.

Jones, Lieutenant-Colonel J. T. *Journals of the Sieges undertaken by the Allies in Spain in the Years 1811 and 1812*, London, 1814.

Kincaid, Sir John. *Adventures in the Rifle Brigade*, London, 1830; and *Random Shots from a Rifleman*, London, 1835; re-pubd. in combined edn. under the former title, London, 1908.

Napier, W. F. P. *History of the War in the Peninsula*, London, 1832–40.

Oman, Sir Charles. *History of the Peninsular War*, vol. V, Oxford, 1914.

Simmons, G. *A British Rifle Man: The Journals and Correspondence of Major George Simmons*, ed. Lieutenant-Colonel W. Verner, London, 1899.

Smith, Sir Harry. *The Autobiography of Sir Harry Smith*, ed. G. C. Moore Smith, London, 1910.

Surtees, W. *Twenty-Five Years in the Rifle Brigade*, London, 1833.

Verner, Colonel W. *History and Campaigns of the Rifle Brigade*, vol. II, London, 1919.

The Berezina

Austin, P. Britten. *1812: The March on Moscow*, London, 1993.

– *1812: Napoleon in Moscow*, London, 1995.

Brett-James, A. *1812: Eye-witness Accounts of Napoleon's Defeat in Russia*, London, 1966.

Chuquet, A. *Human Voices from the Russian Campaign of 1812*, trans. by M. H. M. Capes, London, 1913 (re-pubd. London, 1994), being the English title of the fifth series of the author's *Etudes d'Histoire*. It includes a brief biographical essay on Eblé).

Labaume, E. *Circumstantial Narrative of the Campaign in Russia*, London, 1814.

Marbot, A. M. *Memoirs of Baron de Marbot*, trans. A. J. Butler, London, 1913.

Nafziger, G. F. *Napoleon's Invasion of Russia*, Novato, California, 1988; statistically the most detailed, and with most reference to the actions of individual units.

Ségur, General Count P. de. *History of the Expedition to Russia*, London, 1825.

The following eye-witness accounts are available in translation:

Bourgogne, A. J. B. F. *The Memoirs of Sergeant Bourgogne 1812–1813*, trans. and ed. by P . Cottin and M. Hénault, London, 1899, re-pubd. with intr. by D. G. Chandler, London, 1979.

Roeder, F. *The Ordeal of Captain Roeder*, trans. and ed. by H. Roeder, London, 1960.

Walter, J. *The Diary of a Napoleonic Foot Soldier*, ed. and intr. by M. Raeff, Moreton-in-Marsh, 1991.

Vossler, H. A. *With Napoleon in Russia 1812*, trans. by W. Wallich, London, 1969.

Hougoumont

Clay, M. 'Adventures at Hougoumont', in *The Household Brigade Magazine*, 1958, pp. 219–24.

Dalton, C. *The Waterloo Roll Call*, London, 1904.

Hamilton-Williams, D. *Waterloo New Perspectives: The Great Battle Reappraised*, London, 1993.

Low, E. B. *With Napoleon at Waterloo*, ed. MacK. MacBride, London, 1911.

MacKinnon, Colonel D. *Origin and Services of the Coldstream Guards*, London, 1833; author was the officer commanding the regiment's grenadier company at Hougoumont.

Müffling, F. C. F. von. *History of the Campaign ... in the Year 1815* (pubd as being by 'C. de M.'), ed. Sir John Sinclair, London, 1816; the r/p. (Wakefield, 1970) uses the title *History of the Campaign of 1815*.

Paget, J., and Saunders, D. *Hougoumont: The Key to Victory at Waterloo*, London, 1992.

Siborne, H. T. (ed.). *The Waterloo Letters*, London, 1891.

Siborne, W. *The Waterloo Campaign*, London, 1844.

Weller, J. *Wellington at Waterloo*, London, 1967; includes photographs of the appearance of Hougoumont at that date, including splendid aerial views.

INDEX